BLOOD ON THE BAYOU: CASE CLOSED

BOUCHERCON ANTHOLOGIES

Murder at the Beach (Long Beach CA, 2014)
Murder Under the Oaks (Raleigh NC, 2015)
Blood on the Bayou (New Orleans LA, 2016)
Passport to Murder (Toronto ON, 2017)
Florida Happens (St. Petersburg FL, 2018)
Denim, Diamonds and Death (Dallas TX, 2019)
California Schemin' (Sacramento CA, 2020)
This Time For Sure (New Orleans LA, 2021)
Land of 10,000 Thrills (Minneapolis MN, 2022)
Killin' Time in San Diego (San Diego CA, 2023)
Tales of Music, Murder, and Mayhem (Nashville TN, 2024)
Blood on the Bayou: Case Closed (New Orleans LA, 2025)

DON BRUNS, EDITOR

BLOOD ON THE BAYOU: CASE CLOSED

BOUCHERCON ANTHOLOGY 2025

Down & Out Books
3959 Van Dyke Road, Suite 265
Lutz, FL 33558
DownAndOutBooks.com

Cover design by JT Lindroos

ISBN: 1-64396-427-5
ISBN-13: 978-1-64396-427-0

TABLE OF CONTENTS

AN AVID FAN: THE HUNT FOR "DR. FELL"

Ali Karim

"There must be something else," said the perplexed gentleman. "There is something more, if I could find a name for it. God bless me, the man seems hardly human! Something troglodytic, shall we say? Or can it be the old story of Dr. Fell?"
Chapter 2 [aka The Search for Mr. Hyde]
Strange Case of Dr. Jekyll and Mr. Hyde
by Robert Louis Stevenson

I was asked to pen a few words for the *Blood on the Bayou: Case Closed*, Bouchercon Anthology 2025. This year's convention is hosted in the city of New Orleans, where mystery and horror co-exist with the legends of Hoodoo and Catholicism, mixed into Santeria. It is also a place where it is difficult to separate the stories of the past from the fictional myths that spread along the Mississippi River and into the bayous and swamps of Louisiana.

Like New Orleans, there is a linkage within mystery fiction to the edges of the horror genre, and if we plotted a Venn diagram, there would be authors who would be placed where the circles overlapped and where the literary work is both horror as well as mystery/crime fiction.

Two of the best-known authors who mix horror with mystery/crime fiction are Thomas Harris and Robert Bloch, and where they *interacted* [in the aforementioned Venn diagram] was in the name Dr. Fell.

Let's go back in time.

Dr. Hannibal Lecter fled from the authorities in America at the conclusion of Thomas Harris' novel *The Silence of the Lambs* [1988] when he escaped his locked cell in Baltimore State Hospital for the Criminally Insane. He would reappear over a decade later in the follow-up novel *Hannibal* [1999], disguised as Dr. Fell, the curator of the Capponi Library in Florence, Italy. Thomas Harris did not select the "Dr. Fell" pen name for his insane psychiatrist at random.

Hannibal was a mystery/crime novel that was written in a gothic literary style. The locations and characters striated within this bizarre narrative transformed it into a novel of horror. The name Thomas Harris chose as the disguise for Lecter, namely Dr. Fell, was intriguing, referencing dark literature.

John Dickson Carr's character of Dr. Gideon Fell was featured in 23 novels and many short stories from 1933 to 1976. In Carr's *The Three Coffins*, Dr. Fell details a "locked room" lecture illustrating how apparent '*locked-room* or *impossible-crime*' murders might be committed. It must be remembered that Dr. Lecter escaped his incarceration in Baltimore State's Hospital for the Criminally Insane at the bloody climax of *The Silence of the Lambs* committing murder from his locked cell and ending up in Florence as Dr. Fell.

Robert Louis Stevenson in his Jekyll and Hyde novel references Dr. Fell as something monstrous, perhaps related to the childhood nursery rhyme later referenced infamously by poet Robert Graves in 1926.

I do not like thee, Doctor Fell,
The reason why—I cannot tell;

But this I know, and know full well,
I do not like thee, Doctor Fell

Which in turn is derived from the English satirical Poet Thomas [Tom] Brown who was a student at Christ Church, Oxford, when he was caught doing mischief. The Dean of Christ Church, Dr. John Fell (1625—1686), who later became the Bishop of Oxford, expelled Brown, hence Tom Brown's mischievous ditty above.

Either of those facts above could explain why Thomas Harris chose the name "Dr. Fell" as disguises for the fleeing Dr. Hannibal Lecter, but being the obsessive mystery/crime and horror fiction reader—I felt there had to be something more.

Despite the ubiquity and voluminous information of the Internet, there was no other explanation as to why Dr. Lecter became Dr. Fell.

So, as I sat in my library, looking at my vast array of books, I pondered upon what I should write for the Anthology. I chuckled at my collection of books, amassed over the decades and I thought to myself "what makes a reader of crime, mystery, thriller fiction *become* an enthusiastic and *'avid fan'*"?

An obsessive and inquisitive nature.

My eyes rested on a shelf that contained all my Robert Bloch novels and collections, of which his seminal work *Psycho* [1959] is the most renowned due to the adaptation by Alfred Hitchcock in 1960. On the adjacent shelf were my various editions of the Thomas Harris novels [*Cari Mora*, *Black Sunday*, *Hannibal Rising*, *Red Dragon*, *The Silence of the Lambs* and *Hannibal*].

I knew why these two authors were shelved next to each other in my library. It was due to literary speculation that posited that, without Robert Bloch's novel *Psycho*, there would not have been *The Silence of the Lambs* from Thomas Harris. It is widely conjectured that Robert Bloch based the Norman Bates character from *Psycho* on the real-life serial killer Ed

Gein, as did Thomas Harris when he created Buffalo Bill in *The Silence of the Lambs*. Both writers have been characterised as writers of mystery/crime fiction that is also horror fiction, thus situated in the Venn diagram's centre.

I also thought of Dr. Fell.

One of the benefits of having a vast library of crime, mystery and horror fiction is it allows one to research. In the collection *Robert Bloch: Appreciations of the Master* edited by Richard Matheson and Ricia Mainhardt [1995], I discovered the Robert Bloch story "I Do Not Love Thee, Dr. Fell". It eponymously references the Tom Brown poem/nursery rhyme, but more eerily, its theme foreshadows the authors' most renowned work, *Psycho*. The narrative revolves around the character of public relations man Clyde Bromley, who has professional appointments with the psychiatrist Dr. Fell. It soon becomes apparent that there is no Dr. Fell, as the psychiatrist is actually part of the subconscious mind within the patient Bromley, who has a dissociative personality disorder (pre-dating Bloch's 1959 novel *Psycho* by several years). Bromley's Dr. Fell personality is emerging from his subconscious, not unlike the manner *Mother* would emerge from Norman Bates' subconscious mind several years later.

Curiously, the story "I Do Not Love Thee, Dr. Fell" was Robert Bloch's first story to be published in "The Magazine of Fantasy and Science Fiction" in 1955, by its editor at the time Anthony Boucher, and who coincidently gave his name to the world crime and mystery convention Bouchercon. It is even more eerie that the first Guest of Honor at the inaugural was Robert Bloch (Santa Monica, California, May 29-31, 1970)

Thomas Harris' *The Silence of the Lambs* would be awarded the Anthony Award (also named after Anthony Boucher) in 1989 at Bouchercon XX Philadelphia, Pennsylvania (Oct 6-8, 1989).

It takes a deeply obsessive and inquisitive mind in the crime, mystery and horror fiction genre to be able to track the linkages between Robert Bloch, Thomas Harris and Anthony Boucher to the annual celebration of Crime, Mystery Fiction—Bouchercon.

I'll leave you with an assertion from the incarcerated Dr. Hannibal Lecter to Detective Will Graham, which is useful in contextualising how my own interest in reading Crime, Mystery, and Horror Fiction became something more, transforming me to an *'Avid Fan'*.

"We don't invent our natures,
Will: They're issued to us along with our lungs
and pancreas and everything else. Why fight it?"
—Thomas Harris, *Red Dragon* [1981]

Enjoy the stories contained in this volume.

Ali Karim
Fan Guest of Honor Bouchercon 2025 New Orleans

SIX CYLINDER TOTEM

Eric Beckstrom

God is a bullet.
—Concrete Blonde

He had left her what he could. Her eighteen years of life. Three months' rent paid ahead. A 2012 something or other with a good engine and its title paid in full. The vintage wooden cigar box. The things inside it.

And he left behind the question he'd often asked her:

"What does the universe breathe?"

Alexis would answer the question differently each time.

Each time, he would tell her, "You have a poignant imagination."

When she was five, and briefly Minnesotan, it was, "The universe breathes snow drifts and mittens." When she was eight, her Indiana eyes beamed. "It breathes cicada rattles and tree frog songs." At ten, the year her mom died in red water off New Smyrna Beach, something swimming away with bits of her in its mouth, the universe breathed "teeth and tears." When she was twelve, with Maine crushes, it was, "The universe breathes cute boys and mean girls."

To some answers, her dad had given her especially long hugs, like he knew some truths she didn't.

Today, Alexis did know: The universe breathes some things when you're a kid and other things when you grow up. It breathes some things when your parents are alive and other things after they're gone. Killed in water blooming slow motion blood, or drowned in the brackish, troubled waters of Pontchartrain.

In the cigar box, Thoreau Gustave, her dead father, had placed an old tennis ball, an ink pen with Loretta's Authentic Pralines stamped on the barrel, and a small sheet of paper. On it, written in ink from the pen, was a bulleted list.

Covered by the list, like a game of Rock Paper Scissors, was something else. In her hand, it was heavy with weight, heavy in other ways. It constricted the nerves below her heart, like one of those giant balls of mating pythons they sometimes find in Florida swamps.

Her dad must have seen something coming. Before today, the box always sat empty on the wide sill of the picture window next to two things that were important to him, as ballast is important to a ship at sea. Shark tooth fossils. A dud firecracker with no fuse, holding a childhood tale he'd never shared with her. The tennis ball.

But no dust on that sill. He dusted every week (*used to dust*). A rented house is still a home, he always said (*used to say*). Every *-ed* was a bullet to her heart. From now on, she wouldn't dust the sill. It would be a reminder of his absence. An homage.

This silly poignancy marked a difference between them. Alexis clung to certain pasts. She'd learned that death comes from nowhere, a dark, swirling thing with teeth, judging and tearing. She'd become desperately nostalgic. Agoraphobic with grief and memories, she couldn't leave for weeks.

Whereas her dad siloed the past.

"Learn from the past if you can," he said, "But forget the 'Back Thens,'" as if bygone days were a rented textbook.

He tempered that advice for her sake. "We're the same, but we're different. Keep your imagination and your nostalgia. In *you*, those things are strengths if you live them and don't let them live you."

The items on the sill were exceptions to his rule.

"I keep those things because some lessons are hard to learn and easy to forget. I'm not a slow learner, but I am a fast forgetter."

His tennis ball was a rare 'Back Then' he'd shared with her just this week.

The boy is ten years old. His dog, Chinook, sprints around the field chasing his beloved tennis ball, the boy not far behind. Like the boy, he's ten, but that's seventy in dog years. Chinook twists his ankle. It kinda-sorta heals, but the dog never runs like that again. The boy doesn't know that day in the field, one of hundreds, will be the last of its kind. But his older brother knows, and he keeps the ball.

When they bury Chinook in the same field a year later, he presents the ragged tennis ball to his little brother. "Keep it in on your windowsill, as an homage."

Thoreau doesn't know what an homage is, but it's the kindest thing his brother, Landry, has ever done for him.

Alexis hadn't known why her dad told her the story about him and Uncle Landry, but today, bracing herself for tomorrow's graveside service—there would be no funeral mass—she thought he'd been preparing her for certain possibilities.

At the gravesite on Shrove Monday—"confession Monday," and wasn't that perfect?—Alexis clutched the bulleted list in her pocket. On it, written in her dad's calligraphic hand, were the names of the five people standing across from her on the other side of his casket.

"Cousin Camille"

"Cousin Beno"

"Cousin Augie"

"Cousin Raphi"

And: “Uncle Landry”

It was a kill list.

In front of each name, her dad had drawn an almost photo-realistic .357 round.

“Bullet points. Get it?” Dad jokes from beyond the grave, his voice on the wind.

The moment she’d read the list, things had made sense. Her dad’s unusually frequent visits to Landry’s. His breezing home last week like Sinatra at the Sands.

“Things are about to change, Lex. We’ll own, not rent, and that 2012 is gonna be a ‘26.”

But then, Landry and his brood happened, two-faced as Picasso’s Tête de Femme. That’s what her dad was saying through the list, and she had faith in him, was sure he’d never lied to her and that this couldn’t be a misjudgment on his part. A conspiracy, not only to gain control of the family wealth—which incidentally, included the field where the brothers had buried their dog—but also to hoard the gains from a deal Landry Gustave, his kids, and her dad had brokered. Landry’s weight, her dad’s plan, and this one even above board. For a year now, her dad had been an honest broker, gone legit like Michael Corleone never could. All for Alexis’ sake. Thoreau Jacques Gustave, betrayed and drowned in Pontchartrain on the family land, now Landry’s.

And all the while, Alexis, fresh from high school, considered too young to be looped in, probably protected by that, but hating herself for not seeing her cousins’ duplicity. She wondered now if Landry had killed her grandpa, too. In telling her the story of the dog and the brothers, had her dad been telling her that losing her mother to the ocean was the *second* great loss of his life? Had losing his brother to betrayal been the first? He seemed to have concluded this just days ago, years too late.

After the service, they all offered Alexis condolences, eleven-year-old Raphi in tears.

“Are you going to the parades tomorrow?” Alexis asked.

"Tourists," Landry scoffed. "Never go. You know that."

Even greedy with words. And yes, she knew, but things needed double-checking.

Camille said, "You shouldn't be alone on Mardi Gras, not after this. Please, come over."

Perfect. An invitation.

After they left, Alexis felt their words hovering around her like malarial mosquitos.

Before the reception at Landry's place on Pontchartrain, she stopped at The Happy Crab all-in-one and paid cash for what she'd need tomorrow night if all went well. A filet knife, a hammer, an ice cream scoop, which, for her purposes, would never cool to less than 98.6 degrees Fahrenheit. She thought about evenings on the apartment roof, Dad scooping Rocky Road while the sun, too, melted below the horizon. For what she had planned for her cousins, she would not use the scoop from home. Like the thing coiled in the bottom of the cigar box, it was holy.

The scent of the secret city sun and of Pontchartrain's nearby, algaeic slime, wafted with breezes through the open French doors of the veranda. Alexis, Augie, and Camille sat near the threshold in simple wooden chairs. Beno was getting beer.

Her cousins' repeated condolences made Alexis sick with their sincerity, as if rather than conspiring to drown her dad, they'd spilled drinks on her and felt truly sorry for the mess. Such good actors. Appalling that, until she'd read her dad's list, these people had been friends, not just cousins.

The expensive spring water Alexis was drinking came in an actual glass bottle. If not for the more appropriate ending she had planned for them, she might have smashed it over Camille's head and slashed Augie and Beno's throats with the jagged edge. The others sipped cans of Reasonably Corrupt, which Alexis knew was the only beer they and Landry drank. The lager must be a sweet, dark inside joke between them.

How had she never seen the awfulness in this house? What a difference a death makes.

From the direction of the kitchen, roughly six or seven miles deeper into the house, came Beno, who sat down between Augie and Camille.

"What took so long?" Camille asked.

"Didn't you hear that? A six-foot catering cart fell over. My ears are still ringing. Plates crashing, head caterer yelling at his lackeys."

No one on the veranda had heard a thing. So, even the loudest sounds couldn't be heard from across the vast house. Good to know.

Awkward sips of beer followed, and occasional intakes of breath as someone—never Alexis—began a sentence, decided against it. She figured they must be wondering how you talk to the cousin whose dad you helped kill.

Augie filled his lungs like someone diving into a sinkhole brimming with bull sharks. "Your dad used to play Monster Chase with us when we were little and we were all hanging out," he said to everyone, but speaking to Alexis. "Remember that?"

Beno said, "We'd all run around screaming, and he'd stalk after us saying, 'They're coming to get you, Barbara,' in that creepy voice."

"When I was little, I'd sit on his ankle, and he'd bounce me like I was on a horse." Were Camille's eyes glistening?

Good actors, indeed.

A breeze entered the veranda, mingled with clinking bottles, jangling ice, reminiscing voices.

"He liked each of you," said Alexis, knowing they'd misinterpret her low voice as mournfulness, not outrage.

Beno said, "He knew our dad didn't want kids, so your dad was especially good to us."

"You're wrong," Alexis said.

From across the room came violent gagging. A glass shattered. Ice cubes skittered across wooden planks.

"Daddy's choking!" Raphi cried out. "Someone help!"

The year before, Alexis and her dad had completed a first aid course. Another of his principles was "Have faith, be kind, be ruthless." Learning first aid was preparing to be kind.

And he liked oxymorons. Open secret. Jumbo shrimp.

Kind but ruthless.

Alexis knew the Heimlich maneuver, could have saved Landry by standing behind him, positioning her fist and thumb below his ribs, pulling back and up.

Instead, she stood back, looking helpless with everyone else while Camille pounded Landry's back, the opposite of what you're supposed to do. It made the little orb lodge more deeply in his windpipe.

Alexis believed her dad would have thought what she'd done was imaginative, but unlikely to succeed. She admitted the chances were practically nil. Maybe magic had made it work. The shark tooth tucked in her shoe. The power of the ink on the list in her pocket. Maybe Mardi Gras luck. A fava bean in a piece of king cake.

"Daddy, breathe!" Camile screamed, each palm to his back a killer exclamation point.

Uncle Landry's eyes were hazel. His right one bulged in its socket.

His left eye wasn't in its socket. It had been in his drink. Now, it blocked his throat.

It was a glass eye, landed during a long-ago night of drunken fishing. Bourbon and fish hooks. Bad combo.

During past visits, Alexis had observed how the hazel of Landry's glass eye matched the hue of his devil's cut bourbon and the glimmer of ice cubes. He never took his bourbon neat. And he loved his eye patch, the pirate look, so almost always kept the false eye in a shot glass which sat next to his chair on a prominent mahogany bookcase, next to first-edition novels he had never read. Would never read.

Tonight, when Alexis had held out the glass of bourbon to him, the camouflaged glass eye clinking around with the ice, he'd raised the brow of his real eye.

"Because you gave the tennis ball to my dad."

He smiled a little. A bit sad? A bit mistrustful? Yes, certainly that last.

"I don't know why Dad brought us back here. He didn't like seafood or beignets. He didn't believe in saints, marching in or otherwise. He didn't even like jazz, which I told him was insane. He didn't believe in ghosts, but here we are in the most haunted city on earth, where people—him included—stay above ground even after they die. There's even a street named after the booze he hated. But you love it, don't you Landry? Your bourbon?"

He should have been suspicious, but it was just Little Lexi, right?

As she had walked away to join her cousins on the veranda, he'd been lifting the drink to his lips.

Camille wasn't pounding anymore. No point.

Sometimes a glass eye is as good as a bullet.

Paramedics, cops, the coroner came and went. Alexis made noises of comfort and condolence.

Good actor. LOL. And she almost did.

In the car, she took out the list and the Loretta's Authentic Pralines pen.

She crossed off "Uncle Landry" and drove home.

What kind of father gives his eighteen-year-old daughter a list of people to kill? A list of her own people?

Back in the apartment, Alexis opened the cigar box and looked at the thing that had swelled her throat when she first saw it, like she was part of that ball of writhing swamp pythons, swallowing something better left to a bigger snake.

It was made of blue steel, black walnut, the scent of oil,

family history, family lore. She lifted it from the box, gripped it, ran fingers over wood, metal, inherited memories, sacred family stories.

Huh. Yesterday, reading about swamp pythons. Today, holding the heirloom revolver, a 1955 Colt Python .357, her dad's, his dad's before him, now hers.

She could feel the experiences of grandfather and father spin in the Python's cylinder. Could see those stories shine in its steel. Their hands had polished the walnut grip, oil from their palms sealing in lore from streets, alleys, rooftops, lakeshores. Their sweat, and, in the end, her grandpa's blood, infused the wood with their essence, lent a patina to the gold medallions inset on either side of the grip, one rearing Colt for each of her forebears. The revolver was not an oxymoron breaking her dad's rules about the past being the past. Lore isn't the past. Lore is the past being in the present. The Python had saved her dad's life before he went straight, and saved her grandfather's life before that. Alexis knew that one of those times for her dad had been before she was born, and that one of those times for her grandfather had been before her father was born.

So, without those six cylinders, there would be no present. No her.

What kind of father gives his daughter a kill list?

Alexis thought all of that might hold the answer. And maybe the father knew the daughter would exact retribution anyway. Maybe he was the kind of father who'd taught his daughter she was capable of anything she set her imagination to.

Late the next afternoon, Alexis texted her cousins she'd be there around 8. They could all be together to support each other through this horrible time while everyone else celebrated Mardi Gras. Three thumbs-up emojis appeared.

She left the apartment wearing a nondescript purple, green, and gold t-shirt, with a generic knapsack slung over her shoulder. In it was a harlequin mask, a dark wig from Mardi Gras past, a generic Saints t-shirt, the hammer and the ice cream scoop, rubber cleaning gloves, a flask of lighter fluid. And the Python, wrapped in protective cloth.

In her jeans pocket was the kill list, the pen, a lighter.

Geographically, entering the sacred heart of Mardi Gras and its thirty parades was as simple as donning the harlequin mask and crossing from one street to the next. Charon himself couldn't have made the crossing easier, or the change in atmosphere more dramatic and literal. The music, echoing, cavorting, swelling, swooning from all directions; trumpets, trombones, cymbals, millions of clattering beads; the swirled scent of food, booze, pot, sweat, perfume. Voices singing, laughing, lilting, careening, sneaking, but never whispering, except a soft jazz ballad hushing through a mic inside a café. The groaning, fluttering, rocking, floats. Dancers, standers, stumblers. All of it did something to and through the heat and the humidity. The atmosphere is supposed to be someplace up there in the sky, but on Mardi Gras it's in New Orleans. It descends to earth, pulled into the NOLA vortex, and clings to everything. Becomes everything.

Walls of people pulled Alexis into the crazy Carnival synthesis of Catholicism, voodoo, paganism, souls of saints, spirits of the enslaved, eternal pharaohs and their hybrid gods and demons, a holy distillation of purple and green and gold, the Zoroastrian priest of ancient Persia, the gifts of the magi, all carried through a maze of people and streets on floats devised by new and ancient krewes with names like Rex, Endymion, and Bacchus, Cleopatra and Osiris, and Sobek the crocodile god, thought by ancient Egyptian sects to have brought order or chaos to the universe. No one knew for sure what to believe, except Alexis, who believed her dad.

At some point, Alexis realized she was not seeking or fleeing the Minotaur at the center of this labyrinth, whatever that Minotaur was. Grief, love, memory, faith, retribution. She neither sought nor fled those things because she had become those things. *She was the Minotaur.*

And sometimes the Minotaur must leave the labyrinth.

Strong wind tightened beads around fleshy necks, severed the cords of paper lanterns, freeing them to roam the crowds. That reminded her of something that'd been on her mind since the graveside service. Sometimes you have to cut the cords connecting you to your religion. Those threads, already frayed from generations of family tossing the fabric of religious belief into unvisited corners: you might need to cut those threads once and for all. Become pagan.

Because God is a bullet, and so you must become God.

Changed, Alexis departed the labyrinth. Instead of the horns of a bull, she had the Python, handed down across generations to restore order.

She traded mask for wig at the 6 p.m. prohibition, fake hair covering brows, lips, cheeks. By foot and by stealth, in less than three hours, she was at Landry's, near Lakeshore Drive. If you're around NOLA long enough, in Landry's orbit, her dad's, you can learn where ATM, counter, and crime cameras are, where private cameras are likely to be, and get around without being tracked in ways that stitch together handy timelines for cops. Add masks, wigs, crowds, Mardi Gras beads and boobs, and you can practically teleport from one parish to another.

Nightbirds and moths swam through the dense humidity. In the black distance, the Causeway glided its way across Pontchartrain, carrying imaginary people leading imaginary lives, coming and going between imaginary places. The only real things were in her knapsack.

Alexis stowed the wig. No surveillance on this property. Landry, ever self-assured. She walked around back to the open veranda, where they'd be expecting her. Around the veranda's chandelier, moths fluttered, confusing artificial light with the moon. Like people confusing what's important with what's ephemeral. Things like wealth and power. Things like life.

They were there, drinking Landry's devil's cut.

"An homage?" Alexis asked. She sat down, opened the glass bottle of fancy water waiting for her, sweating in the humidity, dead center on a coaster.

"*En mémoire de*," said Augie.

She offered no condolences.

Beno said, "Lexi, something's been bothering me. Last night, I was saying that Uncle Thoreau was good to Camille, Augie, and Raphi and me, because he knew our dad never wanted kids. Why did you say I was wrong?"

"You were wrong thinking Landry didn't want kids."

Her cold tone made them recoil.

"Landry did want kids, but not because he wanted a family. He was planning decades ahead. He was forming a fucking *gang*. Don't pretend you don't know that's all you were to him. He knew a day would come when he'd need a group of absolute loyalists to serve him and to take over later. For Landry Gustave, wealth was thicker than blood. Ask your mom, if you can find her. Hell, for him bourbon was thicker than blood."

Her cousins set down their glasses, sloshing with shock. This wasn't Little Cousin Lexi.

She unzipped the knapsack, reached in, left her hand there, coiled around the Python.

The others were glass-eyed.

"Alexis, what—"

"You were lackeys. Beno, scurrying after Landry, filling his glass, wiping up the circles on his eight-thousand dollar coffee table because he was above using coasters. Augie, cleaning up God knows what behind his old, dying dog. Camille, pounding his back every time he choked because he wouldn't chew his food like any two-year-old. The pounding killed him, by the way."

Camille's face crumbled. "Lex, please—"

Augie pleaded, "Lex, we didn't m—"

"And together, like a committee, you and your dad decided

my dad had to go. Dad's idea, but Landry wanted it for himself and y'all helped him with that, too. Did you hold him under the water or just help Landry sell it as another Pontchartrain drowning?"

Alexis' voice was all levee and high water now. She stood and let the knapsack fall away from the revolver, pointed the barrel at the bunch of them, now standing clustered together.

Beno: "God damn you, Alexis."

"I do not believe in God. Unless God is a bullet."

Raising the bottle of water to them, a mock toast, she said, "To blood and bourbon."

She dropped the bottle, gripped the Python with both hands like Dad had taught her, and began firing.

She felt the generations of sacrifices offered up to the Python. The grip was hot, like three pairs of hands, not one, gripped it. Like the barrel was a pyre. Like it was fired by overheated Gulf currents feeding impossible masses swirling up from the climate change apocalypse and the dark South magic of the Caribbean, to be gripped tightly by Grandpa and Dad and herself and wielded against her profane cousins.

Alexis pulled the trigger three times, no pauses, so fast the three hit the floor as one.

Blood always wants to escape, to flee veins and arteries. It yearns for unobstructed openings. It coagulates against its will. But better to be a congealed pool on the outside than to flow constrained on the inside.

"To paraphrase Milton's Lucifer," said Alexis.

She snapped open the cylinder, removed the spent shells, flicked it shut. She dropped the shells into the knapsack's outer pocket, and, as blood mixed and pooled nearby, wrapped the revolver and stowed it.

Then she took the bulleted list and the pen from her pocket and crossed off three more names.

Only Cousin Raphi, now.

He had made no appearance. Hadn't heard a thing. The

crashing catering cart had proved that likely. Raphi's older siblings would have put him to bed early, maybe even Benadrylled him to move him into sleep while they conspired on the veranda. He would find the bodies, he would be traumatized, but he would live.

Alexis took out the filet knife, the ice cream scoop, and the gloves. She put on the gloves, picked up her bottle of water, put it in the knapsack.

Then, she pulled the bodies away from the deeper blood. Quick and sure, she used the knife to widen the wounds enough to insert the ice cream scoop. Rotating the scoop in each wound until she heard the dull click of metal on metal, she spooned out the slugs. Good ammo. No fragmentation, just three intact little lead flowers, which she dropped in with the spent shells.

She changed into the Saints t-shirt, wrapped the knife, gloves, and scoop in the other one, and returned everything to the knapsack.

A breeze lifted Camille's bangs from her forehead, discarded them, moved onto the blood and began drawing out moisture, turning it sticky, filling the air with the sweet, coppery scent of retribution.

"What does the universe breathe?" her dad asked, or maybe the breeze.

"It breathes grief, love, memory, and faith. It breathes retribution," she answered.

"They're just four rounds in the same revolver."

"His whole family's dead, except me. Sparing Raphi wasn't kind."

"Have faith, be kind, be *ruthless*."

"Ruthlessness and kindness. Mercy, retribution. Maybe they aren't different things," said Alexis.

She walked to the bookcase by Landry's chair. His favorite shot glass was there at eye level, pretending to be innocuous. His glass eye wasn't there. It would be buried with him. Through the distorted curve of the shot glass, she read the spine of the book behind it, and smiled at the irony of what it said.

"Landry, I don't know why Dad trusted you. I guess you used the desperation you created when you gained control of the family wealth and the land, even before Grandpa died. I imagine you had Grandpa killed, too, right? I think Dad suspected, but was desperate to provide for me, so he threw in with you. And I think Grandpa gave the Python to Dad and not to you all those years ago because Grandpa saw what might be coming, too. I think he wanted to pass it onto someone who understood what it is. What it contains."

"Lots of imagining and guessing, Little Lexi. About as reliable as the wind you've been talking to."

Alexis shook her head, clearing it or in disputation, she wasn't sure which.

"You shouldn't have changed, Landry."

She rubbed her thumb over faded green felt. The old tennis ball, hollow but not empty, filled her hand. She wondered about the tosses, the catches and misses, the beautiful, shattered brotherhood preserved within the little sphere like it was its own world. She felt it all, like memories, though she hadn't lived it. Hadn't even been born.

"You shouldn't have changed, Landry."

Alexis set the ball on top of the shot glass. Now it was a pedestal.

She turned and strode with the breeze past the bodies and the blood, out through the veranda doors. On the shoreline, she wiped down the spent shells and set them on a flat rock with the slugs she'd scooped from her cousins. She smashed everything flat with the hammer, then pitched the brass, lead, hammer, and ice cream scoop into the lake, over the sink hole she knew was there. Then she dowsed the mask, gloves, knapsack, and Mardi Gras t-shirt in lighter fluid, burned the lot of it, and ground the whole mess into the mud.

Looking over Pontchartrain, Alexis took the bulleted list from her pocket. She crumpled it tight, placed it on her tongue, and sucked the ink inscribed there by her dad and by her. She swallowed it like a communion host. She smiled.

She put the wig back on and began the long walk home.

Relatives are always the first suspects, especially the ones with dead fathers who'd been in business with four fresh bodies and had died so near them. Alexis' phone back in the apartment playing downloaded episodes: tonight's text exchange with her cousins, hundreds of happy photos of them together, stored in the cloud, the lack of physical evidence connecting her with tonight, no evidence she'd known about the business between Landry and her dad. Taken together, she figured it had legs enough to let her walk.

She would make her way back through the dwindling Mardi Gras crowds. Cameras would record her, but people and shadows, the wig, the ubiquitous Saints t-shirt, would scrub her into anonymity. She'd be home in a few hours. The final part of her plan would unfold.

Raphi.

He would inherit Landry's fortune. She was a legal adult and his only living relative. They would visibly grieve together. He would beg the authorities for her to be his guardian. Wasn't she the only person in the world he had, after all? And she him.

And when he was older, maybe on his eighteenth birthday, she would make him a Mardi Gras king cake. His birthday was, well, today, actually. It fell near Mardi Gras every year. Cousin Alexis would make him a king cake with sparkles on top. Gold for power. Purple for justice. Green for faith. Faith being most important, as it makes the others possible. Hadn't she just proved it?

She would sit him down on his eighteenth birthday, on the veranda of their house, and they would toast each other with bites of cake. Inside his piece, Raphi would find the traditional Mardi Gras fève, a little Christ figurine. Yes, respectful of tradition and history—important—but the irony was the thing. Dad would love it.

It would also symbolize everything her dad and mom had sacrificed for her, nurtured within her. Everything the universe breathed.

Raphi would find the fève in his cake, so would get the prize. It was tradition.

"Here," she would say. "Happy birthday, Cousin Raphi."

She would slide aside his empty plate and set the old cigar box in front of him. Something heavy inside would shift a little. Maybe it would hiss.

"This is yours now."

SHOES

Jayne Belmont

Jackson stepped off the St. Charles streetcar at Carondelet and waited on the corner to cross Canal. His white t-shirt stuck to him. It wouldn't be much better in the kitchen during the dinner rush later. Six months in Louisiana wasn't long enough to get used to the dense humidity. Had it been that long? He'd lost track of time in the anonymity of the French Quarter.

He avoided Bourbon Street. The drunken tourists, hustlers and lost souls crowding the street made him uncomfortable. He'd been down it once before, looking for a job. Today would be his second, and last, if he could help it. Jackson's destination was a tiny store tucked between two noisy Bourbon Street bars. The crowds would be worse if he went after his shift.

Head averted to avoid broken sidewalks and eye contact, Jackson moved down Bourbon as quickly as he could. He'd seen the dagger in the window of the shop that first time, ducked in to admire the workmanship of the carved wooden hilt. The manager promised to hold it for him. He finally had enough money to pick it up.

He knew Amy would love it. She collected decorative knives, a hobby that intrigued him when they first met. Everything about Amy intrigued him. Her smile, her long black hair, her green eyes. He had no doubt she was his soul mate, would be forever.

A man's fingers partially wrapped around Jackson's forearm as he hurried past. He jerked to a stop, startled from his focus by the physical contact. A leering grin framed multiple gold teeth, jagged white scar engraving the man's right cheek. Jackson's eyes swept down his arm, and the man released him, grin fading but not completely.

"Hey man, bet you twenty I know where you got them shoes." He nodded at Jackson's feet. Jackson didn't have twenty to spare, not even five. But an extra twenty would buy food on his days off. No, he thought, it's a scam, no one would be dumb enough to take that bet. If it wasn't, he lost a quick twenty bucks. Two hours of sweating over dirty dishes.

The man's teeth glinted off the late afternoon sun as Jackson's mind raced. Take the bet. If he lost, walk away. But he couldn't lose. He'd bought the shoes at an outlet store in Lake George Village over two years ago, almost fifteen hundred miles away. With Amy. She'd picked them out. Said they were cute. No way this man could know that.

"Okay, where." The words were out before he thought it completely through. Amy did that to him.

"You got 'em on your feet!" The man slapped Jackson on the arm. "You lost man." He stuck his hand in Jackson's face and Jackson backed off, again startled by the physical contact. He turned, blocked by a large man who wasn't grinning.

"You heard him, you lost." The word 'pay' wasn't uttered but Jackson heard it loud and clear, even over his shock at feeling intimidated. It was a new sensation. He reached his shaking hand inside his pocket, pulled out a twenty, thrust it at the gold teeth and turned away.

He didn't get far. Jackson swung around as his arm was grabbed again, ready to react in a way he knew he shouldn't, to find a ten clutched in the hand of the big man.

"Only twenty, man. We ain't thieves."

Jackson grabbed the extra bill and ran, slowing down as he realized running away made him look like the idiot he'd been.

He also realized he was twenty dollars short. Amy's smile faded in his mind, her disappointed eyes gently mocking him for being a sucker. Bourbon Street, strike two.

Jackson sank down onto an upside-down crate outside the kitchen's back door. Even at midnight the heat was stifling, but after seven hours in a grueling hot kitchen it was a relief. The fans that moved humid air around the dish room were a joke. A busy dinner service had almost distracted Jackson from his humiliation and frustration. Two more weeks before he could pick up the dagger. If he could afford revenge, he'd do it tonight. Revenge was dangerous. He'd have to rely on karma.

Karma picked the wrong target. Two nights later, Jackson stepped on a bent kitchen grate, ripping a long gash down the side of his shoe. Amy made fun of him for owning only two pairs of shoes, one dressy and one for everything else. When he ended up in New Orleans, the everything else pair, the cute shoes Amy had picked out, became his kitchen work shoes. The dressy ones got hocked for rent. The money he'd put aside would take another hit. Amy's birthday was two months off, but the shop wouldn't hold the dagger forever.

The bed in his one room rental sagged under Jackson's weight. The new shoes, purchased from a second-hand store and not exactly new, sat on the floor. He reached forward and pulled the scuffed wooden chair closer, setting his old shoes carefully on the worn seat. Jackson removed the shoelaces, first from the torn shoe and then the other. He slid them slowly through his fingers. The blood stains on the shoes were long gone and the stains on the once white laces had faded, but Jackson could see them clearly, even in the dim light. As he clutched the stained laces in his fist, Amy's face, eyes closed, flashed briefly in his vision. Damn, he missed her. The dagger would show her how much, he was sure of it. He removed the laces from his new shoes and carefully replaced them with the stained shoelaces. He pushed the shoes Amy picked out underneath his bed, then headed to work.

"Jackson! Plates!" Elvis's voice boomed from the line. Another busy dinner service, another beastly hot and humid night. Jackson grabbed a stack of plates and hurried them to the line, where Elvis grabbed them from his hands. There weren't any thanks. Jackson worked under the table and at the mercy of the owner. The cash was the only thanks he cared about.

When he got his week's pay after shift, he stuffed it in his pocket. He didn't need to count it to know he was still short. Rent was due tomorrow. He got change to use the old pay phone on Magazine to call the store, hoping they'd give him more time. He didn't want to disappoint Amy, even though he knew she wasn't expecting a present. He was relieved when they agreed. The Big Easy. So different from home.

It was six weeks before he saved the money back, even while working extra shifts. Barely in time for Amy's birthday, but Jackson allowed himself a small smile picturing Amy's face when she opened it. The perfect present, the perfect surprise.

Even at three p.m. the street was crowded. Jackson figured he could use that to his advantage, skirting clusters of tourists and hawkers just far enough away to keep a hand from reaching out to grab him. He didn't mean to, couldn't help scanning for the gold teeth and white scar, afraid of the anger threatening to explode from the humiliation of their previous encounter. Two more blocks and Amy's birthday present.

"Sorry, man, we sold it yesterday. We didn't have any way to contact you."

Amy's face, sad green eyes, gentle smile, disappointed but accusing, affirming he'd let her down again. It was all Jackson could see. He left the store and strode down Bourbon, mindlessly dodging people as his rage grew. He veered down a side street, his vision obscured by Amy's face, morphing from disappointment into anger. His shoulder slammed hard against the corner of a dumpster, jerking him sideways, and he stopped, shoving the dumpster back against the wall, then again and again and again until his rage began to subside. One final shove and the tears he'd been holding in check for so long gushed down his face as he sank to the ground. A drunk tourist, Mardi gras beads swinging wildly, stumbled toward him, then veered away.

For her, Jackson had changed. Anger management classes, yoga, boxing, whatever it took. And it worked, for two years, until the night a mugger stepped out in front of Amy and Jackson, returning to their car from the gym where they first met, where he'd just proposed. The gun, pointed straight at Amy, exploding into her chest, blood splattering the ground and his shoes. The shoes Amy picked out.

Jackson and the mugger locked eyes. Even in his shock, he could see the mugger was just as surprised as he was. It didn't matter. When Jackson's rage subsided, the mugger lay in a bloody heap at his feet, Amy slumped on the ground behind him. He knelt beside her, brushing her hair back from her face, her dulling green eyes staring straight at him, wordlessly thanking him for getting the bastard who killed her. He didn't deserve her thanks. He'd let her down in the worst way possible. He walked away, Amy's dead face imprinted in his eyes, her blood and the blood of the man who killed her mingling together on his hands, his clothes, his shoes. He kept walking. How he ended up in the French Quarter was still a blur.

The body was wedged behind a dumpster just off Bourbon. The first officer who responded to the call sighed as he pulled out his radio. This one wasn't sleeping it off. Who knew how long the body had been there. The stench of urine mixed with the smells emanating from the bags of trash, exacerbated in the hot, humid air. Another drunken tourist doing his business behind a dumpster, most likely the victim of unfortunate timing by a garbage truck, he figured. When he rolled the dumpster away from the wall, the body fell on its back, eyes staring wide, mouth full of gold teeth, hanging open, a jagged white scar stark against a bruised and bloody dead face. The body was fully clothed except for one thing.

The shoes were missing.

SAINTS AND SINNERS

Don Bruns

John Crouton ran high-end poker games in New Orleans. John Crouton...Johnny Crumbs to those who loved him or hated him, ran low-end poker games in New Orleans. If you were a local, you were a regular, and if you were visiting, you had to ask for an invitation. And the stakes were very high or very low depending on what category game you played.

Sure, there was a major casino in The Big Easy. Caesars, down by the dirty Mississippi, where *gambling* was illegal, but *gaming* wasn't. The government allowed a twist of words to determine the legitimacy of the wagering. But Johnny C was definitely illegal. No license for gambling or gaming. He charged for entrance to the games and skimmed the winnings. Sometimes four or five games a night.

The backrooms of vacant storefronts, seedy offices of a bar or restaurant, Johnny C found the places and catered the snacks and booze. The hoodlum brought young girls into the mix and made some good money on that business, too. Human trafficking in The Big Easy was relatively simple. And very profitable. And there was always some blow.

The cops in New Orleans, hundreds short of their employment target number, had bigger problems to deal with. Drugs, battery, rape, robbery and murder. Johnny Crumbs was a small-time crook. Barely a ripple on the crime wave that plagued New

Orleans. Until he wasn't.

The man pocketed hundreds of thousands of dollars every year. Two years previously he bragged to a cohort he'd pocketed a profit of almost two million. The money was never reported, so there was no way of knowing what the poker king really earned, but he owned a two-story high-end home with a manicured lawn in the Garden District. He drove a two-year-old red Ferrari and always had some brassy blond in a tight blouse and short skirt on his arm. A short, squat man of fifty years, he did well with the ladies. The ones who were attracted to wealth and power.

And he frequented the classy restaurants. Arnaud's, Commander's Palace, Dicky Brennan's, and the private, exclusive Boston Club. What happened to Johnny Crouton shouldn't have happened to anyone. If the cops had done their job, he'd be in jail or prison, safe from a violent end. If the NOPD had the manpower, they would have stopped the criminal in his tracks. But they didn't. Didn't have the time or resources, even though everyone was keenly aware of his nefarious activities. Politicians, krewe kings, and bigshots in the NOPD all knew. Hell, often losing heavily, they were part of thc party, playing the games sometimes weekly. Even the mayor was rumored to be a semi-regular in the weekly games.

And then, he wasn't.

Johnny Crumbs didn't have a backup. It never occurred to him that at some moment in the future, he might not be running his infamous operations. Telling friends that yes, he had his hand in the game, he brazenly tattooed *Bullet Proof* on his left bicep. *Royal Flush* was tattooed on his right. And that was the way they identified his body. His drowned body.

Homicide detective Quentin Archer answered the call and found the body just as it had been discovered by a custodian at MO's Bar and Restaurant, in a broom closet in the rear office of the bistro, head submerged in a mop bucket of foamy water and his chubby naked torso, rear exposed, with the fingers on his right hand cut off. Apparently, the little man no longer had his hand in the gambling enterprise.

"We know who he is," Archer said to partner Frank Barber. "Problem is..."

"He had dozens of people who probably wanted him dead," Barber answered. "What makes it doubly difficult on a case like this is we should celebrate the fact someone finally took care of the problem."

Archer gave him a grim smile. "Equal justice, my friend."

"So much bullshit, Q."

"Have everything dusted for prints, including the bucket and that mop hanging from the wall." Archer nodded to the uniformed officer in the doorway. "We'll interview whoever cleaned up last night and Frank, can you talk to Mo and see if we can get the names of any noticeable customers in the bar at the time of death?"

"On it, Q."

They stepped away from the body.

"The chance of solving this is zilch. However, we need to make an effort. Agreed?"

Barber nodded. "Brass wants to see an effort, we'll go through the routine, Q."

A department photographer was busy snapping scenes as Archer walked back and stared at the obscene pose. A nude man, head in a frothy mop bucket, stretched out on the floor. Johnny Crumbs was a despicable character. He was a NOLA lowlife. There were a hundred of them. But nobody should end up like this. He motioned to the uniformed officer protecting the crime scene.

"Can you lift his head?"

The man looked left, looked right, and said, "Maybe you can do that, Detective. I'm not sure I can. I am certain I don't want to."

Archer reached down, grabbed the man's neck and pulled up the head and examined the deceased's red-veined eyes, open wide with a ghastly expression, his puffy face pasty in the bright light, but the necklace hanging from his neck impressed Archer the most. A silver St. Christopher medal. The character of an old man with a staff and a young kid holding onto his back. The words *St. Christopher Protect Us* ran around the outside of the silver disk.

Well, Chris didn't deliver, thought Archer. Or maybe he did. Maybe the kindly Saint was protecting others by signing off on Johnny Crumbs. Maybe. Archer grew up in a Detroit Catholic family, a cop family that had turned bad. A drug ring run by his two cop brothers had forced Q out of town, killed his wife, and alienated him from his home. And that was the reason he found New Orleans, with its own corrupt police force. And while Archer had never been that devout, he knew Saint Christopher's story. Risking his own life, Christopher had taken the unknown child, on his back, across a turbulent river, never questioning who the youngster was. The fable established the boy as the Christ child. And because Chris had taken him safely to the other shore, he had become the Patron Saint of Travelers. Immortality by saving a kid's life. Not just any kid.

Jesus Christ. Johnny Crumbs. The two JC's at least shared initials, and Archer hoped that was all there was to the coincidence. A simple culprit and victim would be nice. A killer and a body. Cut and dried. But in New Orleans, with its history bathed in the supernatural, its mystic vibes, its voodoo culture and spiritual influences, there never seemed to be a clear path to a solution.

Archer let go of the skin at the back of the man's neck and let his head splash back into the sudsy bucket. There was a lot of work to do in the next twenty-four hours. After one day, the leads dried up, the evidence got sketchy, and witnesses scattered like leaves on a crisp fall day.

"We've got ears to the ground?" Archer asked.

"Some," Barber answered. "You know, Q., as a department

we didn't have the time or manpower to worry about Crumbs. Nobody was complaining, no murders, so we concentrated on the more serious side of crime. Then the fucker ups-and-dies on us. In a rather grisly fashion."

"And now he becomes the serious side."

"And," Barber looked up from his desk, "what are the ears going to tell us, Q?" He sipped his coffee. "Big game gambling...it's a draw. Hardly worth our time pursuing it. Offering women to sweeten the pot, postpone the pain of losing. There are a lot of prostitutes in our city, Archer. Supposedly, the guy was a low-level drug dealer too, offering blow and grass mixed with fentanyl. Our guys should have gone after him on drugs, but he is, was, a minor player." Barber paused, keying in something on his computer.

"That said," Barber looked up from his computer, "*we* may not have been interested in this player, but there are hundreds of players who would have a vendetta...a beef with El Hefe."

"Who?"

"JC. Johnny Crumbs.

"Well, I hope they tell us who stands to pick up the slack. I think it makes sense that there's a strong possibility whoever knocked off Johnny would be interested in taking over the business. A lot of money to be made."

"Yeah. And it could just be someone who was tired of losing. Or a guy who got a bad sandwich at a game. Maybe a drug overdose or someone picked up a disease from one of his hookers. Could be lots of things, or a gambler that just didn't like Johnny Crouton."

Archer nodded. "Could be, but I think it goes deeper than that. This guy ran his game for what? Eleven years? Like an oiled machine. He didn't have a habit of pissing people off. He didn't even piss us off. We let him skate."

Barber shook his head. "We're short staffed, Q. We let a lot of people skate."

"Point made, but no, there's something else."

The two men worked their keyboards, filing individual reports. Half an hour later, Archer looked up and stretched his arms. On his third cup of strong black, he saw Barber taking a slug of his.

"Last game was apparently played a block from MO's."

"So?"

"Place on St. Peter Street, just north of the St. Louis Cathedral in Jackson Square. Used to be The Corner B&G. Bar and Grill. Closed down about six months ago. Now there's a padlock on the door."

"Except there wasn't that night. Right?" Barber cocked his head. "They played a game there? So, let's interview that neighborhood. Let's interview whoever owns the vacant building."

"Our perp may have been at the game. Probably was at the game. May have approached JC, and left him at MO's. So, let's see. Tomorrow, bright and early. Catch them before they're awake."

Archer woke up, an alarm inside his head. He'd never relied on an alarm clock. Tell yourself what time you want to wake up, concentrate on it, then go to sleep. The mind apparently had a timer...or *his* mind did. Six A.M.

Boxer shorts and T-shirt, he stumbled to the small kitchenette and pushed the button on his coffee maker. French Market coffee and chicory. His cottage, a former slave habitat, was at the end of the courtyard where the Cat's Meow was located, the Quarter's famous karaoke bar. Open till three in the morning. Archer used earplugs. Heavy duty earplugs. The off-key singing, the mindless country tunes that were repeated over and over, the crowds screaming...the sound became muffled, and he could usually drift off.

He opened the door, and looked out at the bleak city that hadn't quite gone to sleep and hadn't quite awakened. Gray weathering clouds on the horizon and the sweet, sickening smell of whatever they sprayed on the streets overnight to mask the garbage and vomit odors.

"Quentin, we need to talk."

The detective stepped back and started to pull the door closed. The young black lady in the courtyard pushed back with her hand.

"Quentin."

"It's six in the morning. At least let me get dressed."

Archer scurried to the bedroom and pulled on a pair of jeans.

"What the..."

"You look different. No tie."

A homicide detective rule Archer didn't understand. Always wear a tie. Apparently, you didn't want the murderers to see you as too casual.

"You've got a problem. I have some thoughts."

She stood there, an orange and black scarf wrapped around her hair. Solange Cordray, the attractive voodoo practitioner that had helped solve several of his cases. She was somewhat skeptical of the police, he was skeptical of voodoo, but in the few cases when he'd used her help, things had worked out. Criminals had been brought to justice, and truth be told, in those cases, they would have remained unsolved without her voodoo influence.

"Quentin," she stood in the doorframe, "you are working a case involving the death of a gambler, drug dealer, and sex trafficker. And I am sensing that you are not quite sure how this all fits together."

Two cloth chairs in his small vestibule. He motioned to her to sit on one.

"This just happened. How the hell do you even...never mind. You and I have been involved in enough cases that I shouldn't be surprised. You totally confuse me."

She nodded. "Quentin, the answers in my life confuse me as well. But I woke up last night and had a vision. I have a friend, someone who works at the St. Louis Cathedral in Jackson Square. Janitorial division. His name is Pascal. Pascal Jean-Pierre There's a lot of spit and polish going on in that place. They're on it full time."

"I can imagine."

"Lots of wood, lots of marble. Pascal and I, we talk. A native Haitian, he's a very devout man and strange as it seems to some people, the voodoo and Catholic faiths have a lot in common. Our gods and your saints, one supreme being...in fact, many Haitians practice both voodoo and Roman Catholicism." She paused. "Pascal also believes in the voodoo religion, so he and I have a very strong connection. A lot to talk about. He's used my services in the past."

"Keeping the option open?" Archer took a sip of his coffee. "Solange, what was the dream? The vision? I've got a dead body, and maybe hundreds of people who may have had a reason to kill the guy. Possible prostitution, sex trafficking, drugs and gambling. I've got a lot to sort out."

"Pascal was in my dream."

"The custodian?"

"Sometimes living people come to me. I felt that he represented the church, the spirit of Catholic saints. It wasn't anything specific, but there was a sense. A sense about your murder victim."

"Solange..."

"The deceased," she stood and walked to the door, "John Crouton, in his own way was a religious man. Possibly, probably for his own gain. Maybe praying for more wealth, more power or possibly salvation."

"And?"

She turned to him.

"I called Pacal. Late last night. I would never have bothered him that late, but he was part of my dream, vision. I simply asked if he knew the deceased."

"And your janitor friend was aware of the..."

"No, but when I told him about my dream, he initially was hesitant. He questioned my knowledge. He was somewhat apprehensive. When I told him that I was moved by a dream, he finally admitted he had a passing knowledge of John Crouton. Apparently played cards at some of the man's games."

Archer sipped his coffee, his eyes a little more alert.

"This guy, Pascal? He actually knew Johnny Crumbs?"

"Quentin, was the victim wearing a medal? A coin? Maybe the protection of a saint?"

He hesitated. "Pascal told you this?"

"No. He'd seen him. Never met him. I sense this. The medal."

"You are amazing. Truly amazing."

"Yes, no?"

"St. Christopher. A St. Christopher medal. Around his neck." Archer shook his head. The young lady always surprised him with her insight, with her vision.

"The patron saint of travelers? The saints are watching, Quentin. The voodoo gods are paying attention. There's something very sinister that has happened, and it directly involves the two faiths. That's all I have at the moment."

"If you are right, it's more than I had ten minutes ago."

"Bring me the medal," she said. "Even inanimate objects have energy."

"It might be wrapped up as evidence and…"

"Bring me the medal, Detective. Please. Let me hold it. It's part of the process."

She turned the handle, opened the door, exposing the courtyard and the pink glow of the French Quarter sunrise, and then she was gone.

Archer took a sip from his mug. The brew was cold and tasteless, and he tossed it in the sink and went back for a quick shower.

***

Barber and a team were bright and early, knocking on doors, asking questions and getting nowhere. Archer palmed the medal in a plastic baggie. If you knew someone in the evidence room, things were possible. An early seventy-eight-degree temperature and low humidity encouraged a morning hike, and he walked into her shop at nine a.m., surprised she was open that early. Her collection of voodoo dolls, candles, incense, and spiritual books surrounded him. The fragrant air smelled of olive oil and cherries, lemons and California oranges.

Appearing from the backroom, she smiled. Her wraparound cotton dress was patterned with streaks of sky blue and sunlight yellow. She wore it well.

"Detective. You brought the Saint Christopher medal."

"Very perceptive."

She smiled. "I may, I may not, sense the energy, but this is the medal the man wore when he was drowned?"

"It was on his neck when we found him."

"His body is..."

"With the coroner's office."

"You stole the necklace this morning? After we talked?"

"It's only the medallion, and what I did is confidential information, Ms. Cordray."

"I feel good about this, Quentin. Give me the medal."

Archer handed her the clear plastic bag, and she opened it, pouring the silver disc onto a small wooden table.

"Please, sit." She gestured to a gray, worn, cloth bench, and the detective sat down, watching as she studied the silver coin.

"There is energy in inanimate objects, Quentin. And if the object, this St. Christopher medal, was intimately involved with the subject as you say it was, then St. Christopher may have captured some of the victim's energy as well. It happens. Eventually, we are all a part of the universe, and good or bad, evil or upright, we leave a mark."

"I'm not sure I believe or understand your philosophy, but..."

Solange Cordray held up her hand and stopped him.

"In many cases, even I don't understand. But hear me out. I believe that in the smallest, most intimate ways, every action has an effect. Everything that happens has an impact, Quentin. A pedestrian steps on a cricket, and the carcass washed away by street sweepers. One less piece of food for the white ibises. And that bird has to find another meal. Every action, even unintended actions, cause consequences. And every consequence changes the dynamic of the universe." She paused. "We are not aware, but everything you do, everything I do, changes history. It's a hard concept to understand."

Archer shook his head.

"Seriously? A cricket? All I want is information on our killer." He stood. "Solange, I won't, I don't pretend to comprehend what you believe. But if you feel that this piece of metal, this charm bracelet trinket..."

And as they both focused on the silver medallion, for a moment it seemed to glow. A flash of yellow. Archer would swear later that his eyes had misted, maybe an allergy, maybe dust in the air, but the pendant had a brief golden hue. With a burst of color, a fraction of a second, it glowed yellow, then was simply a silver disc lying on the wooden table.

Solange picked it up.

"Warm, Quentin. Almost hot. You saw the glow?"

"I don't know what I saw. Maybe a..."

"You, detective, are a moving target. The more you learn about this case, the more dangerous it becomes."

Archer threw his hands up.

"I know nothing. How am I a target?"

"I only know how to deal the cards, Quentin. I don't always know what your hand will be."

"I'm a target? Because I'm working this case?"

"You are Catholic. You have St. Christopher, a saint who appears to be an old man with a cane. Your travel saint. We have our supreme god, Papa Legba. An old man with a staff.

The spiritual guide of voodoo."

"And?"

"Be careful, my friend. They are both concerned about you."

"We need to talk to Pascal, your connection in the church."

"He's coming in. He has information and will meet you at French Truck Café on Magazine. At ten this morning."

"How the hell do you..."

"Detective, I'm trying to help." She stared into his eyes. "He's not happy about the meeting. Very nervous, very suspicious."

"Why?"

"That's up to you to find out."

Archer shook his head, turned and walked from the dark shop into the early morning sunrise. The gold-fringed clouds reminded him of what had appeared in Solange's store. A glow of yellow from the St. Christopher medal. The vision had to be his imagination. Inanimate objects were exactly that. Inanimate.

He saw the bald man at an outside table, a steaming cup of coffee already in front of him.

"Pascal?"

"Detective Archer?" The slender Black man cocked his head.

"Thank you for coming."

"I'm not in trouble, correct?"

"Not that I'm aware of," Archer pulled up a chair.

"My spiritual advisor said I must meet with you. I don't want to prolong this meeting. I gambled. I played. Some of the smaller games. I mean, I kind of knew that it wasn't on the up-and-up, but..."

"You're not in trouble. Trust me."

"Well, that's a relief."

"Solange Cordray suggested that I—"

"Yeah, yeah. Listen, Detective Archer, I have to be kept off the record here. I need your word."

"You've got it."

"I wouldn't be here..." he hesitated, running a hand over his head, "she saw me in a dream."

"She told me."

"In a dream, Detective. I don't want to be here, okay? There are things...I'm not comfortable with. But my spiritual advisor told me to be here."

"Pascal, as far as I know, the information I have, you are not in trouble."

The man seemed to shudder.

"Crumbs ran a low rent game."

"And a high rent game."

"That one is above my pay grade. So, I'm in these games with some dirt-poor players. Ten bucks here, maybe twenty tops." He shrugged his shoulders. "People who can't afford to lose even that amount."

"And you?"

"Oh, hell yes. I've lost the grocery money a number of times."

"And the high-end players?"

He sipped his coffee, swirling the beverage in his mouth.

"MO's is five hundred, a thou. I heard some games have no limits, but again, I can't sit at that table, so I don't know."

"What about drugs? Prostitution?"

"I never saw it. Honest to God, Detective. I heard that he was running some of that in the high-end games. Young girls, some blow, but believe me, I was only there for the sport."

"So, why am I talking to you?"

A frizzy-haired girl with green, red and yellow tats from her wrists to her shoulders walked up, looking down at Archer.

"What'll you have, hon?"

"Chicory coffee, black."

"Coming right up."

"You have no information about the high-end stakes? The game that Crumbs probably attended last night?"

"I don't float in those circles, Detective. However, I told Solange this, and I want you to promise me you will never reveal the source."

Cops had to lie. To solve a crime, to coerce a witness, to obtain evidence. No worse than any person in any walk of life. You had to fudge on the truth once in a while.

"I promise," Archer said.

The black custodian folded his hands on the table and closed his eyes.

"Detective, I don't talk much. But I listen. In my job, I hear things that I'm not supposed to hear. Understand?"

"No."

"People say things around a Black janitor. They're nice folks, but I mean, what the hell does a dumb Black custodian care about the business of this church? So, they can talk, share information right in front of me, not worried at all that I might figure some things out."

"And you do care—"

"I care because it's my job, my profession. And I love my church."

"And what did you hear?"

"I'm not comfortable telling this. But every week, there's a donation in the range of ten to fifteen thousand dollars. From the same anonymous source."

"Substantial."

"Half a million a year. Always in a brown manilla envelope. Usually slipped under the rector's office door. Been goin' on for several years."

The waitress set the cup in front of Archer.

"Anything else, hon?"

Archer looked up and shook his head. He watched a green and yellow snake slithering up her arm.

"So, it's a donation from John Crouton."

"Seems to be the consensus." Jean-Pierre ran his hands over his smooth head then folded them again on the table. "People have seen him, middle of the week, sitting in a pew, walking around the building."

"So, he's buying salvation, paying for his sins. I imagine the church is grateful. It's a nice chunk of change."

"No law against it. Just a man supporting his church. Quietly. I understand, Detective."

"So now," Archer sipped his coffee, "now that he's gone, the cash flow stops."

Pacal nodded. "You see, Detective, the cash flow stopped about two months ago."

"So, Crumbs had a falling out with the church? Maybe the games weren't paying out like they had been?"

"Here's the rub," the custodian said. "I listen, Detective. And people say that Johnny was still showing up, still sitting in a pew, walking through the church, still lighting candles." He nodded. "Hell, I've seen him there."

"Just not dropping off the money?"

"It seems to some that he *was* dropping off the money. It's just that the money wasn't being collected by the church."

He met Barber for lunch at Alberto's on St. Peter. They ordered sandwiches at the busy counter, the menu scrawled on a blackboard and the smokey smell of grilled beef and chicken in the air.

"Got some background, Q, but nothing substantial. People say that there's a regular game at the boarded-up grill, and they have recognized some of the people who are seen walking in and out."

"Like?"

"I mean, hearsay, like a prominent councilman, a TV weather guy, even some actor who was filming a movie here a couple weeks ago. Local celebs."

"And you talked to Mo?"

"He's in early this morning. Didn't work last night. He's

going to bring in the evening crew to see if they noticed anything, but I get the impression we won't get much."

"And I have no idea what I got this morning." Archer moved his coffee as the waitress put the grilled turkey sub in front of him.

"And the roast beef for you," the young lady placed Barber's plate on the table.

Barber took a deep breath, smelling his meal.

"They make a good sandwich."

"Frank, I met with Solange Cordray this morning."

Barber nodded.

"I know, I know. Everyone is skeptical. However, we've solved cases with her insight."

Barber nodded, chewing a bite of sandwich.

"She introduced me to someone from the church who claims that Crouton was a major donor."

"Paying back some of his ill-gotten gains," Barber wiped his mouth with a paper napkin.

"Only now it appears that someone is stealing the money he donates. Johnny was bringing cash in a manilla envelope during the week and sticking it under the rector's door. This guy says in the last month, the money has been coming up missing."

"And what, pray tell, does the church have to do with the death of Crumbs?"

"Johnny was giving a sizable donation to the church. All of a sudden, the money is gone. I don't know."

"So, you've got squat."

"So far, yes, but I think that the church thing might lead to something bigger."

"In the meantime, Quentin, I'm visiting thirteen hundred Perdido Street."

"City Hall?"

"Councilman Tom Hill is there this afternoon. Seems he has been known to visit the game on a regular basis. Maybe the night of the murder."

"Good luck."

"We'll start with some questions, offer him immunity, and if he won't give us names, activities, we'll threaten him."

"With?"

"The drug thing could be a big deal. But if we can suggest he might be involved in underage prostitution..."

"And you've got nothing."

"So far, yes. But he doesn't know that."

"Touché. Get what you can, Frank. The faster we can get this covered, the better."

And there she was. Outside the restaurant in her wraparound blue and gold-streaked dress.

"My French Quarter stalker," he said.

She smiled, her perfect white teeth contrasting with the attractive dark face.

"I'm returning your medal, Detective."

"So, no energy? No information?" Disappointment.

"Quite the contrary. I received some strong energy. I prayed on it."

"And?"

"I believe the Christopher medal was a gift to the victim. Someone gave the medal to John Crouton, possibly to ward off evil, to protect him, to lead him to righteousness. If we find the giver, it could be a break."

"But you have no idea who the giver might be?"

She brushed back her coal-black hair and shook her head.

"Quentin, would it be that there were definitive answers in any religion. The gods, the saints, they give direction. They send signs, but often those directions and signs cause even more questions."

Archer nodded. "I get it. Investigating a murder is pretty much the same. Witnesses, leg work, pure luck can give us direction, but there are always more and more questions."

"And I know you well enough to know what your question is. Over and over. Why?"

"Why is the gift giver important to this case?"

"I don't know. I lit a candle, made an offering of...it's not important what I offered, but I feel strongly that Pascal Jean-Pierre has answers. He may not know he has answers, but I believe he does. That's all I can tell you."

"He's your friend. You're his spiritual adviser. I think you would be better—"

"Quentin," she grabbed his hand and squeezed it, "you know better than anyone. It's not always about spirits and saints. It's not always about prayers and supplications or offerings." She stared into his eyes. "Oftentimes, it's just a human connection. Talk to him. Talk to him."

Her intense stare scared him.

"And ask why. Ask why." She turned and walked away.

The domed cathedral was awe-inspiring indeed. Above the gilded altar was a huge, colorful mural of Louis IX, Saint Louis, surrounded by men, women, children and a legion of soldiers underlined with some Latin script, something about Louis and the crusade. He knew some of the history, but realized he should have done a little more background on this magnificent church.

Five people sat quietly scattered in the polished wooden pews, three were over by the candles and the offering box, but there was no sign of Pascal. Prayer, candles, offerings. Solange Cordray had mentioned all three.

Archer walked out into the mezzanine and into a hall leading to rooms on either side. He saw the man down the corridor, mop in hand, next to a metal bucket on wheels.

"Pascal."

The custodian turned, staring down the hallway.

"Detective Archer? I told you what I know. Please sir," he

set the mop against the wall, "I'm working. We can talk later."

Archer slowly walked down the hall and Jean-Pierre backed up.

"Pascal, did you know that John Crouton wore a St. Christopher medal?"

"I saw the man here. I saw him once or twice at a game, but I did not pay attention to his jewelry. Please, Detective, I've got a job here."

"There's something you're not telling me."

"I told you." He glanced behind him, then in a whispering voice, "I told you there was money possibly missing. I know nothing more."

"You saw Johnny Crouton here, in your church."

"I did. Several times. I told—"

"Did he have a manilla envelope? The one you said contained cash?"

"Not that I recall."

"You lost money at his card games, am I right?"

"I told you that in confidence, Detective Archer." He ran a hand over his smooth scalp. "I didn't steal any money. I'm an honest man."

Archer persisted. There was something else. He could feel it.

"Was the man alone? Did he ever come in with anyone else?"

"I don't know, sir. When I saw him, he was..."

"Was what?"

"Mostly by himself."

"Mostly?"

"I shouldn't even mention this. It's nothing. But once or twice I saw him talking to Deacon Elroy. They'd spend some time together. The Deacon was the only one I ever—"

"Elroy?"

"Church deacon."

"A deacon is..."

"Someone who volunteers in the church. Not just a volunteer, I mean a volunteer pastor who can perform some of the sacraments—like wakes, funeral services, witness marriages, even do baptism."

Archer knew the role of a deacon. He'd been exposed to it in his church in Detroit, but his memory was a little rusty.

"You know this Elroy?"

Pascal turned his head, squinting his eyes. He paused, then turned to Archer.

"I don't. I mean, he says hi to me, nice enough. Used to own a car dealership upstate, I believe. Retired."

"He was friendly with the victim?"

"Detective, I don't know. They talked. I saw them laughing one time, like a joke they shared. I shouldn't have said anything."

"You paid attention to Johnny. You recognized him when he would enter this building. Do you know every local who walks into the church?"

"For Christ's sake, Detective. I lost money to the man. He was a part of my life, and not in a positive way. Of course, I paid attention."

"I've got to ask, Pascal, did you have a reason to want Johnny Crouton dead?"

"What? Seriously?"

The man grabbed the mop propped up against the wall. He held it in front of him, like a cross to ward off a vampire. "I don't believe what I'm hearing. I gave you all the information I had and—"

"Pascal, I had to ask."

"Did I like him? No. But I had no reason to kill him. The gambling problem is mine. I take responsibility for my addiction."

"Is Deacon Elroy here now?"

"I don't know." The man dropped the mop and threw up his hands. Obviously frustrated, he said, "Damn, you got to let me get back to work."

***

Archer answered his cell.

"Hey, Frank. What's the story?"

"Your church story may be something. Councilman Tom Hill is a little shook up that we've identified him as a player."

"He gave you names?"

"A couple. He recognized a fire chief, a reporter from a television station, but nothing that really jumped out."

"Yet the church story caught your attention?"

"That night, Hill sat next to a custodian from the cathedral. This guy apparently played the last game and lost a lot more than he could afford to."

Archer was silent.

"Quentin?"

"The son-of-a-bitch played me, Frank. That custodian is my source from the church. Said he never played the high-end game."

"Hill swears this guy was there. Black, bald..."

"That's him."

"Hill said there's an unspoken code among the players. What happens at the game doesn't leave the room. They even collect cell phones at the door. Word gets back that you snitched, you are permanently banned. Besides, no one wants to be accused of playing the game or participating in the extracurricular activities."

"So, Hill met this custodian, and because you pressured the councilman, he is willing to give up names."

"No, no. It's not like it's a social where everyone wears a nametag. He knew who they were because of his position. He recognized the fire chief, the television reporter, and several others because he dealt with them in his business. But it's a rule at the game. Absolutely no names are supposed to be used."

"So, how do you know about the custodian?"

"Hill says a deacon he recognized from the cathedral told

him who he was."

"A deacon?"

"Hill sees him at the cathedral. Guy has been a pastor for maybe three, four years."

"Name?"

"As I said, they don't call each other by their names. Secrecy and privacy seem to be the way these games were played. But Councilman Hill, he knew this guy. I was intrigued because you said the church might be linked to—"

"What's the name, Frank?"

"It doesn't necessarily mean anything, Q. I go to mass and see him a couple of times a month. Seems to be a very devout guy. But, he apparently plays on the edges. Elroy. Deacon Jameson Elroy."

Archer assumed the hours of employment at the church were from nine to five. Since it was three in the afternoon, the custodian should still be working. And as he walked into the magnificent cathedral, he again stood in awe of the architecture. The domed ceiling with the brightly painted murals and the hallowed chapel where Pope John Paul prayed in front of the statue of Our Lady of Prompt Succor, patroness of New Orleans. He didn't know a lot about the church, but what he'd heard was impressive. The history, the religious significance, the oldest Catholic cathedral community in America. In a fleeting moment, he thought about visiting a mass. Just to see if anything kicked in. Probably wasn't going to happen.

Archer checked the halls, but there was no sign of Pascal. His footsteps echoed down the empty hallway and as he walked, he heard voices, raised voices in a room down the corridor. He stepped up his pace.

The voices were loud, like two people arguing, now screaming at each other.

Two rooms down, the door was partially open.

"Yes, I knew what you did. I saw you. That didn't mean I was going to tell anyone about..."

Archer paused. It was Pascal's voice. Then another voice shouted back.

"You saw what you weren't supposed to see. I took your accusation as a threat, and I paid you back, asshole. I got you into the big league. I fronted you so you could play high stakes and win back your losses. But you told Johnny."

"I didn't threaten you. I simply told you I saw you take the envelope. And I didn't tell Johnny. I swear I never mentioned it. I don't really even know the guy."

"He accused me. Somehow, he knew, and he said he was going to expose what I've done."

Pascal again. "You stole his donation. I watched you. What? Twenty-five thousand? You had the key to the rector's office. But I didn't tell him. Didn't mention a word to Johnny. I think he figured it out for himself."

"Well," there was a long pause, "he's not going public with that anymore, is he? Now there's only one person who knows what happened."

"Jameson, honest to God, you don't want to do this. They'll tie you to Johnny, to me..."

"I fell a little short, that's all. Didn't have to come to this. He knew a little too much, you know a little too much."

"It didn't have to come to *this*?" Pascal's voice. "You robbed Peter to pay Paul, and you didn't think Johnny would find out?"

"It ends with you. No one else knows."

"I know." Archer stood in the doorway, Glock drawn. Shit. The Deacon had a gun in his hand as well. "Drop the weapon," Archer said. "Now."

Elroy didn't miss a beat. He spun around and fired. One shot, then another, the explosions ricocheting off the walls. Archer felt a bullet rip through him, the searing pain as he lost control and the gun fell from his grasp. Heaving a hoarse rasp, he crumpled to the ground.

"You just shot a cop. Jesus Christ, Deacon, do you know you just shot a—"

"And now I'm going to shut you up, too."

"For an envelope full of cash?"

"It doesn't matter why," Elroy said. "There may have been some other transgressions that I'm not proud of, but it's no concern of yours. On the ground, now. Head by your bucket. Close your eyes. You are about to be baptized."

Pascal laid on the cold marble floor beside the mop bucket, staring up at the man.

"You actually equate baptism to what you did with Johnny?"

"I tried to save him." The gun was pointed at the custodian's head. Directly at his head.

"From what?"

"From the hell he had created. I gave him the Saint Christopher medal to guide him. He was leading a lot of people into an evil life of sin and degradation."

"Like you."

"Like *you*. We are all weak, Pascal. The disciple Peter denied Christ three times, yet he was one of the most devout Christians in history."

"You are comparing yourself to Saint Peter? You really are crazy. You gambled, you lost a lot of money, and what? You bought the women, you bought the drugs? Is that it? Your reputation was about to be destroyed? Tell me. How bad was it that you had to kill Johnny?"

"The devil lives in all of us, my friend. But no longer in you."

The blast shattered the stillness. The deacon's eyes were wide with surprise as he took one step, stumbled and fell headfirst into the mop bucket of soapy water.

"Fitting," Archer muttered, as he released the Glock and passed out.

***

"Quentin. Q. Paramedics are on their way."

Archer blinked, seeing a blurry Frank Barber.

"Shot to the shoulder and the second shot apparently missed altogether. You're going to be okay, buddy."

"What are you doing here?"

"I knew you were going to talk to the janitor, and I thought…"

"What about the deacon?"

"Shot to the heart. According to Pascal, you're lethal, even in an injured prone position." He kneeled and put his hand on Archer's wounded shoulder. "You saved his life, man. Saved his life."

He woke at five a.m. Had nowhere to go, nowhere to be. A little rest and relaxation while he recuperated. He'd done some reading, some research on the internet and was bored out of his mind. Still two or three weeks before he was cleared for duty.

Archer made the coffee, pretty much one-handed, and set it on a table by the entrance. He opened the door to the courtyard that had been filled with music and bad singing just hours ago.

"Quentin. I just happened to be passing by," she smiled.

"You are never 'just passing by.'"

"Still taped up, arm in a shoulder sling."

"It comes off next week," he said. "And if I didn't say it on the phone the other day, 'thank you.'"

"I am thankful. I sent you on a mission that could have gotten you killed. You solved the murder and survived."

"You saw things, you had premonitions, you are an amazing woman."

"You put it together, and one more sinner is off the street. The gods and saints were with us, Quentin."

"Come in. Have some coffee. I've got loads of free time."

She shook her head. "Heal yourself, Detective. Physically and spiritually. You've thought about going to mass at the cathedral."

"How do you..."

"Go." She stepped off the stoop. "Say thanks for the saints that saved you. Saint Christopher, who led you to the deacon. And say thanks to the voodoo spirits who interacted as well."

Archer turned and picked up his coffee cup from the table. When he looked back at the doorway, she was gone.

GREEN-EYED MONSTER

Reed Farrel Coleman

Deacon Brand didn't get into "the business" to do this tripe, but who does? Every aspiring stage actor dreams of doing Hamlet on Broadway or the West End. Dreams of putting their unique spin on *Alas poor Yorick or To be or not to be...*For Deacon it was not to be. Never to be. Never ever, especially after landing the gig as host of the Travel Log Channel's *Informal Paranormal: Freaks, Phantoms, and the Fantastic.*

It hadn't been a direct plummet into the abyss of reality TV. *Reality TV, indeed!* What a load of horse manure. Now there was a subject Deacon Brand knew about, chapter and verse. Deacon had grown up working on farms in and around Louisville, Kentucky. Working being the operative euphemism for mucking stalls. But shoveling all that shit did two things for Deacon. It sculpted his body into a form worthy of museum display, and it prepared him for the crap he would have to wade through to finally "make it" in the business. On days like this, days when mucking those stalls seemed like good, honest work, he remembered the nauseating stench of sweat-lathered horses and of their foulness on his boots.

"What is it, Deacon?" she asked, sitting up in bed, pressing her bare breast against him. "Last night was amazing."

If she was expecting him to echo her sentiment, she was in for disappointment.

She was Melody Delhomme, his new production assistant and most recent conquest. Or as Pete Carney, the show's sound engineer, referred to the people Deacon bedded, his most recent distraction. Distractions weren't ever the issue for Deacon who, once he'd moved to New York, traded in his shit shoveling exercise routine for two-hour daily sessions at the gym. But it wasn't so much his V-shape and cut muscles as his gold-flecked green eyes, flowing auburn hair, and angular jawline that made people swoon. Everyone from stagehands to dressers to lead dancers—male and female—hit on Deacon and, depending on how much he'd had to drink, their hits often landed.

As his first agent at CAA told him, "You got the looks, kid, a voice like an angel and that big head of yours is perfect for the screen."

His then agent was referring to the physical size of Deacon's head in proportion to the rest of his body, but he might as well have been referring to his client's ego. An ego that grew in inverse proportion to his career arc. *Arc!* It wasn't so much an arc as a flat line with the occasional upward blip.

"What is it, Deacon?" Melody repeated, reaching her hand down to take hold of him. "Let me make it better, whatever it is."

When she bent over to replace her hand with her mouth, he pushed her away, almost knocking her off the bed.

"Go shower," he said. "I'm still sore from the grooves your teeth left on me last night. You need to have someone teach you how to do that right."

Melody wrapped the blanket around her and ran into the bathroom to hide her tears.

Deacon could be cruel, *was* cruel. Many people grow up in tough circumstances, people who battle just to keep their heads above water, yet somehow manage to bring light into the world. Not so for Deacon. He was a light swallower, a dark vacuum following in his wake. He felt he was owed. It wasn't clear by whom he was owed or what he was owed exactly. He knew in his marrow he was owed by God, the universe, and by just about anyone who had the misfortune to cross his path. And Melody, she definitely owed him, particularly after sleeping with her. For his legion of faults, though, he wasn't stupid. He realized he'd better make nice with Melody. Not out of guilt, not out of #Metoo fears, and certainly not out of kindness, but out of necessity. For as much as he loathed to admit it, he needed her, at least until this episode was shot. So, he got out of bed, shook the tension out of his body, did his deep breathing, and trailed after her.

On his way, he laughed to himself about the absurdity of his plight. How he had gone from shit-shoveler to a rising star to almost was to has been to hosting the most unreal show in all the realm of reality TV. Even a high school dropout from Louisville, Kentucky got the irony involved in calling a show about every cockamamie woowoo claim reality TV. In three seasons, they had done two episodes about vampires, one on death cults, one on devil worship, two on alien abductions—one in New Mexico, of course, and one in Maine—three on bigfoot, six on various ghosts, one on sin eaters, one on gargoyles, two on goblins, two on possession and exorcism, several on serpents and dinosaurs continuing to roam the planet, and seven on his least favorite topic, humanoid animals. Oh, how he hated those episodes. Why? Because you had to be a moron to buy the copy he was forced to read, and by his own estimation, he was no moron.

He could hear his breathless, dramatic voiceover describing his always close encounters with these creatures. It was a mystery, but somehow Deacon and his crew never actually had the chance to directly confront the targets of their episodes. Always glimpses, blurry photos, pixelating images, distorted night vision footage, shadows, silhouettes...Always rustling in the woods, weird noises, screams and screeches, howls and roars. Some of the humanoid animals like the Man-Wolf of Manitoba were said to simply be genetic mutations, others, like the Rhino-Man in Lesotho, were alleged to be the result of nefarious experimentation—think The Island of Dr. Moreau—by twisted individuals or amoral government agencies looking to create a more perfect soldier.

Do you hear that mournful wail? That's neither wolf nor man, but the tortured baying of the Man-Wolf of Manitoba. Here are some images we captured on the cameras we mounted on trees in Riding Mountain National Park. See how, unlike a wolf, the creature's hind legs are much longer than its forelimbs. That is a feature of human beings...

The thing about it was, it was all as much horse shit as the stuff he shoveled back in Louisville. To give Deacon plausible deniability, he was never officially let in on the setup. *As if he were clueless!* Even before Pete Carney confessed in a drunken stupor at a Bangor, Maine bar, Deacon knew that the blurred images of Bigfoot used in all three episodes were from a staged photo shoot featuring a former NBA benchwarmer dressed in a Chewbacca costume. That the ghostly images were sometimes as simple as flash powder or, if the budget allowed, CGI generated. And it seemed every production assistant he'd bedded couldn't wait to spill their guts about how they were going to pull off this week's scam. They always whispered it to him as if they were revealing the nuclear codes.

As an inside joke with Deacon and a middle finger to the show's producer, Pete Carney would use Deacon's voice in post-production, distorting and filtering it to create the requisite sound effects for that week's episode. To date, Deacon's voice had been used to create the squeal of a bat, the roar of a T-Rex, the screams of a ghost trapped in a castle dungeon, and Pete's personal favorite, the baying of the man-wolf.

He rapped on the bathroom door. "Melody, I'm sorry. Sometimes I just say cruel things because I get tense and, well...I'm more insecure than you think. If you let me in, I'll let you do whatever you'd like or let me do to you whatever you'd like. Last night, you mentioned wanting to try something in the shower you always wanted to try."

"You promise? *Anything?*" her voice crackled with excitement.

"Anything."

Deacon heard the shower turn on and he knew he had her.

Still a little giddy and sore from their early morning session in the shower, Melody could barely contain her excitement when they got off the airboat. Deacon could barely contain himself from vomiting up his lunch. He had no love of seafood, and that crawfish boil was about as appetizing to him as eyeballs floating in pig's piss soup. He could not help but think of crawfish—which weren't fish at all—as insects on steroids. It was bad enough that he had to choke down the grilled alligator medallions in comeback sauce as a starter. Fighting back the urge to puke his guts out, he thought, comeback sauce a very appropriate appellation.

Never mind the food, there wasn't anything he'd ever experienced that kicked his motion sickness into gear like the twenty-minute airboat ride. Even with the earplugs to deaden the din of the huge pushing propeller, his hearing was screwed and his legs rubbery. The final straw was the earthy stink of decay in the bayou. All the oppressive moisture and heat worked on dead and dying things like a kind of slow-motion acid. On the other hand, it helped things like moss and fungus and mosquitos thrive. Twenty seconds after stepping off the flat-bottomed, aluminum boat, his feet sinking into the wet, muddy ground, Deacon dropped to his knees and de-lunched himself.

The reason he had subjected himself to it all, to Melody's voracious sexual appetite and unskilled technique, to the rancid food he had just given back to the bayou, and the stomach-turning boat ride was the chance to finally have a real encounter with the subject of an episode, not one of his crew or a hired hand dressed up in an olio of old monster costumes. No more near misses for Deacon Brand. It was so important to him to find something genuinely unique in the world instead of the phoniness of reality TV, that he had done this trip with Melody on the sly, footing the expenses himself.

He'd done it because he had heard the rumors. He was about to get the axe; the show's producers having grown weary of his unending complaints and his obvious lack of enthusiasm for the job. What the producers didn't know was that getting fired suited Deacon just fine. He had been offered the role of Macbeth in a new film version of Shakespeare's Scottish play and it would have been impossible to continue with the show and do the movie. This secret mission was meant to be a final "Fuck you!" to the producers. Deacon's way of saying, "I'm going to do what you never managed to do with your phony bullshit. I'm going to give you the real deal."

The idea had been unknowingly dropped in his lap by Melody at her welcome to the crew dinner in LA. This was before Deacon had sampled her wares and was in seduction mode. Melody was certainly attractive enough with her dark complexion, long dark brown hair, and blue eyes. She was a little curvier and bigger breasted than was his preference, but there was something mysterious about her. There was a look in her eyes that was beyond desire, beyond hunger. It was almost feral, and then there was her scent. Her perfume was something he had never smelled before. He couldn't have described it other than to say hers was herbaceous and sweet all at once. They had bumped into one another outside the restrooms and lingered, Deacon turning on his charm.

"If you keep staring at me like that, Mr. Brand—"

"Deacon, please."

"If you keep staring at me like that, Deacon, I may not be able to keep my secret."

After some prompting, a deep kiss, and her breathless shuddering, she told him about Gator Boy, the Green-eyed Monster of Plaquemines Parish. He swore her to secrecy on the spot.

That was two weeks ago during pre-production meetings for season four. He had kept her at arm's length, putting off sleeping with her as an inducement to keep her secret and to travel with him during their week off before filming began.

"This is going to be just between us, Melody. I'm going to trust you to do the filming and sound. Do you think you can handle it?"

"Of course. I went to USC for just these things."

"Great. It'll be quite a feather in your cap if we pull this off."

Somehow, standing there on shaky legs, his breath stinking of vomit, his shoes and pants muddied and wet, none of it seemed worth it. All he wanted was to get back to the Hotel Monteleone, brush his teeth, shower, and then drink himself blind at the famous carousel bar. What Deacon didn't need to add to his misery was Melody's cousin Jean Paul, whose airboat they'd just come in on, busting his chops. At least he promised to carry the video equipment.

"Oh, wha's a matter der, *monsieur*? When we Cajuns say *laissez les bontemps rouler*, we don't mean coughin' up your *dejeuner*." Jean Paul, a big doughy man of forty, wacked Deacon on the shoulder, laughed, turned to Melody. "Hey little cousin, talk about your boss here. He pretty and all like Adonis, he cut out for de bayou? Whatchu t'ink?"

Melody looked away, not wanting Deacon to see her smile. Then, in an accent that shocked Deacon, Melody said, "*Allez, allez*, Jean Paul. We go to Reine Marie's."

Deacon shook his head. "You're just full of surprises, Melody."

She shrugged her shoulders. "You scrubbed the Kentucky out of your voice. I can hide the Cajun when I need to. And don't worry about your stomach," she said in her LA voice. "Reine Marie will have an herbal tea to soothe it."

After a few minutes walking, Deacon said, "You're not the first Cajun woman I've met, you know?"

Melody stopped in her tracks to face him. "Are you kidding me, Deacon?"

He raised his right hand. "I swear. Most beautiful woman I ever met, Odile Belladonna. I think she came from someplace west of here, Avery Island."

Jean Paul turned, smiled. "Sure t'ing, that over by New Iberia. We Delhommes got *famille* dat way."

Melody was curious. "Tell us about her, this Odile."

"It was when I first got to New York City. I met her at an audition for an Off-Off-Broadway play. We both got the parts. She was the only woman I think I ever loved. God, she was like a force of nature, that woman. Sapphire eyes, black hair, pillowy lips and kind, so kind. We were engaged to be married."

Jean Paul was curious too. "What happened *avec les deux amants?*"

Melody said, "That means the two lovers."

Deacon lied. "She got scared and broke it off. We lost touch.

The truth, as it can often be, was much uglier. What happened was that Odile and Deacon both auditioned for parts in a revival of Arthur Miller's *A View from The Bridge.* She got the part. He didn't. He was so sick with envy that he set it up for her to catch him in bed with the male choreographer from a musical they'd done together. That was bad enough, but afterwards Deacon told her he'd only asked her to marry him because he felt sorry for her, that she was pathetic, and that he preferred any man to her in bed. That was a decade ago.

They walked the rest of the way to Reine Marie's cabin along the bayou in silence. That was all good with Deacon, who had no desire to discuss the subject of Odile or his time in New York any further.

"This Reine Marie, she will take us to the gator boy?"

"*Oui*, dis the Queen Marie she will do," Jean Paul answered Deacon.

Melody knocked on the cabin door. "Reine Marie, it's Melody Delhomme and the man who's come to meet the boy."

When the door pulled back, a frightening-looking woman

dressed in a dazzling array of colored lame robes came into view. She had a head of wiry, steel wool hair, black lashes like spider legs, neon blue eye shadow, a pointed nose, and thin red lips. Between those thin lips, she clenched a pipe in yellow stained teeth. Her black-painted fingernails were getting so long that they curled at their tips. She stared past Melody and Jean Paul, smiling broadly at Deacon.

She waved them inside. "*Entre, entre, mes cher.*"

Reine Marie and Melody did the European kiss kiss thing. Jean Paul simply kissed Reine Marie on the cheek. When Deacon extended his right hand to her, Reine Marie wagged a finger at him.

"You kiss your Reine Marie," she said. "My, you are as handsome as Melody has said. To look at you...*beau regard, non?*"

Deacon did as he was told. He had come this far to meet the gator boy. Melody had vowed with her life that the gator boy was the genuine article.

Reine Marie took hold of Deacon by the biceps and gave him a tilted head stare. "You've been ill, *monsieur.*" She clucked her tongue. "Reine Marie will make some tea for you that will make you feel like you have never felt."

"Then I can meet the boy?"

She winked at him. "I guarantee that once you've had some tea, he will be very close to you and you to 'im."

Jean Paul put the case with the video equipment down and sat opposite Deacon on a rustic chair fashioned out of fallen tree branches. Melody chose a wicker chair next to the sofa on which Deacon was seated. The cabin was dank, the lighting dim, but Deacon said not a word about it. Jean Paul did most of the talking in his barely comprehensible Cajun patois, directing his conversation to Melody concerning some relative or other.

Five minutes later, Reine Marie appeared with a tray of four mismatched teacups. She served them all individually. Taking special care with Deacon's cup, fussing over him. They drank in silence. Although his tea tasted like dirt, Deacon once again summoned up the strength to hold his tongue. He'd endured Melody's unending appetite for him, the drive down, the bad food, the boat ride, the hike through the bayou. He wasn't going to let a terrible tasting cup of tea stop him now. Getting his meeting with the gator boy was the thing.

He let a few minutes go by as he listened to Reine Marie, Melody, and Jean Paul prattle on. Deacon figured he'd let enough time go by and was growing impatient. The time had come to meet green-eyed gator boy. He tried to open his mouth to tell Melody to set up the equipment, but his mouth wouldn't move, it wouldn't open wider or close. The teacup fell out of his hand. He noticed his breathing had slowed. When he told himself to get up, he couldn't. Not even his eyes moved. He couldn't blink. He could still see. Still hear. He could think, though his processing was sluggish at best.

Melody, Jean Paul, and Reine Marie stood from their chairs and surrounded Deacon. Jean Paul looked to Reine Marie. She nodded. As soon as she did, Jean Paul slapped Deacon across the face with a meaty open hand.

"You felt that, *non*, *cherie*?" Reine Marie asked. "This you should know, you will not be able to move, but you will feel it all, everything."

Melody stepped into Deacon's line of sight. "You know, Deacon, you never asked for Reine Marie's last name. Can you guess? Wait, you can't answer. *Quelle domage*!" She squeezed his crotch hard until tears came out of his eyes. "Tears, *mon dieu!* He is almost human, but not for long."

Melody stepped aside and Reine Marie knelt before him. "I once had a beautiful girl, *ma belle fille*, Odile. She kill herself, but this you know, Deacon Brand. For the love of you, she kills herself. Now you will pay. Odile's *frere*, Jean Paul is going to take from you what you have taken from *sa soeur,* his sister. But smile because I will keep my promise. You will be as close to Gator Boy as is possible."

***

Ten minutes later, stripped naked, Deacon's wrists bound together by rope, he was suspended by a tow truck hook above a fenced in inlet off the bayou. His feet dangling a yard above the murky water. He was still unable to move but felt the humidity on his skin and the stings of invisible insects.

"You know who live 'ere, Deacon?" Jean Paul asked with a laugh. "Gator Boy. He not full grown yet, only twelve feet, but he a 'ungry gator. We don't let 'im eat for a few month now."

Melody and Reine Marie cackled.

When Melody got control of herself, she said, "Do you know how gators eat? That's right, you can't talk. So, I'll tell you. They clamp their jaws around part of their prey, their teeth digging into the flesh to grip. Then they spin their bodies as fast as they can, using their weight and momentum to tear away chunks of their prey. Those chunks they swallow whole."

"*C'est vrei, cherie*. But you will bleed out soon enough after he take a leg or two," gloated Reine Marie. "We cut your leg a little so Gator Boy he can taste it in the water. The pain will not last long. My pain has lasted me much longer. We feed all of you to 'im, but your eyeballs. Those..." She couldn't continue for the tears over her dead daughter. "*D'accord*, Jean Paul, lower 'im in."

With that, Jean Paul leaned into the cab of the tow truck, turning the key to start her up. Certain the engine was running steady, he moved to the controls at the rear of the truck and pushed the handle that lowered the tow hook. When Deacon's feet were submerged, Jean Paul let go of the tow hook control. It didn't take long for Gator Boy to take notice of the blood and movement in the water. Much to the delight of Odile Belladonna's family, it took longer for Deacon to bleed out than anticipated.

***

Melody Delhomme called the New Orleans PD three days later to report Deacon Brand missing.

"The last time I saw him, he dropped me off around the corner from the bus station. My cousin, Jean Paul, picked me up there to drive me to see family on Avery Island. When I got back to the hotel today, I noticed housekeeping had cleaned the room, but that Deacon's things were untouched from the day we left. I checked with hotel management, and after checking the card swipes, they told me no one had been in the room since the day Deacon dropped me off. All my calls to him went direct to voicemail. I'm very worried."

In the months that followed, Melody had done several more phone interviews with the NOPD. When the police investigated her alibi, thirty family members and friends swore she had stayed with family on the island. She had, in fact, gone to the island with Jean Paul after they watched Gator Boy feast. The cops didn't quite believe her story, but they couldn't shoot any holes in it. No, she didn't know why Deacon had rented video equipment or what had become of it. Yes, she had come with him because they were casual lovers and since he was paying, she was thrilled to see her family for the first time in three years.

Another handsome Hamlet wannabe, Maurice Vidal, an actor with Haitian heritage, was hired to take Deacon's place as host of *Informal Paranormal.* The first episode of season four was about celebrity disappearances. It featured a half-hour segment on Deacon's vanishing into thin air somewhere in or around New Orleans. A good part of the segment was a tearful interview featuring the show's production assistant, Melody Delhomme.

Two men in sweat-soaked camo tee shirts, the words Montana Museum of Oddities written across their shirt backs, got off the airboat. Holding their ridiculous matching bucket hats against the damp breeze, they trudged to Reine Marie's cabin door. She was expecting them and stepped outside to greet them.

"Dis way to your purchase gentlemen," she said, walking them around back.

They could not contain their enthusiasm at the sight of the thing, a twelve-foot-long stuffed alligator with green eyes, human eyes. But it was the stuffed human arm sticking out of the gator's mouth that sent them over the top with excitement.

"D'ere he is, jus' as in de pictures, my green-eyed monster you have acquired."

"Those are his eyes?" One of the men was skeptical. "How'd he get 'em, you suppose?"

She shrugged. "*Je ne sais pas.* Maybe he is a more envious alligator than the others. Who can say?"

THE FAR END OF BOURBON STREET

Larry S. Evans II

"Well, I'm still sort of working through—'*SHE KILLED HIM WITH BEE TOXIN!*'"

The knot of people exploded in laughter on cue. He might as well have had an applause sign over his head.

Townsend Marlowe still knew how to play his audience.

Allison winced. She'd lost count of how many times she'd heard the anecdote this month. Well, at least this venue had a bar in the back.

There'd be another few minutes of 'when you first started out' questions before the autograph session proper. Allison put in an order for a Manhattan for Town, confident that it would be as low octane as her too icy mojito. Best keep him off the rocket fuel as long as possible.

She'd been his publicist long enough to know his reputation as a hard-drinking womanizer wasn't entirely true.

She'd been his wife long enough to know it wasn't entirely false, either.

The drink arrived, suitably diluted, with the final round of applause. She collected it and skirted the meandering crowd by the signing table. Town was pressing through those hoping to 'have a moment' as he left the stage.

"Your libation, my liege. Assumed you'd be thirsty."

"Thanks, Lis. Not too bad a crowd for midweek."

"Well, a bookstore-cum-speakeasy is right up your alley. I'm surprised there's only the one in NOLA, and it's new."

"'Speakeasy' is the new black..."

"Apparently..."

They arrived at the signing table where there was already a considerable queue. Allison saw to it there were a number of pens laid out, and that the booksellers managed the line and three book maximum limit. She pulled back, snapping the occasional pic for social media. The fans had an expectation. Town's performance had not yet ended for the evening.

Town was working the watery shallows of his second Manhattan as the line ebbed. The overall crowd in the place was transforming from bookish to speakeasyish already, and Allison was hopeful they'd be able to make it an early night. It was a vain hope.

One of the straggling autograph seekers offered to buy Townsend a drink. This wasn't new. There's one or two in any crowd who want to keep that prolonged contact, hoping for some private secret insight that no other fan (and aspiring writer) will have.

"That's awfully generous, but we do have that signing at the B&N in the Garden District tomorrow..."

"Oh, now c'mon, Lis. He *wants* to buy me a drink. What's the harm of *one* drink? After all, the fans are why we're here."

Allison knew well enough when to pick her battles.

"Just *one*..."

Townsend plopped down at the bar like he had just dropped anchor. Sure. Just one.

"A Blanton's double. Neat."

Allison saw the fan visibly pale at the thought of how much a double pour of the premium bourbon was going to run in a place like this.

"Hey, friend, why don't we get this round. Barkeep, make that two, please." She glared at her husband, who grinned sheepishly.

"Enjoy. I'm going to take care of our tab," she told him pointedly. Allison settled up, and made a great show of putting the credit card in her purse for Townsend.

"I'm going to head back to the hotel. One of us needs to be up early tomorrow."

"I'll be along shortly."

"Get a cab."

She knew full well that the fan would insist on getting at least one round. Town wouldn't 'want to upset his fans'. With any luck, the guy wouldn't be dumb enough to try to keep up with her husband's consumption. Either way, by the time he was 'along shortly' he'd be well in his cups and had no business walking through the Quarter at night, even if it was only a few blocks.

Allison made the perfunctory thank yous and goodbyes to the staff and stepped into the early evening. She was tired and had little interest in weaving her way through the stumbling crowds of drunken tourists, enthusiastic hawkers, buskers, beggars, and homeless that were part of the night scene along Bourbon. She made her way over to the more subdued Royal Street, and located a car to take her back to the Hotel Monteleone.

Allison closed the door and shed the day behind it. She poured herself a white wine from the bottle next to the nearly full bottle of whiskey that Town insisted be delivered earlier. She moved toward the bathroom, started the tub, and disrobed.

Let him have his fan time. He'd pay for it with a fair hangover at least. The event at the B&N was bright and noisy. She'd make sure of that. She topped off the wine and slipped into the tub. Each of them had their means of playing at the marriage game.

She was deep asleep when the phone rang.

"Lish, 'm in jail."

The slur was almost comical. Was he pranking her?

"Goddammit, Town! I told you to take a cab. Did they catch you pissing in someone's doorway aga..."

"Sayin' I sh-shot..."

She snapped fully alert.

"Say I killed th' guy."

Townsend pulled the page out of his vintage Underwood and sank back into the chair. He took a mouthful of Basil Hayden and savored it as he read.

Something was...*off*.

Names.

Those people don't have any names.

Why don't they have names?

They're not important.

No. No, that's wrong. They *are* important.

Why?

Because...one of them is dead.

And another one of them is the killer.

They have to have names.

Town had barely begun to crumple up the page when behind him a voice roar-whispered.

"But *you're* the killer!"

He jerked upright in the bed and immediately regretted it. Twin knitting needles pierced his temples and then exploded into flames. His gut bubbled up to burn his throat and he couldn't stop the spasm.

Miraculously, there was a pail or a bucket there. Eventually, the shaking stopped. He felt himself being lowered back onto the bed. A warm cloth sponged the vomit from his lips. A moment later, a welcome cooler cloth covered his eyes and forehead. He surrendered to the inviting oblivion.

Robert Morton, age 64, married, two kids...of...um...Buffalo, New York...

Married? Divorced? Widowed? No, married. Has to be. Someone has to grieve for the victim. If he's that old, the kids are grown, so there has to be someone for the reader to connect with. A reason to care.

But what if he was a bastard?

Deserved to be killed? *Hmm.*

That's a way to go. Meatier than the innocent bystander.

Besides, if he was a bystander, who was he standing by and why was someone trying to kill them?

But then why were they trying to kill Bob Morton? Who'd he piss off? *Where are those damned names?* Someone in the bar? Someone in the audience?

Town couldn't concentrate. His head pounded. He emptied the glass and refilled it. Damn. He was going to need to order another bottle from room service.

He felt the whiskey burn enough into his gums as he swirled it back and forth. Now...why couldn't he think clearly. If those people in the next room would be quiet...

There were voices in the next room. *Who were they? What were they saying?* He strained to shake off the coils of sleep.

"Robert Mercer, from Niagara Falls. Early 60s I think. In town for a conference. Not sure why he turned up at the signing...maybe he saw something on the web."

Who was that? The voice was familiar. Town knew the voice. Brent? Brad? Brick? (Brick? Really?) No—Breck. Breckinridge Andrews. US Attorney. What was he doing here?

"So, there's not really anything to connect him...nothing that might indicate a motive, I mean?"

The wishy-washy voice was Harvey's. Harvey was here from Houston. Of course. Allison would call him first. He was a good lawyer...if you needed a contract written. He was no criminal attorney. But then, Townsend hadn't *needed* a criminal attorney.

What was Allison saying?

"God, do we really think he could have shot somebody?"

"No. Look, what we think won't matter. If they can tie him to the gun..."

"What?"

"On a good day, the right judge, stars aligned, maybe manslaughter. He'd still do time, Lis. Like, in Angola hard time."

Townsend pulled himself up and pitched forward, landing hard against the jamb of the bedroom door. He was slurring badly.

"Din do it. Diddun kill an- anybody."

Allison was there, guiding him back to bed.

"We know you didn't, honey. Sleep. We'll talk when you can manage to get pants on."

He tumbled back onto the king mattress. She pulled the duvet over his bare backside. Blackness swirled and then consumed him.

Wrongfully accused. What a trope! He might as well be watching Perry Mason. Framed by the usual suspects for a murder he didn't commit. Don't forget the requisite red herrings in the second act. How had he gotten here? He was supposed to be writing international intrigue. That's what got him the publishing contract, a couple of successful series, and the adulation of fans worldwide. Why was he back writing this tripe?

He ripped the page up and threw it at the trash can. It hit the top of the second empty bourbon bottle and fell onto the floor with the other wadded or ripped pages. *Didn't they ever clean this place?* He rubbed his throbbing temples.

Long fingers rested on his right shoulder, while another perfectly manicured hand offered him a filled glass. He took it, leaving the hand free to join its mate that began working the stiff muscles of his neck. He swallowed deep and leaned back against the softness. It was nice. Town took a deep breath of her perfume. A husky voice whispered behind him.

"You're the killer, darling. You get to decide who lives. Who dies."

Something was...off.

Why couldn't he think? He couldn't remember ever being this hungover.

"Chloral hydrate."

"What?

"Chloral hydrate. Back in the day, they called it a Mickey Finn. Tranquilizer that doesn't play well with alcohol. I'm surprised with all that spy stuff you write you haven't heard of it."

Harvey was notoriously into film noir. It was one of his more endearing qualities and his personal library had been a tremendous resource for Town.

"Anyway, you're lucky it was that. You were too out of it for the police to properly question you, and Breck was able to convince the magistrate to let Allison take you back to the hotel."

Town gradually realized they were in the suite's living room. He was propped sloppily on the couch, mostly covered by one of the hotel bathrobes. Not designed for big guys, he guessed. A quick glance down confirmed that he had -somehow- managed to put on pants.

"How'd he do that?"

"While I don't doubt having the US Attorney show up at three a.m. probably got their attention. He told them about vetting you for that Homeland Security think tank. Guess they figured you probably were not the type to go shooting strangers outside bars in the Quarter. So, they let you go until you could sober up enough to Mirandize. Took your clothes, though, and probably did a swab test for gunshot residue. They can do that apparently. Exigent circumstances, according to Breck."

Harvey's tone changed.

"So, we're not out of the woods yet, son. They could be back tonight or tomorrow with a warrant. And I'm not so sure we have anything we can do about it."

He leaned forward from the overstuffed chair facing Town.

"Big problem with chloral hydrate is memory loss. You're probably starting to notice. Even as much of a Hemingway-style drinker as you are, I bet you don't usually black out."

That was frightening. He was right. Townsend could not piece together what had happened after the signing wrapped up. He'd gone over to the bar. Allison had left. And then...

And then?

He snapped up in the bed. The room was pitch black. How had he gotten back here? He experienced his senses slowly wake up to the room around him. There was the sound of the street outside. Sirens. There were always sirens. Were they getting closer? Someone was lying there next to him. Someone there in the dark. He breathed in. Perfume.

Something was...off.

Why was Harvey babysitting him? Where was Allison? Dealing with the press, probably. 'Big time thriller writer shoots fan in drunken rage'. Oh yeah, he'd dumped some crap on her over the years, but this was a new one. But she'd been there. Next to him in the bed. Hadn't she? Was that earlier?

"Oh my God!"

"What?"

"That's *her!*"

Breck leaned forward. Harvey was straining to see what Allison had found on the phone that had upset her.

"That's -Nicole!" The name dripped hatred.

Breck had moved around behind her chair. He squinted at the woman in the picture of the autograph line.

"Allison, I don't..."

"That's her."

Harvey managed to get the phone away for a moment. The picture was not great, and it had been nearly fifteen years. But underneath the bleached hair and behind the Botox, he could see enough of a resemblance to understand what set Allison off.

"If she was there? If she came back after you left?"

Allison didn't want to think about it. She couldn't not.

"Goddam that bitch..."

Nicole finished massaging Town's rigid neck and moved her hands down his chest.

"You need to take a break."

"Deadline. I'm way behind."

She leaned further over, her softness pressing in as he turned to inhale that perfume. Her hands went lower.

Well, an hour or so wouldn't wreck the schedule *that* much more.

Darkness. Sirens. Someone lying there next to him. That smell. Strong. What was it? Sirens were coming closer. Did he smell perfume?

Still. Still...something was...off.

Allison was yelling something at him. He'd drifted off again. The pounding of his pulse in his ears quieted. He was still there on the couch in that silly robe.

"How could you, you son of a bitch? How could you do that *again*?"

Harvey was pulling her back away from him. *What was he being accused of?* He couldn't remember.

"Plural vibrate..." he managed to stammer.

"What?"

"Gabe me plural vibrate. Mickey mowsh."

"Allison, he's still drunk. Or drugged. She could have put something in his drink, you know?"

Allison paused. She was still plenty pissed, but it was possible. She had seen Town drunk off his ass a number of times, but never this...this stupid.

"We should probably get a blood test. The police will order one, anyway."

Allison was in control of herself again. Harvey felt the tension drop and let go of her arms.

"We need to find her."

It read like bad exposition. Nicole Adams. The femme fatale. The other woman. Breaker of happy homes. A dame who knew what she liked and knew how to get it, and then used it to get some more.

It had never really been that simple. That would have been easier. Townsend Marlowe had created a character that connected with the zeitgeist of the mid-90s. It had made him rich and famous, and with that, came temptation. Allison was busy keeping him in the public eye. Nicole was willing to stroke his ego, among other things.

Town had been better at writing about secrets than keeping them. The affair lasted a little under a year before Allison found out. He stopped seeing Nicole almost immediately. Then he and Allison spent another year deciding if they hated each other enough to get divorced or loved each other enough to put it behind them. In the end, they paid Nicole an ungodly amount to shut up and go away, a solution that appealed to her type of person, and gradually moved on.

Her type of person, though, seemed, at least to Allison right now, the sort who would frame Town for murder. Proving that, well, that was a different thing.

The bookstore speakeasy was profoundly busy. A possible murder on your doorstep involving a famous writer was tailor-made publicity for the venue. Allison suppressed the urge to accuse the owner of that. Then she cursed herself for wishing she'd thought of that as a pitch.

The bartender didn't remember seeing that blonde woman. Could she have been there? Sure. It was busy. Did he see anyone else talking to Town? Like he said. *It was busy.*

Town and the dead guy had been there till close. And a bunch of other people. She might have been there, might have not. They did the last call, bouncer sent everybody out and had locked the door when they heard the shots. He called 9-1-1.

By the time the police got there, Town had passed out with a body next to him. There was a gun there on the sidewalk. Where the hell did he get a gun?

"Of course I have a gun. I write international spy novels. Being into guns is part of the gig."

Breck rubbed his eyes. This was not helping.

"Town, did you have a gun with you tonight?"

"I'm not sure."

"How can you not be sure?"

"Well, um...from what Harvey said, there's some gray area here."

"How so?"

"Technically, you can't legally carry a firearm into a bar in Louisiana."

"That's correct."

"But you can carry it into some place like a restaurant that serves alcohol. Which is kind of confusing."

"So?"

"Well, was I at a bar that has a bookstore in it, or was I at a bookstore that has a bar in it?"

"That's splitting hairs, Town. Did you have a gun or not?"

"See, that's the problem. If I tell you, and it turns out that was illegal, you, being an officer of the court, have to disclose it. With Harvey, it's privileged."

Breck saw the trap, relented.

"Okay. At some point, you will be asked by the police if you had a firearm with you. In a *purely hypothetical situation*, would you have had a firearm that was legally registered to you, or to Allison, or the corporation? Anything that could prove that the gun they found with you was *your* gun?"

"Hypothetically?"

"Hypothetically."

"Don't tell him anything else, Town. That bastard's done enough to damage your reputation."

They were sitting in the US Attorney's Office. Breckinridge Andrews pushed his glasses back and glared at the woman.

"I'm sorry you feel that way." He turned to Townsend.

"Mr. Marlowe, I cannot, in good conscience, allow your application for the DHS Intelligence Project to be approved. My investigation shows you have a history of alcohol related incidents, some questionable financial transactions, and..." he turned to the woman next to Town, "you cheated on your wife. Under those circumstances, you are at risk of being leveraged by various terrorist elements, foreign nationals, and other bad actors. Your participation in the project could compromise the security and safety of the process, participants, and their findings. Thank you for your interest, but we will not be contacting you further."

"It would've looked so good on that book, honey. Maybe there's a way to still spin it."

Town laughed bitterly. "Oh, yeah. I'm sure she's gonna want to do that."

"She'll do whatever makes her money. That's why she won't give you a divorce."

"Jesus, Nicole! It's Texas. Community property. If we divorce, she gets half at least. That includes half of all the books and the royalties."

Maybe that's why she'd agreed to what Allison always called "the blackmail". Once she found out Townsend was only going to be half his bank account, Nicole looked at him like he was half a man.

So why the hell was she back now? Was she even behind this?

Allison gave up at the speakeasy. The crowd was building, and she needed to get back and relieve Harvey. He still needed to get Townsend a local criminal attorney to rep him if there was an eventual arraignment. God, she hoped he'd sobered up enough to deny seeing that bitch again.

But if he hadn't? If it wasn't her…at all?

Why the hell could he not stop at just one drink?

Town ripped the page out of the Underwood. This was all over the place. Yes, okay, sometimes, *sometimes*, the characters take you places you didn't think they were going. At least he'd heard that at so many writer's conferences and panel discussions. Killed with bee toxin. Sure. Why the hell not?

"Deadlines, baby. Get me another drink, will ya?"

Damn that perfume. He'd have to remember to take a shower before he left.

There in the dark, someone was lying next to him. Gradually, he could hear again. Sirens. Coming closer? That smell so strong. It was like it was all over him. He should have taken a shower. He rubbed his temples. It hurt. Something hard. Something in his hands.

Why couldn't he remember? Why didn't it add up? Was there something in the drink? If he could just open his eyes. Why couldn't he open his eyes?

Something was...off.

"It's okay, honey. I forgive you."

When had she said that? Had she ever said that? Was it Nicole or Allison? Had either of them ever said it?

"You can't assume it didn't hurt her, Town. I hate the bitch, but I can't assume it didn't hurt her."

No, that's not what was said.

"You can't assume *you* didn't hurt her."

But he had, hadn't he? He'd always assumed he could write his way out of it. As long as those keys kept clacking, he'd wiggle on out of it, never mind who it hurt. Never mind how many bodies were left lying there.

He *was* the killer, after all. He got to *decide* who lived and who didn't. And who did it.

He'd pat himself on the back and have another drink.

Then he'd take a shower and get the smell off him. He smelled like a whorehouse. Like a distillery. Like a -insert colorful writer's cliche here. He must have broken the damn bottle somewhere. A bottle of something. This smell was awful. What the hell was it?

***

"Barium nitrate."

"What?"

"Barium nitrate. Lead styphnate. Antimony sulfide. It's gunshot residue." Harvey leaned in. "They found it on your clothes, Town. They found it on your hands. This does not look good."

He got quiet, then close to Townsend's ear:

"I need you to tell me now. Did you have the gun, or did she bring it with her?"

He looked down. He was in handcuffs. *Why was he in handcuffs?*

The sirens were so loud now. The smell made him gag. He vomited, but it didn't stop the pain in his head. He went to rub his temples. There was something hard. He remembered being in handcuffs. When was that? No. No. It was just...*something*, there in his right hand. He relaxed the palm. Let it drop. Heard the rattle as the gun hit the cobbles of Bourbon Street. There was a body lying next to him.

Open your eyes. Open your eyes, God damn you.

No. Oh, God, no.

It was Allison.

SOURLANDS

Michael Ferreter

The nightclubs of Bourbon Street beckoned me to join them: all flashing lights and noise and ebullience. But the pounding bass of the discotheque and the raucous joy of Dixieland weren't for me. Not tonight.

I kept walking northeast along Bourbon, away from the shouting fraternity types and screeching bachelorette parties, until the neon signs disappeared one by one and the neighborhood's classic balconied buildings were replaced by modest one-story structures. I stopped in front of a bar not too far before Bourbon dead-ended. The place had no cover and no drink minimum. Just right for my budget this evening. Lucky's, the sign said in black and white, surrounded by dancing quarter notes and a cartoon Dalmatian that looked more rabid than lucky. The chalkboard sign on the sidewalk didn't have a musician's name on it, just said "PIANO."

The doorman—I can't even call him a bouncer, he was so slightly built—nodded at me. Probably because we looked alike: over-the-hill black men in a racially divided city. But also because we felt alike: invisible, worn down by life, luckless at Lucky's, baffled by the combination of bad choices and circumstance and fate that brought us to this moment.

About a dozen people occupied tables in ones and twos in a space that could hold a hundred. The room was low-ceilinged and claustrophobic, with a slightly elevated stage in one corner. A piano trio played as I got a bottle of beer, whatever was on special. Most of the people were on the left side of the room, where they could watch the piano player's hands. I circled around to the right side, where I could see his face.

I only heard the band play three songs. The first was a pleasant mid-tempo number that sounded vaguely familiar, like the original pop version had been in a TV commercial. Someone in the audience with a cell phone might have had the same reaction and found the answer on the internet. I kept waiting for the piano player to sing a line, to jar loose the lyrics from my mind, but it was an instrumental.

The second song knocked me out. It started with solo piano, a series of dissonant, twisting lines that trailed upwards like questions. The pianist tapped individual keys high up on the keyboard, less notes than pleas. Then the bass and drum kit joined in, and the piano man finally sang.

It was a ballad about a poor farmer who had been chased off his property by a mob and eventually killed. There was a line in the chorus about sweet lands turned sour. The bandleader sang with such clarity and such pain that I knew it was a true story. His playing got louder, angrier, indignant. The ending of the song mirrored the beginning with the same melodic theme, except now the pianist thumped the lower keys with his left hand, the questions of the introduction turned into angry exclamation marks.

The audience clapped louder for this song. I looked down and saw my hands pumping like pistons.

His closing song was an upbeat boogie-woogie number, a nice way to send the people home happy. The moment the music ended, the bass player and drummer bounced off their stools and darted for the dressing room. The piano player stayed at his bench, not doing much of anything. Just caressing the keys, reveling in the moment. The few remaining audience members headed for the door or to the bar to settle up.

I grabbed my beer and approached the stage. “That was nice music,” I said.

The piano player looked up and looked me over quick-like, with an instantaneous judgment that I must pose no threat.

Up close now, I saw him differently. We could have been cousins. We were about the same age, our skin the same tone of mahogany. He had lost more hair, just a slim horseshoe of curls roaming from ear to ear. He grew his mustache in the 1970s fashion, thick and wide, whereas the wisps of my 1940s style could have been drawn with a mascara brush. He wore a creamy velvet jacket the color of butterscotch, so thick I started sweating just looking at it.

“Buy you a beer?” I asked, though I barely had money for another one myself.

“Club soda?” His speaking voice was raspier than his singing voice. It was confident, not apologetic, and I knew he had been through battles with the demon rum. I nodded, and we walked back over to the bar. He told me his name was Harlan Washington III.

A beer and a club soda cost the same as my first beer. I tipped the bartender, a white kid who looked like he belonged in law school, what I thought a club soda cost.

With drinks refreshed, I couldn’t help but ask. “That ballad, the second-to-last song. That’s a true story, isn’t it?”

He scoffed, a sound more bitter than humorous. “It’s late at night, this place is closing down”—he swept an arm across the emptying space—”and you want to talk about that song of all songs.”

“You don’t have anywhere to be,” I said, “because you joined me for a drink. I ain’t got nowheres to go, neither. I reckon you might oblige me.”

“It’s a damn sad song, friend.”

“And I’m sure it’s a damn sad story, if you’re willing to tell it.” Harlan sighed, his shoulders falling a few inches, and after a moment, took a sip of his drink.

"My grandfather was a sharecropper in Florida in a backwater place called Chickahatchee County. The biggest town had maybe 2,000 people. Two hours away from the tiniest dot on the map. Well, he saved up his money and after a while he bought himself a right proper farm of his own. Not much, but his land, in his own name. Part of a development called Sweetlands. He farmed it for a time. Got pretty successful, too." He paused, his chest clutching as if the next part was too painful to voice. "Too successful for the white men in the county. They tried to run him off his land. Burned down his barn and poisoned his horses. He wouldn't give up. He wanted to leave this land to his son. Create a legacy. When all that didn't work, well, one night they got a posse together and put him in a tree."

The tale was basically the same as I'd heard it before, but with a passion that could only come from being passed down generation to generation within the family.

"What do you call your song?"

"Never said it was mine, but I suppose that part is clear as day."

He winced, like biting into a lemon. "'Harlan's Lament'." He had narrated the history with a dry detachment, an accountant describing a tax provision. But this, saying the song title, he had an ache in his voice.

"Harlan was your grandpappy, wasn't he? And you are named after him."

He nodded, a slight dip. "That's right."

"What happened next?"

"My grandmother left Chickahatchee County in a hurry, feared for her life. She took my father and his baby brother and resettled in Alabama. My father met my momma, and they didn't like Alabama much, and before I came along, they moved to Mississippi. That wasn't much better for me, so I ended up here. My daughter lives in Houston." He chuckled softly. "At this rate, my great-grandchildren are going to end up in California, and then what after that?" It was the only time he laughed all night.

"And the mystery of the killing was never solved?"

"It wasn't no mystery, friend. It was a lynching, and in Chickahatchee County, Florida, 1922, the white man got away with it."

"Do you ever wonder about what happened to the man that organized the killing of your grandfather? Him or his descendants?"

He made a growling noise, fierce and guttural. "I don't wonder, I know. They stole our land and built it into something bigger that made them damn rich."

"Have you ever been back to Chickahatchee County? Or been at all, I should say?"

"Only once. Went to attend the funeral of a great-aunt." He pronounced it the proper Northeastern way, like "ought," not like the bug. I liked that. "Held my breath the entire time I was there. Didn't sleep a wink at night. Didn't relax until I crossed the county line into safer ground."

"The white man still holds that much power there?"

Harlan's shoulders shook, almost a shiver. "Don't like to think about it. But the answer is yes. Family named Blaine runs everything in that county."

I felt I had asked enough questions to make a man curious, if not suspicious. I took a sip of beer when I heard a wooden clunking sound behind me, and turned to see the bartender was now out in the main room, flipping chairs onto tables. The whole music area was dark, with only the bar light above us shining.

I looked back to Harlan. "You ever wonder what became of John Blaine?"

His eyes narrowed, looked at me differently now. "You ask an awful lot of questions for a guy who walked in and only heard three songs." Then he recoiled in a double take. "And how do you know the name of John Blaine?"

I met his gaze and nodded at him in a smug and knowing

way that made me feel like George Clooney in *Ocean's Eleven*.

"You ever wonder what became of John Blaine?" I repeated.

Harlan shuffled in his seat. "No, sir." But the intensity of his eyes spoke otherwise.

"John Roberts Blaine, born 1865, died 1949, took the land he stole from your grandpappy, and four other black farmers in Chickahatchee County, and became the biggest crop producer in three counties. When the soil turned and more people started moving to the area, he shifted to real estate. Built apartments for the new folks. If it were the big city, he would have been called a slumlord. But this being where it is, they called him the King of Chickahatchee County."

I waited for Harlan to interrupt or ask a question, but he was a patient man. Like me. I looked quick and confirmed the barkeep was gone.

"J.R. called his company Blaine Living. Radio commercials of the day sang out, chirping like a bird: don't settle for plain living, choose Blaine Living." I took a newspaper clipping from my pocket, an article I found in the microfiche at the public library. "This is the ribbon cutting of his first apartment complex." I put it on the bar. Harlan kept his eyes fixed on me.

"He ran the company until just before his death and handed the reins to his son, John Thomas Blaine. J.T. expanded the family operation into grocery stores. Today any man in Chickahatchee County wants to eat something besides his shoe, he gotta get it at a Blaine Grocery. They drove off anybody that tried to open a store in their territory. And I mean to tell you, J.T. ran the playbook his daddy taught him."

Now I saw Harlan stiffen, his chest tighten like he dared not exhale.

"Junior finally died of cancer three years ago." I took a newspaper obituary out of my pocket, laid it on the first article. "Then John David Blaine got the keys to the kingdom. The seed must have corroded through the generations, because J.D. was the worst of them. Ripping off workers' overtime, union busting, illegal contracts, bribing officials for new developments, you name it. Seven Blaine employees died of 'mysterious circumstances' in only three years. Seven people. All black folk. The apartments, the grocery stores, none of it satisfied him. He wanted a casino. Being the new King of Chickahatchee County wasn't good enough for him, he wanted to be emperor. All built on the stolen fruits of your grandpappy's farm.

"Four days ago, J.D. Blaine caught a bullet between his teeth." The newspaper clipping I pulled out next was recent, a blazing front-page headline. "Nobody seems to know what happened. The sheriff is looking into rumors that he was running up gambling debts. Maybe he owed money to some bad people, maybe the Mafia. Where those rumors came from, no one can rightly say, but they're out there."

Now I pulled out a Polaroid. Set it on the bar and turned it right-side up to Harlan. The photo showed a heavyset man on his back, blood and gray matter pooling out of what used to be the back of his head.

"But I know the truth. Because I took that photo. And now two people know the truth."

Harlan picked up the photo, examined it close-up and further away, set it back down.

"I'm sorry it took one hundred years to set things right," I said.

"You of all people got nothing to be sorry for, friend." He licked his dry lips. He had been singing and playing for a full set, probably an hour and a half. I noticed he had barely touched his club soda.

"Feels good to finally get one over on the white man, doesn't it?"

Harlan didn't say anything to that. He looked back and forth between the image in the Polaroid and the face of the person responsible for it.

"Do I owe you something?" His eyes were now locked on mine.

"After what was done to your family, you don't owe nothing to nobody." This was the moment that should feel so good, and yet it always burned with the bitter knowledge what was done could never be enough.

He shook my hand with a fierceness and intensity that can only be summoned in a moment like this. His muscular, ropy fingers reached all the way to the pulse point of my wrist. A piano player's fingers.

"I don't suppose I can ask your name and thank you proper."

I nodded downward at the bar where the photograph sat.

"No, I suppose not," Harlan said.

A fat white man appeared from the back room. "Hey! Boy!" We both looked up. "Come get your pay and get outta here!" Harlan made no move to get up. I sat up straighter. *Show some damn respect. This is Harlan Washington III!* That's what I wanted to say, but the words got caught in my throat and the fat man disappeared. Especially in the South, I found it hard to talk back to a white man. Unless my gun was doing the talking, of course.

"So, is he Lucky?" I asked, my feeble attempt at a cross between small talk and a joke.

"I don't suspect any of us here tonight is." Harlan slipped the Polaroid and clippings into his jacket and eased off the barstool. He looked at me, hard and gentle all the same time. Then he turned and headed to the dressing room to receive his wages. I'd already received mine.

The doorman was long gone when I stepped out into the cool, breezy night air and paused. Silence engulfed me. The merriment of the French Quarter was far behind me, as only a stray shout or laugh bouncing and echoing along the narrow corridor of Bourbon reached my ears.

I thought about Auntie Patricia and the stories she told on her deathbed, the happy ones she told everyone, and the darker ones when we two were alone. I thought about why she told me, and only me, of evil things done a century ago and what she expected me to do about them.

I thought about the Washington family's state-by-state westward migration, away from Chickahatchee County, their own private Manifest Destiny. I was out of money and out of mission. *West sounds good*, I thought. I turned to face where I remembered seeing the last light of the darkening sky, and started walking.

THE EXTRAORDINARY LIFE AND SUDDEN DEMISE OF FRANKLIN ANDERSON

Barry Fulton

My big brother, Frank, dead five years. Silence from Washington until the registered letter arrived at my law office in downtown New Orleans. Addressed to me, Peter Anderson, Esq., with the enigmatic return address of Cryptographic Associates, Washington D.C.

"Your presence is requested at ten in the morning on the fifth of July. Please call for instructions." Sounded formal—and weird.

July fifth. The date grabbed my attention, so I phoned. An unnamed woman with a chilling voice invited me to a private ceremony to honor my older brother, Franklin Anderson. She said they wanted me to describe his life "to be recorded on video for posterity." My younger brother, Stevie, received the same invitation, the same instruction.

Police uniform smartly pressed and shoes spit-shined, Stevie was standing at the entrance of the Hale Boggs Federal Building in New Orleans when I arrived. He spotted me and stepped forward with a pride that reminded me of our big brother.

"Hey, Stevie, you look like a crime show cop, all muscle and attitude."

He thrust out his chest in an exaggerated motion and embraced me. "Trying to keep up with you, Peter, although you've slowed down a little."

"Slowed down? After the ceremony, come over to the sports center, and we'll see who's slowed down. In the meantime, what do you know about the Washington big shot who's coming here?"

"Nothing. And the woman on the phone said it's all hush-hush. Cosmic Top Secret. No friends. No press. Just the two of us and two nameless Washington types."

A young man in a charcoal pinstripe suit—he must have been waiting and watching—walked toward us. Six-foot-something with a serious face and hard eyes. "You the Anderson brothers?"

"Yep," Stevie said, smiling. "We call ourselves Law and Order. Peter's a lawyer, and I'm a city cop."

"I'm Thelonious Jefferson," the man said. No handshake. No smile. "Follow me to meet Admiral Northcote. Our video tech is setting up to record your memories. Then the admiral will present the medal honoring Franklin's service."

Jefferson led us up the stairs to the third floor and down the hallway. A uniformed guard opened a locked door and took us into a brightly lit recording studio. A woman wearing a headset stood behind a video camera. No acknowledgement from her. An older gentleman with white hair and rimless glasses strode toward us and extended his hand.

"Peter and Stephen, I trust. I'm Admiral Roland Northcote, chief of the unit your brother so ably served." His slight stoop and furrowed face suggested he had retired from the Navy years before.

I shook his hand. "Good to meet you."

Stevie also shook his hand. "My pleasure, sir."

"Let's get started. I understand you'll both speak. Who's first?"

I held up my hand and walked to the lectern in front of the

camera—to speak of the kid with a secretive career and tragic death.

Frank Anderson, our big brother, was born in a Minnesota farmhouse south of Saint Paul, followed three years later by me and then a year after by Stevie. Our dad scratched out a living on a thirty-acre sheep farm while Mom raised us and ran the house. She prayed a lot and insisted Dad accompany her to what she called "the little church in the meadow." He was a peaceful man, drank very little, swore only occasionally, but often returned from Sunday service in a white rage. "People speakin' in tongues and hootin' and hollerin'," he would say, "ain't nothin' about that in the Bible." But Mom was one powerful influence, so seven days later, we'd witness a repeat performance. Don't know if Dad's anger or the preacher's shouting killed her at the too-young age of thirty-four. Her funeral service was the last time any of us entered that wretched church.

I looked over at Stevie, sitting ramrod straight. He nodded, which I interpreted as his approval. I glanced at the admiral and then faced the camera again.

After that, I never saw Dad angry. He must have missed Mom terribly 'cause he became a man without feeling. Frank said Dad still loved us but kept it hidden inside. It wasn't till years later I realized my big brother had become a substitute parent for Stevie and me.

Frank graduated from high school in 1968 as valedictorian and gave a speech about honor. The words hit a nerve with Dad. First time I saw him cry. Frank's plan to attend college ended the day he received a letter from Selective Service drafting him into the Army. They told him to report to Fort Polk, Louisiana, in forty-five days—a world away for a Minnesota farm boy.

The Vietnam war was raging, college students were protesting, and our boys were dying in the jungle. Dad said honor be damned, go to Canada. But Frank said it was his patriotic duty to serve. He came home after boot camp for a quick visit before leaving for Vietnam. Our big brother, all of eighteen years old, had become a soldier practically overnight. I remember his deep tan and the sharp creases in his khaki trousers.

"I'm proud of you," I said, maintaining my composure.

Frank sent a letter every week. After dinner, Dad would open the latest envelope and begin to read, but usually stopped and asked me to continue. I read the letters out loud, although I stumbled over the Vietnamese names. That made Stevie laugh.

Stevie's sober face broke into a smile.

Not Dad, of course, who had not smiled since Mom's death.

Close to Christmas, the weekly letter did not arrive. And by New Year's, the next letter was also missing.

"Holiday backup," Dad said. But the letters never resumed.

Three months later, we still ran to the mailbox when the mailman's dusty old Ford approached. Nothing except catalogs, grocery store flyers, and the occasional greeting from Aunt Lillian in North Dakota. Week after week, our hopes faded. Finally, a letter from the Department of the Army: Private Franklin Gunnar Anderson was missing in action.

Dad stopped eating. Suicide by starvation, I called it. "Frank should've gone to Canada," he said over and over until he passed. Only a few people attended the funeral—two guys from the pool hall, a salesman from John Deere, and a big-boned woman from Mom's church. Stevie said the Army lost Frank and killed Dad.

With help from our uncle Fritz, Stevie and I worked the farm while attending high school. Nearly a year after Dad's death, another official letter from the Army appeared in our mailbox. I read it first, and like Dad, I cried. Then, I read it to Stevie. Frank was alive. They'd found him wounded in some village and sent him to a military hospital in Japan to patch him up. The letter said he'd lost a limb. Lost a limb? Couldn't they tell us if it was a leg or an arm?

Within a week, Frank called. Sounded like the brother we knew. High spirits and raring to come home. "It'll be awhile," he said, "because they're going to fit me with a prosthesis and teach me to walk again." The energy drained from his voice when I told him of Dad's passing. We didn't tell him why. Nothing he could do about it, anyway.

Stevie said, "That'd be cool, Frank coming home with a wooden leg."

When Frank arrived months later, we organized a celebration. Twenty or so people showed up, mostly guys he'd known in high school. And there he was, in his uniform, standing tall and strutting around to show off his new leg. We were so proud of him, but surprised he wasn't being discharged. "No," he said, "they've treated me okay, promoted me to sergeant, and they're sending me to school in Monterey to study Russian."

While Frank was enjoying the California coast, I struggled with my senior year in high school. And my kid brother struggled with drugs, his eyes vacant much of the time.

I glanced at Stevie, covering his eyes with his hands.

After Dad's passing, Stevie hung around with a rough crowd. Once he nearly landed in jail for defacing a police car. The Minnesota winters seemed even bleaker, and work on the farm more grueling, as Stevie and I became sheep herders. The day I graduated, I abandoned the farm, said goodbye to Saint Paul, and headed south toward a warmer climate. Took Stevie with me, hoping to keep him out of trouble. I told him those needle marks on his arm were a death wish and reminded him of Frank's sacrifice.

Five days later, we arrived in Baton Rouge. We chose Louisiana because the Army had sent Frank there for basic training. He told us it was plenty warm even in the winter.

I got a job driving a forklift in a warehouse and helped Stevie enroll in school. Within a few years, I advanced to warehouse manager, and Stevie earned a degree in forensic science from

Shoreline Community College. He moved to New Orleans, where he's now a respected member of the city's police force. The kid said he never misses the freezing winters of Minnesota.

"No way," Stevie grumbled, out of camera range. "I couldn't go back home."

I nodded. Me, neither. I moved to New Orleans a few years later.

None of this would have been possible without Frank, who continued to look out for us—frequent letters and brotherly advice. After Monterey, they sent him to Moscow as an interpreter for the Defense Attaché. And from there, he traveled all over the world. I envied his time in Paris and Rome, less so in Abidjan and Karachi. He wouldn't talk about his job. Still in the Army, but no longer a sergeant, he'd earned a commission and been promoted several times.

Frank retired from the Naval Air Station Joint Reserve Base in New Orleans after twenty years in the military, but never slowed down. Not sure who he worked for, but always on the move. Never stayed in one place long enough to get married until he met Louise. Within a few months, they were engaged.

As I continued to speak to the camera, I tilted my head toward Stevie.

When neither of us got invited to the wedding, I questioned his marriage. Not like Frank to leave us out. His explanation—his bride chose the guests—didn't cut it with me.

I still don't know why he married her. Loneliness? Dazzled by her personality?

Stevie said, "Maybe she has big tits." He scowled when I shot him a glance. I grinned.

It wasn't long before Frank and Louise moved from his modest condo in New Orleans to an upscale home in Lake Vista.

Stevie's turn now. He knows better than me what happened next.

* * *

Stevie walked to the camera, cleared his throat, and began.

Admiral Northcote and anyone looking at this video, I'm the kid brother. Now a cop, as you can see from my uniform. And damn proud of it.

I'm not used to public speaking, but Peter insisted I talk about my visit to Frank and Louise's mansion in Lake Vista.

I received an invitation to dinner months after the wedding. Frank greeted me like a long-lost brother, which wasn't far from the truth. He said Peter was out of town, but would visit when he returned. Then Louise took over to show off their riches. Stunning architecture and expensive furniture—but artwork that even a cop wouldn't have bought at a yard sale. She didn't get the joke when I asked if she'd seen the painting of Elvis on black velvet at the New Orleans Museum of Art.

The house tour ended in the dining room. She claimed a visit to Versailles with her first husband had inspired the blue fuzzy wallpaper. I wondered how many others there'd been before Frank. We ate in the kitchen. Muffulettas from Central Grocery on Decatur Street and wine in Waterford goblets poured from a jug of Carlo Rossi red blend.

After dinner, Frank walked me to the car and said my visit was a blessing. When I teased him about marrying a rich widow and living in a castle, he didn't smile.

His back stiffened, and he gave me an icy stare. "Do you remember Dad saying the neighbor woman was so poor she didn't have a pot to piss in? Just like Louise on the day of our wedding."

I glanced at Peter, who was nodding in agreement. He must have recalled Dad's description of our neighbor.

A no-class bitch—sorry about my language—but that's not the half of it. Louise treated me with a contempt that made my skin crawl. And even worse, poor Frank looked like a beaten dog. They say you can sense danger after years on the force. By the time I left for what turned out to be the last time, my sensing circuits were overloaded. I should have spoken to

Frank, warned him that “somethin’ wasn’t right.”

Frank had been a faithful correspondent, but that, too, ended. He answered my occasional emails, but had little to say. I was surprised when a FedEx Envelope arrived, requiring my signature. FedEx from my brother, living ten miles away?

He reminded me he would celebrate his seventy-second birthday in a few weeks. Passed his recent physical, he wrote, with flying colors. The doctor said he’d never seen a one-legged man in such good health.

Frank had updated his will and rented a safe deposit box. He enclosed a key and concluded his letter with these grim words:

If anything happens to me, get yourself over to Lake Vista and open box 317 at the Gulf Coast Bank and Trust. Besides the will, you’ll find a letter with your name. I’m also sending a key to Peter to ensure one of you opens the box at the earliest possible moment. It’s important.

I tried calling, but heard nothing more from Frank, unless you count the email from the Turks and Caicos with a picture of him and Louise lying on the beach. “Wish you were here,” he wrote.

They hadn’t been married a full year when I received a text from Louise: *Call me as soon as possible.* I phoned immediately.

“Frank died of a heart attack in the middle of the night,” she said.

“What?” I stammered, trying to sound composed. “Was there any warning?”

“No, nothing,” she said, “hardly enough time to plan a decent funeral.”

After a few more words, Louise excused herself and hung up. I drove to the bank to open Frank’s safe deposit box.

“I didn’t know they rented boxes that big. Full of photos, certificates, passports, and medals—and right on top was a large white envelope with our names and the words ‘open immediately.’”

Inside the envelope, I found a single typewritten page.

Call (202) 555-0179. Let it ring until someone answers. Then ask to speak to Warren. They may put you on hold for a few minutes, but be patient. He will ask for your case number. Tell him 303199470.

I called from the bank. After a few minutes, a man came on the phone and asked my name. He said he would arrive at the Louis Armstrong New Orleans International Airport on the next flight out of Washington.

Before he hung up, he asked for the name of the funeral home.

The safe deposit box had hundreds of old pictures and two versions of Frank's Last Will and Testament. The first, prepared soon after his marriage, gave everything to Louise, including the house and an impressive portfolio of tech stocks.

Suspicions confirmed. Louise married him for his money. And that explains the second will that left everything to Peter and me. Frank must have prepared it when he recognized her motive for their marriage.

Peter nodded as I looked toward him seated to the right of the camera.

Louise, who knew nothing about the second will, used his death as an opportunity to entertain her friends. She planned a huge reception after the funeral and—get this—even hired a society photographer to cover the event. I asked her if Frank would be buried with a flag and military honors.

She shook her bleached-blond head and said, "That would be tacky."

That pretty well sums up Louise, doesn't it? And for what followed, I'll turn it back to Peter.

Stevie relaxed his shoulders, patted the perspiration on his forehead, and exchanged places with me.

We got together that evening after a phone call confirming the stranger from Washington had arrived. He asked to meet

Stevie and me over breakfast the following day. I assumed it had something to do with Frank's military service. Perhaps a guy from the VA with some honor or an American flag to place on the casket?

Stevie and I were the first ones seated in the restaurant when it opened at seven. The waitress arrived with menus and two cups of coffee as we discussed the new will and the mysterious man from Washington.

"I bet Frank won the Publishers Clearing House Sweepstakes," I said, "and this guy's coming here to give us twenty-five thousand dollars a month for life."

"Or Frank might be in debt to the Mafia," Stevie replied, "and he's here to collect."

I nudged Stevie and pointed to the man standing in the doorway. Dark glasses and rumpled suit. He looked around the room and walked toward us.

"Pardon me, are you the Anderson brothers?"

"Yes, and you must be..."

"I'm Agent Warren Fitzgerald. From Washington." He opened his wallet and flashed a badge.

"Wait a minute," Stevie said with all the authority of a uniformed cop, "that's not an eagle on your badge."

"You're absolutely right. It's an osprey, the only bird of prey found worldwide. Take a closer look at the badge. You'll see we're USG all the way."

Stevie and I looked at each other, both skeptical but eager to hear why Fitzgerald had flown to New Orleans from Washington. He studied the menu while the waitress poured his coffee and warmed ours. He ordered a stack of pancakes and two eggs, sunny side up.

"You're wondering why I'm here," he said.

"You knew our brother, Frank?" I guessed.

"No, never had the pleasure." He offered a bemused smile. "I'm here to retrieve his leg."

"His leg?" I said. "What the hell?"

Fitzgerald raised his chin and nodded.

"They send him to Vietnam, blow off his leg, keep him in the Army for twenty years, and now they want his prosthesis back." This didn't seem right. I must have been channeling Dad's temper when I let loose on this bureaucratic bastard.

"This is a fucking outrage," Stevie added. "I see why you have a bird of prey on your badge. You're swooping down to pick his body apart."

I glanced over at Stevie. Grimacing, hands clenched on the edge of the chair.

Fitzgerald swallowed a gulp of the coffee, so hot it appeared to scald him. Deserved it and worse, I thought. Frank had been dead little more than twenty-four hours, and the Feds were already demanding their piece of him.

Fitzgerald patted his lips with a paper napkin. "After retiring from the Army as a lieutenant colonel, he signed on with us."

"With us? Who?" I asked.

He leaned in and lowered his voice. "If you look closely at his ID, you'll see a faint overlay of an osprey."

"Uh-huh," Stevie interrupted, with the look he must have reserved for drunken drivers who claimed they had only one beer.

"CIA? NSA?"

Fitzgerald shrugged. "I'm not at liberty to say."

Then, he asked us to meet him at the funeral home at noon. "They're expecting us," he said.

Fitzgerald was waiting when Stevie and I arrived. One classy place with politeness that spilled over to unctuousness. The funeral director said he understood what Mr. Fitzgerald requested, but Mrs. Anderson had said no, insisted Frank would not hobble around heaven on one leg.

Fitzgerald opened his briefcase and withdrew a peculiar-looking flashlight. He said the prosthesis belonged to the federal government. "Let's see the leg," he said, "and I'll show you."

The undertaker clapped his hands. A young guy came running, received his instruction, and returned with the prosthesis. Fitzgerald pointed his flashlight at the disembodied leg, turned on an ultraviolet light, and exposed his proof. “Property of the US government,” accompanied by an image of an osprey.

He said he could take the leg with him or get a court order that would postpone the funeral. After a phone call, the undertaker told us Mrs. Anderson had agreed. Fitzgerald reached in his briefcase, removed a black nylon case with a carrying handle, inserted the prosthesis, and headed for the door. My brother and I trailed him to the parking lot.

“Mr. Fitzgerald,” Stevie said, “you’d be downright rude if you run off like that.”

“I don’t get it,” I said. “What do you want with a used prosthesis? Aren’t they custom-made to fit the amputee?”

Stevie’s stern expression in his police uniform seemed to prompt Fitzgerald to offer an explanation. “For our ears only.”

We walked to a garden behind the funeral home and sat on two facing wrought iron benches. Fitzgerald asked if we had seen anything unusual in the safe deposit box.

“Yes,” Stevic said, “a bunch of medals and several passports, all with Frank’s picture, but with different names.”

“You two must have suspected what the passports revealed. He served our country by listening and reporting. Operation Osprey. Now that we’re away from other eyes and ears, I’ll explain the leg.”

He sat on the bench before continuing. “The prosthesis is full of high-end chips and electronics for listening and recording. Among the most sensitive devices in our arsenal. It’s still operational. Hears everything we say, even a whisper. Probably picking up the bees flying around that lilac bush twenty feet away.” He nodded toward it.

“Holy shit,” Stevie said.

“My agency will download the recording and then decommission the leg. Most of the voices will be the everyday humdrum of life. But some will be golden, because of the company your brother kept—swindlers, crooks, spies."

I took a deep breath. Then I had my Eureka moment and asked Fitzgerald if we could hear Frank's voice just before he died.

He said that would be impossible. "Contrary to our rules, no exceptions, unless..." *He paused. Thinking? Maybe improvising.* "...unless there were an overriding interest—or suspicion from a law enforcement agency."

"Agent Fitzgerald," Stevie said, using his command voice, "Join me at the police station. And bring the leg with you."

"Yes, Captain," Fitzgerald said, "and the techie who accompanied me from Washington will download everything from twenty-four hours before Frank's death to this moment."

Stevie said he was sorry I couldn't join him. "Police business," he said with a wink. Same impish look as I saw on the black and white Kodak picture he found in the safe deposit box. The entire family—Mom and Dad, with Frank and me looking deadly serious and Stevie bubbling over with mischief.

I drove back to my apartment with that picture imprinted on my mind. Frank, our role model, now dead. Stevie, then in trouble with the law, now he is the law. He promised to call me as soon as he learned something from the recording.

Hours passed. Called his cellphone two or three times. No answer. Only the usual recording, "leave a message."

It was dusk when Stevie finally phoned, said he'd meet me in an hour. I could tell from the catch in his throat, the slight break in his voice, that he was shaken. When he told me what he heard, I lost it.

Stevie arrived early at the church the following morning. Said he was touched to see Frank's widow kneeling at the casket before it was closed. He thought she was praying. Then he watched her remove his cufflinks and stash them in her purse.

My brother and I were seated in the second pew from the front when the service began at mid-morning, he in dress blues and I wearing Levi jeans and a flannel shirt. We'd decided to honor Frank in our own way and stand apart from the society crowd. The minister undoubtedly said all the right things, but I didn't hear a word. Between praying and pondering the idea of a glitzy reception, I felt alone. Stevie must have heard my rapid breathing. He leaned over and whispered in my ear, "Not to worry. My men know their business." I nodded in response.

After the service, stylishly dressed young women passed flutes of Champagne while servers offered steak tips, grilled shrimp, and miniature drumsticks from some exotic birds. *Ospreys?* A photographer captured smiling mourners. A string quartet played softly at the edge of the lawn.

Frank's widow—in her funeral finery of somber black with way too much jewelry for grieving—stepped up to a platform on the center of the lawn. She bowed her head, waited for the crowd to quiet, and thanked all for their support in her "time of grief." Stevie nudged me and said he hoped the photographer was on his toes.

Without warning, two uniformed police officers pushed through the crowd of mourners. The taller one stepped on the platform and announced in a booming voice that still resonates, "Louise Anderson, you are under arrest for the murder of Franklin Gunnar Anderson." The only sound I remember was Louise calling for her sister, who was also being handcuffed by two other cops.

Agent Fitzgerald, standing beside me, said he'd be returning to Washington shortly. "Gotta take the leg with me," he whispered, "but I'll get you a transcript of the recording."

I broke down again when I read the transcript. Here it is, word-for-word, as Louise spoke to her sister at four a.m. on the morning of the fifth of July.

It's kinda creepy looking at him lying there, all quiet and still. Listened for breathing and checked his pulse, like you said. He's sure enough dead. Dumb bastard never had a clue. I had to push a little to get him to join me in a glass of sherry. He wanted a Guinness, but I told him it was his patriotic duty to celebrate the Fourth with a little sherry—just like George Washington. Except, of course, Martha never added a pinch of fentanyl.

I could go on all day about Frank, but I hope this satisfies your instructions. A damn shame that a man who so influenced Stevie and me had to die at the hands of this money-grubbing bitch.

I nodded so they'd know I'd finished and closed my eyes for a moment. I couldn't believe Frank didn't see it. Imagine doing all the amazing things he did and being taken in by her? Goes to show that everyone had their weaknesses. Including Frank.

Admiral Northcote stood, signaled to the camera operator to stop recording, and invited Stevie and me to join him. We followed him to a small office adjoining the studio and sat around a conference table.

"Thank you," he said. "We'll fire up the camera again for the medal presentation, but first you should know why your brother was murdered."

Stevie and I exchanged a glance.

"Not for money." He paused. "But to protect a Russian asset from disclosure."

"Russian asset? You mean—a spy?" Stevie asked, sitting up in his chair. "Someone Frank had identified?"

The admiral removed his glasses and leaned forward. "Yes, Ludmila Poteyev, born in Russia, immigrated to the States in 1968, and enrolled in the College of Engineering at Tulane, where she was known as Louise Phillips." He paused. "Convicted five years ago, she's serving a life sentence at the Big Sandy Federal Prison in Kentucky."

"Louise? Frank's wife?" I said, unable to wrap my mind around it. "But...she's there for murdering Frank."

Northcote nodded. "True enough. No reason for us to identify her as a Russian spy at that time."

Stevie's mouth fell open. My heart raced. Words wouldn't come.

Northcote continued. "She directed two other sleeper agents, Russian nuclear specialists. Frank followed them for months, including frequent trips to the Waterford 3 Nuclear Generating Station in St. Charles Parish. Louise coordinated the effort along with her so-called sister."

"Frank learned this after the wedding?" Stevie frowned.

"No. He knew well before the wedding—the fake wedding we planned to compromise her. However, when her colleagues were arrested, she suspected Frank knew her true identity."

I could hardly breathe. Stevie maintained his professional cop look, but I could feel his foot tapping beneath the table. "Admiral, am I to understand she killed Frank to save her hide and return to Moscow?"

"Return to Moscow? No. She'd have been disgraced for failing to shut down Louisiana's power grid."

The admiral stood and invited us back to the studio for the award presentation. He read a long citation, held up Frank's medal, and concluded with a handshake and a farewell. "Next time you flip a switch, thank your brother when the lights come on. Without his work, New Orleans would have fallen into darkness for months."

PINES VILLAGE: A JONATHAN GRAVE SHORT STORY

John Gilstrap

Jonathan Grave knew they were close to finding Anita Ortega. She'd used the ATM card she'd stolen from Herbert Ansell to get two hundred dollars from a machine at a bodega on the outskirts of the French Quarter, and then again in the neighborhood that called itself Desire. That was yesterday, and unfortunately, neither of those machines had working security cameras, so Jonathan and his team couldn't tell whether fourteen-year-old Logan Ansell was still with her.

"This is taking too long, Boss," said Brian Van De Meulebroecke, aka Boxers. Larger than most door frames, his callsign Big Guy said it all.

Jonathan didn't reply. This would take as long as it would take, but Big Guy's concerns were one hundred percent legit. With each hour that passed after a kidnapping, the victim's chances of survival plummeted exponentially.

"I'm sure that Venice is doing everything she can," said Gail Bonneville, the third member of Jonathan's 0300 team—hostage rescue team.

Venice Alexander (pronounced Ven-EE-chay, because... reasons), was a slayer of electrons, the computer genius who handled all of Security Solutions' cyber intel operations.

Anita Ortega and three masked cohorts had snatched Herbert and Grace Ansell's son during a home invasion in the suburbs of Houston the night before, along with a duffel bag full of electronics and personal belongings while holding the parents at gunpoint and ultimately knocking them unconscious. When they awoke, instead of calling the police, Herbert called his attorney, Nathan Frisetti, who in turn reached out to Jonathan through a previously established back channel.

This was not the first time Jonathan and his team had been called upon by Frisetti, whose clients tended to have lines of work that proved unattractive to most law firms.

Security Solutions, Inc., of which Jonathan Grave was the sole owner, was a private investigations firm that often worked in gray areas of its own, delivering information to some of the world's largest companies via means his competitors hesitated to employ. While not always on the right side of the law, Jonathan liked to boast that his team was always on the side of justice—on the side of the angels. He hated bullies and bullies came in many forms—many sporting boards of directors and ensconced in skyscrapers. Jonathan took pleasure in leveling the field on behalf of the victims of such bullies, and he employed a staff of a dozen investigators who shared his worldview.

None of those investigators knew of the secret side of the business—the dark side of the business that brought Jonathan and his team to New Orleans tonight. In fact, only a handful of people in the entire world knew that Security Solutions was in the hostage rescue business. For nearly two decades, he and Boxers kicked doors and rescued people on behalf of Uncle Sam when they were part of the Army's elite Unit. Gail had honed her skills with the FBI's Hostage Rescue Team. They were good at what they did.

With the proliferation of terror cells and cartel-related gangs, kidnapping had become a business along the southern tier of the United States. Hostage takers knew it was a reliable way to extort cash from wealthy loved ones. They also knew that with the criminal penalties for kidnapping and murder being identical—life without parole—the smart move was always to kill the hostage in the end and thereby eliminate their most damning witness.

Jonathan and his team were geared for quick and decisive action. When they took a case, their job was to rescue the victim by whatever means and at any cost. They surveilled without warrants. They entered without knocking. If bad guys surrendered, they lived to tell a harrowing story, but if they touched a weapon or made a threatening move, they died. Jonathan was neither an assassin nor a negotiator.

Nothing started, though, before they knew where to look.

The team had set up its command post in a two-room hotel suite paid for in cash. It was a place to stay out of the heat and review yet again the little evidence that they'd been able to gather.

Security videos from inside the Ansell's home had given them their only break, and it was a good one, recording the entire home invasion from several angles. Initially, all the attackers wore balaclavas as they stormed the TV room where the family was gathered, but in the struggle, Logan had stripped the mask off one of them—a female, whose image Venice had been able to run through facial recognition software she'd gained illegally from Uncle Sam and Bingo! They had Anita Ortega, a frequent traveler through the Texas criminal justice system, but mostly for small stuff. Thirty-four years old, she'd done time twice, once on a drug charge that cost her a couple of years, and then a six-year hitch for assault and battery. Both of the convictions were tied to the activities of a street gang called the Kowboy Kings, whose tactics and activities had grown progressively more violent in recent years.

"It looks like the kid was the target from the beginning," Boxers said, pointing his beefy finger at the 14-inch laptop screen resting on the coffee table. "They go right to him." Logan looked ready for bed, barefoot and wearing sweats.

"Mom and Dad don't fight very hard, do they?" Gail asked.

"You never know how people will react to that kind of

fear," Jonathan said, though he couldn't imagine not dying to protect your own child.

The computer dinged, announcing an incoming message from Venice. Jonathan tapped the keyboard and Venice's face took over the top left-hand corner of the screen. Below her image was a refreshed image of Anita Ortega, and below that appeared a Louisiana license plate. A map dominated the right-hand side of the screen, and below that a picture of a beaten-up blue Subaru.

"We got another hit," Venice said through a smile. "Twenty minutes ago, our gal Anita picked up lunchmeats, frozen pizza, a twelve-pack of beer, a six-pack of soda and some bread at the Quicky Mart located at the corner of Werner Drive and Route Ninety in the Pines Village neighborhood."

"I've heard of that place," Jonathan said.

"Think Harlem in the sixties," Venice said. "Or South-Central LA, but without the charm. The plates trace to a Ford Bronco owned by Sheila Stanton of Metairie, Louisiana."

"They changed the license plates," Boxers observed.

"Smart move," Jonathan said. "What about the amount of food? Is she feeding herself or an army?"

"I can show you the whole security video if you want, but it looks like six, maybe seven loaves of bread. That many packages of bologna or whatever and a stack of frozen pizzas. Extrapolate from that what you will."

"I read that as a houseful," Jonathan said.

"They must be holed up nearby," Boxers said. "It wouldn't make sense to drive long distances to pick up that kind of stuff."

"There aren't many businesses around that neighborhood," Venice said. "Even convenience stores aren't convenient, if you know what I mean."

Jonathan leaned in closer to the screen. "But look at the geography. South of Route Ninety, there's nothing. Interstate Ten is kind of a natural boundary to the north, and I-510 kind of forms a boundary to the east. That gives us that long east-west strip between Dwyer Road on the north and Route Ninety to the south. I bet they're in that strip somewhere."

Gail gave Jonathan a curious look. "Are you suggesting that we cruise the neighborhood looking for the car?"

Jonathan shrugged. "Why not? Better than sitting around here. We can take the weapons and comms gear with us."

Venice said, "Let me translate for all of you. Digger is getting bored."

"Damn straight," Jonathan confirmed. "You gave us a starting point—Werner and Ninety. Do you have a compass direction to help us know which way they went when she left?"

"No."

"Look at the bright side," Boxers said, unfolding his enormous frame from the chair he'd been sitting in. Furniture always looked three sizes too small for him. "There's only three hundred sixty degrees on a compass."

"Mother Hen, I have a question for you," Jonathan said, invoking Venice's callsign. "Does Louisiana allow LPRs?" License plate readers.

"Yes, they do," she said, "and I've already tapped into their network. If the Subaru's plate is spotted, I'll get a ping."

License plate readers were a controversial passive reconnaissance tool that consisted of cameras mounted on the hindquarters of police vehicles that continuously read license plates. When a plate came up as stolen, or the owner associated with the plate came up with a warrant, the fact of the recognition served as probable cause for the police to make a stop.

Ten minutes later, the team and their gear were loaded into their rented black Suburban and heading east out of the French Quarter toward Pines Village. Boxers drove, Jonathan rode shotgun with Gail in the right rear. Never much of a party boy, and generally not a fan of heat and humidity, Jonathan had never understood the attraction of the French Quarter. The street music was great, but the food in the most famous restaurants was overrated, and the sheer number of grifters and pickpockets put him on edge. Throw in the urine and puke that flowed in rivulets down the gutters to the storm sewers, and he didn't understand the popularity of the place.

The portable radio on the center console broke squelch. "Scorpion, Mother Hen."

Jonathan pressed the transmit button without lifting the handset. "Go for Scorpion."

"We got a ping from an LPR," Venice said. "Wilson Avenue and Dwyer Road. Not far from the last place we saw her. I've sent it to your GPS. You're heading in the right direction. Looks like you're still four miles away."

"How old is the ping?" Jonathan asked?

"I hacked into their system to send it to me right away, so less than a minute."

"Were cops alerted too?" Boxers asked.

"Not that I can tell," Venice replied. "Who pays close enough attention to their license plates to notice if they'd been stolen?"

"Does your alert come with a picture?" Jonathan asked.

"Negative."

"All right, then," Jonathan said. "At least we know we're heading in the right direction."

Route 90—Chef Menteur Highway—took them across the Danzinger Bridge into a non-descript straight patch of industrial installations and architectural malpractice. It wasn't till they crossed under Interstate 10 that industrial morphed into residential—old houses with all the same well-worn, single-story post-World War II design. With a little imagination, Jonathan could picture when these were the dream homes of the original owners, but now, Pines Village and then Plum Orchard had the sad, desperate vibe of hopelessness and poverty. Jonathan hadn't done the research because it was none of his business, but if past was precedent, he'd be willing to bet real money that the scourge of drug addiction lay at the heart of the misery.

Jonathan pointed ahead and to the left. "There. That's Wilson Avenue. Mother Hen said Wilson and Dwyer. We'll start there and then cruise the neighborhood to see what we can find."

"Oh, the neighbors are gonna love that," Gail scoffed. "Big black Suburban driving slowly and having a look."

"I kinda hope they try to carjack us," Big Guy said. "Just to see the look in their eyes." Boxers had never been one to walk away from a fight. In fact, starting and finishing fights were among his favorite things to do. When he got to employ explosives, he was fully self-actualized.

The streets in the neighborhood were laid out in an asymmetrical grid pattern, with street, drive and avenue suffixes assigned seemingly without purpose or significance. When they first started their tour, hardly anyone was outside their homes, but as ten minutes moved on to fifteen and then twenty to thirty, word had spread, and more people appeared in their yards and at the end of their driveways.

"You were right, 'Slinger," Jonathan said. "We're drawing attention."

"I make 'em as gang bangers," Boxers said.

"Or just concerned homeowners," Gail countered.

More were armed than weren't, but there was nothing illegal in that, and in a neighborhood known for its violence, Jonathan thought it made a lot of sense to have a pistol on your hip. If nothing else, it would make a potential bad guy think twice about making you his next victim.

After about thirty-five minutes, it was Big Guy's turn to point through the windshield. "I spy with my little eye a blue Subaru that looks very familiar."

"Indeed you do," Jonathan said. "Slow down, but don't stop. 'Slinger, can you get a picture as we pass so we can zoom in on the license plate?"

"Sure." She crawled across the bench seat to take a photo with her phone out the back window on the driver's side.

The Subaru sat parked on a concrete slab that served as a common driveway between one of the ubiquitous single-story houses and the only two-story brick house they'd seen so far in their tour of the neighborhood. Like most of the residences, the two-story structure—number 4949—sported expanded metal burglar proof cages over the windows and front door, but this one also had a six-foot steel fence running down its green side—left side.

"Don't like the fence, Boss," Boxers said. "Big fences mean big dogs to me."

"You just don't want to climb anything," Jonathan teased.

"That's the car," Gail announced, holding out her phone. "Plates match."

When they got to the end of the block, Jonathan told Boxers to turn onto Prentiss Avenue and stop the vehicle.

"We need a plan," Boxers said.

"We need intel," Gail added. "We don't even know if Logan Ansell is still with them."

"I'll do you one better," Jonathan said. "We don't know which house Anita is in. That's a shared driveway."

"I think it's the big one with the pillars and the fence," Boxers said.

"I do, too," Jonathan agreed, "but thinking and knowing aren't the same."

"Do you have a plan?" Gail asked.

"Of course I do," Jonathan said. He shared it with them.

When he was done, they stared back at him. "This is where you say, *ha, ha, just kidding*!" Boxers said.

Jonathan smiled and winked. "Time to go shopping."

They parked the Suburban a block and a half from the target house and walked the rest of the way. The order of the day was to act as normally as possible, but on the best of days, it would be clear to everyone that they were not a part of this neighborhood. Throw in the fact that one third of the party was pushing seven feet tall, and there was no escaping that they were going to draw attention to themselves.

The mission was simple: knock on the door and hope that they'd see a familiar face or hear a sound that would indicate that Logan Ansell was inside. Unless things went terribly sideways, there'd be no attempt to rescue him now, not during daylight hours. That would come later, in darkness and with the benefit of night vision and an arsenal of weapons. For now, Jonathan's total load-out was his Colt 1911 .45 on his right hip, plus two spare magazines on his left, all of it effectively covered by the denim jacket he wore over his khaki-colored shirt. While he'd never been a cop, it seemed impossible for him not to look like one.

Gail looked more like an off-duty lawyer in her jeans and white blouse under a blue jacket that concealed her Glock 19. Between what was loaded in the gun and her two spare magazines, she could throw over fifty rounds down range if things went to shit.

The two of them would go to the front door together while Boxers took a position in the rear. Jonathan slowed his approach to the front stoop, awaiting word from Big Guy that he was good to go.

"All set on the black side," Boxers' voice said through the bud in Jonathan's ear. They communicated through hands free encrypted radios.

"Copy," Jonathan said. "Heading to the door now."

A spauled, degenerating concrete path linked the sidewalk to the front door. Jonathan and Gail walked together, almost in step, as they approached. It felt strange to make an approach like this into potential enemy territory and not take any stealthy precautions. The metal mesh over the glass inset of the front door showed signs of rust, but it extended all the way over the door latch, making it more difficult to breach.

Jonathan opted to knock with the knuckle on his left hand, keeping his right hand free. In his experience, if an encounter went to guns, the escalation happened fast.

Beside him, Gail held an apple pie that they'd picked up from the same shop where they'd seen Anita buying food.

He was about to knock a second time when the door pulled open to reveal Anita Ortega herself, her face a mask of nervous confusion. Her hair was a bed-head tangle.

"Who are you?" Anita said. Behind her, deeper in the house, Jonathan saw shadows moving, clearly observing, but not edging closer.

Jonathan pasted a big smile. "Hi. I'm Jerry Porter, and this is my wife, Dorry. We live down the street and go to St. Timothy's." He stopped at that because he wanted to see the reaction. The interior of the house revealed itself to be an unkept mess. Living area on the right, steps to the second floor on the left, just inside the door. The center hall terminated in the back at a kitchen, and Jonathan surmised from the overall design that a family room and dining room occupied the back half of the house.

"Can I help you?" Anita said, her head cocked.

"We brought a pie," Gail said. "It's apple. I wish I could say it's homemade, but I'm really not much of a baker."

"A pie." Anita seemed to taste the words.

"To celebrate the new addition to your family!" Jonathan announced.

Anita recoiled from the words as Gail held out the gift. "What the hell are you talking about?"

Jonathan feigned confusion. "We were told that you adopted a boy. Are we wrong?"

Anita looked like she'd been slapped. She didn't know what to say.

One of the shadows in the background approached the front door. "Thank you," he said when he was still a few feet away.

"That's very kind of you." Now that Jonathan could see the man's face, he could see that it showed no pleasure or happiness. "Take the pie, Anita."

As Anita reached past Jonathan to take the pie from Gail, the newcomer locked Jonathan with a glare. After she retreated, pie in hand, the glare remained. Jonathan kept his features set in a pleasant smile.

"Tu hablas Espanol?" the man asked.

"Si."

In Spanish, the man said, "Who are you really?"

"Just a concerned citizen," Jonathan replied, likewise in Spanish.

"If you are playing a game, it is a dangerous one. It can get you killed."

The smart play was to look unnerved, frightened, but Jonathan couldn't bring himself to go that far. "Were we wrong about the boy?"

"You don't want me to see you again," the man said. Then he closed the door.

"That went well," Boxers' voice said.

Jonathan and Gail turned and headed back toward the street. "At least we got the bug inside," he said. "Planting it in the pie plate was a good idea."

They'd ignited exactly the level of shit storm that Jonathan had been hoping for. They'd barely made it back to the Suburban when Venice patched the audio feed from the listening device to the team's radios. The occupants of the house sounded angry, desperate as they spoke all at once in a random mixture of English and Spanish.

"...pie in the trash."

"Who are they?"

"...like cops to me."

"...if they were cops, they'd have to identify..."

"...get out of here. They know. Somehow, they know."

"Okay, everybody shut up. Settle down." Jonathan recognized this as the voice of the man he'd spoken to at the door. "This isn't a time to panic."

"What it is, is the time to kill the boy and get out of here." That was the lone female voice in the mix—Anita.

"Now you're just being stupid. People know about the boy. They know about us. We kill the boy, they know we killed him."

"Well, what do *you* want to do?" This, from a third voice.

"I want to wait and follow the plan. When Ansell shows us the money, we show him his kid. When we have the money, we decide what the next step is."

"But he's already told the cops," Anita said. "He broke the deal.

"Those weren't cops," the guy from the door said. "If they were cops, there would have been more than two of them. There would have been two *dozen* of them."

"But still, they know."

A fourth voice: "They know *something*, Filo. And something is more than anyone should know. Someone betrayed the plan. I say we cut this whole thing short, kill the boy, burn the house and get out."

"No one cares what you think, Manny. If we do what you say, Emiliano will say *we* betrayed *him*. I don't care to be castrated and have my eyeballs burned out. Do you?"

After fifteen seconds of silence, Anita said, "Filo is right. We gave Ansell till ten o'clock tomorrow morning. I agree that we should stay with the plan."

"But what about the police you say were not police?" Manny pressed. "What do we do about them?"

"Shoot them if we see them again," Filo said. "Meanwhile, we stay alert. I'll call in some friends to help guard the house tonight, just in case. We hold out for a few more hours. Then it will be over."

"Suppose Ansell does not meet his deadline?" Anita asked.

"Then we will deliver young Logan to Emiliano, and he can decide what to do with him."

"Maybe we should bring him up from the basement to keep a closer eye on him." Jonathan wasn't sure which player said that.

"No, he is secure where he is," Filo said. "I don't care to see his eyes or hear his voice if we get the order to kill him."

The final 0300 plan—the rescue plan—wasn't complicated as these things went.

Venice had downloaded the original construction plans for the target house from the property tax office. Built in 1969, the layout was exactly what Jonathan had thought it would be—a standard colonial with rectangular rooms, with the first-floor plan more or less duplicated on the second floor. Given the age of the house, it was entirely possible that walls had been shifted and modifications made, but there was only so much you could do to the bones of a house.

Electrical service entered the house from underground, via a meter located on the Red side of the structure—the right-hand side, looking at the front.

"Standard procedure," Jonathan said. "We kill the power first. 'Slinger, that'll be on you."

"From where?" she asked.

"I'm not sure yet. The bad guys talked about reinforcements. That's the wildcard. Big Guy, you'll float Roxie before we pull the pin so we can get the lay of the land, and then we'll adjust and finalize. No matter how it goes, it's gotta be fast, hot, and loud. Plan two minutes, max, from start to finish."

"Rules of engagement?" Boxers asked.

"Anyone who points a gun dies," Jonathan replied. "The PC is the mission." Precious cargo. "We press forward to the basement, wrap him and snatch him. Big Guy, you'll have the extra vest. Make sure the carrier has plates."

"How old is this kid? The vest is gonna be heavier than he is."

"We'll carry him if we have to."

"What about police?" Gail asked. "We can't get involved in a shootout with cops. Mother Hen, do you have a plan?"

Venice had been monitoring the conversation over the computer link. "I do," she said. "I tapped into the security system at the Big Easy Club in the French Quarter. There's a band competition going on down there. When you tell me you're at T minus one, I'm going to set off the fire alarm, and then I've got multiple bots ready to call in reports of an active shooter. That ought to draw every police officer in the state away from you."

"We only need to buy a few minutes," Jonathan said. He looked at his watch. "We go at ten-thirty."

Boxers could fly anything that had wings or rotors. His most recent toys of choice were drones, all of which he named Roxie. They offered the most fundamental increase in the team's capabilities since the invention of the four-tube NVG arrays. Night vision goggles.

From five blocks away, they launched the four-rotor mini aircraft at 10:10, and with Big Guy at the controls, they reviewed the tactical landscape they would soon be facing. Flying at 300 feet, the enhanced imagery provided by Roxie gave the impression of being nearly on the ground.

"This Filo guy is no rank amateur," Gail said, pointing at the laptop screen. "What is that, eight guys guarding the exterior?"

"That's what I count," Jonathan said. And each of them was armed with either a shotgun or a variant of the AR-15 rifle platform.

"Plus, we have to count on more being inside," Boxers said through a smile. "This is gonna be a gunfight." Big Guy lived for gunfights.

"The only way to win this thing is by surprising the shit out of them," Jonathan said.

"Like you said before," Boxers said. "Fast and loud. With all that steel on the doors and windows, we'll have to breach with GPCs. That ought to wake 'em up." A general purpose charge—a GPC—was a homemade skeleton key composed of about a third of a pound of Composition C4 with a tail of detonation cord—a plastic tube filed with PETN. It was a great tool for opening doors and blowing holes in walls.

"Shoot our way in and shoot our way out," Gail said.

"Nah," Boxers said with a dismissive wave. "If we do the job right shooting our way in, we won't have to shoot our way out."

"Okay," Jonathan said. "We go Wild West on these assholes."

"Seems appropriate for a gang that calls itself the Kowboy Kings, don't you think?" Boxers quipped.

Five minutes later, Roxie was home, put away in her box, and the team was ready to go. Kitted out in black, from their balaclavas to their boots, Scorpion and Gunslinger both carried suppressed H&K MP7s as their primary rifle, while Boxers stayed with his standard HK 417, a long rifle chambered 7.62 millimeter, in case they needed to reach out and touch someone at a distance.

After last-minute safety checks, Jonathan radioed, "Mother Hen, Scorpion, how do you copy?"

The bud in Jonathan's right ear popped. "Loud and clear."

"Okay, we're at T minus one. Work your computer magic and let us know when you're done." Then to Gail and Boxers, he offered a thumbs up. They'd been doing this together long enough that the pep talk could remain silent.

The radio broke squelch again. "Scorpion, Mother Hen. NOPD is dumping everything toward the club. You're good to go."

As if to emphasize her point, the night lit up with the sound of faraway sirens.

"Tally ho," Jonathan said.

The Suburban coasted down the street with its lights off, a black shadow against lighter and darker shadows. The only illumination on the street came from dim yellow porch lights. As the target house came into view, Jonathan took inventory, his NVGs allowing him to see details with nearly as much clarity as if it were noon. The bad guys outside hadn't moved far, still mingling in the yard.

"Stop," Jonathan ordered. "We'll hoof it from here." He'd considered speeding into the front yard, but that would risk getting their exfil vehicle shot up and then stranding them in enemy territory.

Once parked, the team slid out silently and joined at the front bumper, where Jonathan reviewed the plan one more time. "'Slinger, the clock starts when you kill the power. I'll go in the front. You and Big Guy go in the back and beeline to the basement. You'll need to deploy the GPC fast."

Boxers patted a pouch in his vest. "I'm all set."

"Remember," Jonathan reminded. "Two minutes from first shot to exfil."

As the rest of his teammates split off, Jonathan crouched low and advanced on the shooters assembled in the front yard. He wanted to be as close as possible when the balloon went up. He moved slowly in the darkness, aware that humans became far more sensitive to movement after darkness fell—an evolutionary adaptation to having poorer night vision than the predators that fed on our ancestors.

At fifty yards, he stopped. Jonathan brought his MP7 to his shoulder and thumbed the infrared laser sight. Invisible to the naked eye, his NVGs showed brilliant greenish white light that cut through the lightened darkness and lit up the men who soon would die. To his right, through his peripheral vision, he saw the IR lasers from Big Guy and 'Slinger likewise paint the night.

"Three seconds," Gail's voice whispered in his ear. "Two...one..."

On the cadence that would have been *zero*, he heard the suppressed crackle of a short burst of gunfire. The electric meter sparked and darkness swallowed the house.

The guards out front jumped at the sound, turning in unison toward the red side of the structure. Jonathan dropped the farthest target first, nailing him with a bullet through his eye. Then he worked his way forward, drilling the others with double taps at their centers of mass. All four dropped where they stood. The entire gunfight, such as it was, lasted less than five seconds.

It was time to move. "Going in the front door," he said, sprinting across the yard and closing the distance to the porch. He'd just arrived at the bottom step when the door pulled open to reveal one of the kidnappers—Filo, the one he'd addressed at the same door hours before. He brandished a rifle and looked angry as he pushed open the expanded metal cage that would have been a storm door in a better neighborhood.

"What the hell is—" The kidnapper saw Jonathan, but it took an instant too long for him to react. He was still bringing up his rifle when Jonathan shot him twice in the chest. The body fell across the threshold, preventing the metal door from slamming shut again.

"Five tangos sleeping," Jonathan reported for the benefit of the others. He darted up the stairs and stepped over Filo's body, into the living room.

"Three tangos down in the backyard," Boxers reported. "Fire in the hole."

Jonathan dropped to a crouch and looked away an instant before the world shook from the detonating GPC.

"Door's open," Boxers said. "'Slinger's with me."

"Advancing down the center hall," Jonathan reported.

The building plans showed that the stairs to the basement were accessible via a door in the kitchen at the back of the house. As Jonathan approached the back wall, the ruined door flew open to reveal Boxers and Gail entering together.

"Gunslinger, you hold the hallway," Jonathan commanded. "I haven't cleared the second floor, and I don't want to take the time. If anyone comes down—"

"I know the drill, Scorpion."

Of course she did.

Jonathan led the way down the stairs to give Boxers an opportunity to shoot over his head if it came to that. It was like descending into a grave. The six-foot ceiling forced them both to squat as they advanced. The place smelled like mold.

"Logan Ansell!" Jonathan yelled. "We're the good guys. We're here to take you home."

The stairway bottomed out at a wall with two closed doors on either side.

"I'll go right, you go left?" Boxers offered.

Before he could answer, Jonathan heard movement behind the door on the left.

"I heard it, too," Big Guy said.

Jonathan turned the knob on the left-hand door and let the panel float inward.

From beyond, deep inside the room, a female voice said, "Stay where you are if you want to see this boy alive."

Jonathan said nothing. He was not here to negotiate with Anita. In the darkness, he and Boxers had all the advantage. To make noise or try to open a dialogue would only give his prey a direction to shoot at.

The darkness down here was so absolute that his NVGs barely had enough light to magnify. He solved that problem by turning on the IR flashlight mounted to his weapon's Picatinny rail, bringing daylight brightness that only he and Boxers could see.

Anita had retreated to the back of the room, up against a

washer and dryer. She held Logan Ansell tight against her body, the point of his chin nestled in the crook of her elbow, a pistol pressed hard against the side of his head, in front of his ear. The boy looked terrified.

Still not uttering a word, Jonathan scanned the rest of the unfinished basement with the beam of his IR flashlight. A single sweep revealed everything he needed to see. Only one kidnapper remained.

"I know someone is there!" Anita yelled, as if to be heard far away. Her frightened eyes glowed green in the infrared light.

They'd drilled on this scenario dozens of times. Both he and Boxers had clear shots at Anita's head, but with the muzzle of her pistol pressed against the Logan's head, even a sure kill shot wasn't worth the risk. She looked like she already had a couple pounds of pull on the trigger. Two dots of green laser light danced tiny circles on her forehead as both rescuers awaited the chance to shoot.

Boxers tapped Jonathan twice on his shoulder, an alert that he was going to move. Jonathan braced himself, drawing the buttstock of the MP7 deeper into the soft spot of his shoulder.

Behind him, Big Guy jumped off to the side, intentionally making too much noise.

Anita reacted instinctively, moving her pistol away from the PC's head to aim at the source of the sound.

The instant the muzzle cleared the boy's head, Jonathan fired a single shot into the bridge of Anita's nose. As she fell, she brought Logan to the floor with her.

The boy yelled—the sound of raw panic and fear. No words necessary. Jonathan let his rifle fall against its sling and darted to Logan, lifting him by his armpits. The panicked yelling crescendoed.

"Logan, hush!" Jonathan snapped. "We're the good guys and we're here to rescue you. Your parents sent us. I know you can't see anything, but we can see everything. We're not out of danger yet. You need to do exactly what I tell you."

The boy didn't respond, but Jonathan felt confident that his words had gotten through. If nothing else, he quieted down.

Jonathan reached out his right hand and Big Guy gave him the extra vest they'd brought along.

"You need to wear this," Jonathan said as he dropped the heavy Kevlar garment over the boy's head. It was so oversized that he didn't bother with the Velcro closures. "We're going to get you out of here to a vehicle that will take you to safety."

He didn't wait for a response. "The PC is in hand," Jonathan announced. "Beginning exfil. 'Slinger, what's your status?"

"Nothing to report."

"Okay," Jonathan said, "We're exiting out the black side in less than ten seconds."

"Roger that."

Logan didn't fight the effort to get him up the stairs, but he didn't cooperate, either. He seemed stuck in a mental neutral gear, operating as if in a dream.

Gail was waiting for them at the top of the stairs, still facing the front of the house to cover their exit.

"Big Guy," Jonathan said, "You take the PC. I'll clear the route out the back door."

"Scorpion, Mother Hen," Venice said over the air. "Be advised that police and fire are both en route to your location." She'd been monitoring the emergency frequencies.

"Copy that," Jonathan said. Rifle up and ready, he scanned the backyard with the IR flashlight. Three men lay dead in the grass, but he saw no other hazards. "Backyard is clear."

"Coming out," Boxers said.

Jonathan didn't look back. He kept his eyes forward, leading the retreat to the Suburban, confident that Boxers would have a firm grip on Logan Ansell and that Gail would keep her sights on the target house, continuously scanning for additional hazards.

Neighbors had spilled out of surrounding homes, no doubt drawn by the sound of the explosion. Some noticed and pointed, but no one made a move to interfere or intervene. Several darted back inside after a glance.

"We've been made," Gail said.

"Don't engage," Jonathan said. "Pick up the pace. Big Guy, how's the PC holding up?"

"Physically, I think he's fine," Boxers said. "Otherwise, he's scared shitless."

They'd just reached the parked Suburban when Jonathan heard the first approaching siren. He opened the passenger side back door in time for Boxers to lift Logan onto the bench seat. Gail followed immediately afterward, sprawling her body on top of the boy's.

That's when the panic set in again, and the boy rediscovered his voice.

Jonathan closed the door, slid into the shotgun seat and lifted the night vision array off his head. "Lights on," he told Boxers as they pulled away from the curb. "Drive normally. Last thing we need is to get stopped for a moving violation."

Once he settled down, Logan Ansell didn't have much to say through the five-hour drive to the predetermined drop-off location in Beaumont, Texas. That was fine with Jonathan. There wasn't much to talk about, anyway, once they established Logan could never know the identities of the operators who had rescued him. Mostly, he slept.

At 6:54 a.m., Boxers piloted the Suburban into the shopping center parking lot and pulled into a space in front of the Walmart Garden Center.

"What are we doing?" Logan asked. His voice sounded groggy.

"This is the end of your adventure, young man," Jonathan said. "We're here to meet the man who will take you to your parents."

"Who is he?"

"Nathan Frisetti. A lawyer." As if on cue, the door of a Mercedes opened and out stepped a thin graying man wearing crisp jeans, a button-down shirt and a sports coat. Per the agreement, a Dallas Cowboys baseball cap topped his head, and he carried a newspaper in his left hand. "In fact, that's him. Let's go." He pulled on the handle to open the door.

"I don't recognize him," Logan said. Fear had returned to his voice. "Why aren't Mom and Dad here?"

"It doesn't work that way," Jonathan said. "I promise you can trust me. I've worked with Nathan Frisetti before. He will take you back home."

Logan's eyes reddened and his lip started to tremble. "I-I don't understand any of this."

"I'm sure you don't," Gail said. "I'm not sure any of us do, but I promise that you're safe now."

Frisetti had stopped his advance and was standing a few feet from the bumper of his Mercedes.

Gail said, "We need you to just get out, walk over to the man, and he'll take you home. Then this will all be over."

Logan's eyes darted from Jonathan to Gail and out to Frisetti. He looked like a trapped animal.

"You've got to do this, Logan," Gail said in her softest voice. She reached past the boy's chest to open his door. "We promise everything will be fine."

Jonathan could almost hear the kid's brain whirring as he tried to think of a reason to stall, but ultimately, he came up empty. He nodded once, then slipped out of the vehicle and onto the ground. "Um, thanks," he said. Still barefoot, he walked tenderly over to Frisetti and allowed himself to be ushered into the Mercedes. He gave one furtive glance back to the Suburban before he took his seat and closed the door.

As they watched their PC being driven off to safety, Gail said, "Chalk up another win for the good guys."

Something didn't feel right, though.

"Hey, Boss," Boxers said. "I know we've done business

through Frisetti before, but have you ever met him? Like, face-to-face?"

Jonathan felt his stomach drop. "No. Only over the phone."

"Huh," Boxers grunted. "So, you don't really know what he looks like."

Jonathan closed his eyes and sighed. "Shit."

"Yeah." Boxers dropped the transmission into Drive. "I guess we're following a Mercedes all the way to Houston, aren't we?"

THE GAME OF LIFE—AND DEATH

Heather Graham

"It's easy, it's fun! And it's so Halloween! And it's going to be the best game ever!" Julie Johnston announced.

And inwardly, Connie Braxton sighed. She was here, she would do it. But maybe she had too much respect for the history of the place or maybe even the dead. Sure. It was perfect for a pre-Halloween party. Decaying elegance might well describe the cemetery with its lush growth of towering trees and brush, creating eerie sounds as the branches moved with the night breeze. The tombs, mausoleums, and in-ground graves were touched with all the wear of age. The few lights from a far-away street, along with the half-moon and spattering of stars in the sky, created deep shadows so that it was almost as if an eerie mist had set over the place!

"A scavenger hunt—in an old, old, creepy cemetery!" Julie continued, a mischievous smile on her face. "And of course, it's only possible because my father—a guy I *do* truly adore—is the caretaker here. My backyard leads right into the cemetery, and Dad, whom I love so much, happens to be off for a week to visit my brother! Not only are you specially invited to play a great game, but you also get to run around one of our venerable 'cities of the dead' at night. Okay, no, we're not at St. Louis #1, #2, or #3, but our cemetery in our little city by the bayou is almost as old as St. Louis #1! No one had to be dug up because way back when, it was far enough from the big populations not to bother anyone. And while it's been deconsecrated, my dad keeps up the abandoned church that allowed for all the creepy, cool, wonderful things you'll find here. So, you're off!"

George LaRue, one of Julie's carefully selected guests, let out a loud laugh. "Wait! We're running around a cemetery—trying to find dead people. Isn't that a given?"

"Certain dead people!" Jay Johnston corrected, grinning. "Come on, guys! The Catholic Church owns the major cemeteries, and other people keep 'em locked up at night, too, so…you don't get a cool, creepy chance to run around a real city of the dead at night—on a scavenger hunt no less!"

"A scavenger hunt in a haunted cemetery!" Someone cried excitedly. "Incredibly cool! You go, Julie!"

Connie tried to keep smiling as others laughed and spoke and teased each other and made monster noises.

She really needed to give in and embrace the game. Everyone else seemed ready to do so.

After all, Julie had been her best friend since they'd been kids. And she wasn't particularly spooked-out by the cemetery—the two of them had slipped through cherry hedges that were the line between the caretaker's property and the cemetery itself often enough as kids, delighting in scaring one another with ghost stories.

But this…

A scavenger hunt in a creepy old cemetery? As ridiculous as she had thought it sounded—not to mention the fact that Julie's father would be furious if he ever found out about it—Julie was convinced it was an incredible, wonderful, and unique event for a pre-Halloween party. Very few people in the *entire world* could carry it off, and *Ray* had thought it an amazing plan!

And that was the main reason Connie would have never been able to talk Julie out of it—Julie was, of course, madly in love with Ray. She and Ray had carefully planned the "random" pairing of their friends to go out on the hunt, and they were sure they had created the right twosomes for the project. Julie was still playing innocent about having made sure Connie was partnered with Jonah Jackson.

There was nothing wrong with being with Jonah. She didn't know him well; he was a senior at the university, and she was a junior. But from the few conversations she'd had with him when they'd both happened to be around Julie and Ray, he seemed like a decent enough guy and more.

Jonah was, stereotypically, a hunk. He was gorgeous, the guy every girl in any class at the university would want to be with. Supposedly, the ten guests Julie and Ray had chosen for the event had simply drawn names to pair up so that best friends or couples weren't together for the game.

Random. Sure. And Julie had determinedly pulled this off because she and Connie were best friends. Ray and Jonah were best friends. Julie wanted Jonah and Connie to become a couple, but…

People didn't become "a couple" in one night! And they might like one another well enough, but they both had plans of their own.

Jonah was truly "Mr. Big" at the university. He was incredibly good-looking as well as the quarterback of the football team. Everyone knew he was certain to be drafted by the NFL when he'd finished his degree.

As close as they were, Julie didn't really understand Connie's dead-set determination on getting where she wanted to go.

She was hell-bent on being an investigative reporter in New Orleans, if possible, or anywhere else if need be. She spent her time working hard at her classes at the university, which was expensive. But thankfully, she had managed a hefty scholarship. She and Julie had been friends forever, and when Julie had wanted to throw the small party, she'd wanted to be as supportive as possible.

Julie was used to being in the upper realm of all that was social. So, of course, she had picked her guests carefully. Nine others besides herself, Ray, and Julie—all who were among a well-known group of students—the "in" crowd.

"So!" Julie announced. "You have your lists on your phones! You need pictures of a family mausoleum, interments in walls, family plots, and a great pic of a handsome length of the cities of the dead, as in one of the rows of family mausoleums. Also! The markers for the man whose dog was interred with him after he died, a Union soldier, a Confederate soldier, and the grave of the 'Vampire of Meadow Bay' and that of Belinda Broussard, known to be the zombie of the place since she wasn't dead when she was buried in 1826! That's nine pics, and you must stick together as a couple. Do not group up for the pics!"

The cemetery was known for being haunted, Connie thought wearily. But then again, everything in the City of New Orleans and environs was said to be haunted. But they weren't kids anymore! She knew a lot of the sad history of the place.

They were also not quite in the city—far from the craziness of the French Quarter, down by the river in a little area that had really been the outskirts when the city had been founded. There were stone walls around the place and a handsome metal gate. But since they were far on the outskirts, it was also extremely darker. The cemetery was one typical of many in this section of Louisiana. Many little mausoleums held family members long gone; there were some in-ground burials, some interred in the thick stone walls, and some individual tombs between the rest. And while Julie's father did his best as caretaker for the place, lush foliage and trees filled it as well.

She had told herself she didn't get creeped out by the cemetery!

And she didn't. But it was very dark that night. They had their phone lights, and of course, they were supposed to use them along with their phone cameras, and still...

Ten of them, out in the darkness!

It wasn't a game that Connie liked!

"Break, go, get out there! Winners take all! Oh! One more thing—watch out! We are coming up on all Hallow's Eve, when every creature might be out there. Who knows not who, but *what* you might find in the cemetery!"

"Oh, wow!" Lily Patterson, one of the guests who had "randomly drawn" another of the university's football players, cried softly. "So scary—not just the dead, but a zombie and a vampire out there!"

"I'll protect you!" Lance Cartwright, her football playing partner, assured her.

Connie groaned softly. "Let's do this. I can find what she wants," she told Jonah.

"All of that?" Jonah asked, grinning as he turned to Connie. He really was striking with his dark hair and flashing eyes and football body.

She smiled in turn and shook her head.

"We can't really be doing this, can we?" she asked Jonah.

He shrugged, still smiling. "I guess we can. And I'm lucky. I'm with you—you know this place! We can follow her list quickly and get the hell out of here!"

"That's a plan. Okay, let's start with the dog that is buried with his beloved owner—New Orleans' own version of Greyfriar's Bobby! Others will have a tough time finding it. It's an in-ground burial over by the far side of the old church!"

"Let's do it!"

Connie didn't mind when he caught her hand, drawing her through one of the little breaks in the hedges.

It was as if the lights from Julie's house faded almost immediately. Before them stretched an alley—a little roadway that passed through a line of family mausoleums.

Reaching the end of the little street, she stopped so quickly Jonah crashed into her back, grabbed her and began apologizing. She spun around to look at him, angry and a little disturbed—but not with him! Jonah hadn't done anything; and he was proving to be nice, polite, and he certainly seemed to be...

Caring, as well.

"Are you all right?" he asked her worriedly.

"Julie and Ray got a little bit carried away with this. Look up."

He did so and saw what she had seen—a life-size skeleton hanging from one of the trees.

"I guess you didn't see the bodies," he said dryly.

"Bodies?" Connie asked, staring at him with a horrified frown.

"Yeah, two of them, thrown by the side of the last little mausoleum," Jonah said. "They seriously must have bought out a prop shop for this party. But you know what? I hope they had fun because they are going to have one major clean-up after this."

"Her dad would have a fit!" Connie said, shaking her head. "Anyway…picture of the row of family mausoleums. Picture of the pup and his master. Oh! Our vampire is over here. Come on!"

"Watch it!" Jonah told her.

"What—oh! Another one! Oh, man, really! Julie must have bought out every Halloween costume and prop store in the south of the state!" Connie said, sliding by the "corpse" Jonah had pointed out. "Really, this is too much. Let's finish, quick."

"Yeah, we can get out before the clean-up. Go somewhere not this crazy. Maybe go watch some great jazz or see some local acts on Frenchman Street. I mean, if you'd like. If you wouldn't mind."

Connie smiled at him. "No—I'd like very much! I love the history of this place, Jonah, not so happy about…all this! I mean, there are incredibly sad stories—the Union soldier and the Confederate soldier brothers. They both survived the war and made up. And the Union soldier came home to see his family who were struggling during the Reconstruction period, but forgave him, and he was able to hold his brother in his arms when he died of a war injury in 1867. And the family were the first to demand that those who had been slaves in the city could have a monument in here and have their own family mausoleums or be buried or interred here as they chose. And the fellow with the dog—he became one of the first advocates for Civil Rights, and his dog went with him everywhere. It goes on, Jonah, so many wonderful people buried here, along with some who lost their lives tragically, and I…I just don't like this!"

"I understand!" Jonah assured her.

They heard the others screaming now and then, coming upon more of the props Julie and Ray had apparently set up all over in the cemetery.

On the one hand, she had to admit that she was grateful. She was glad she was with Jonah for the ridiculousness of it all! He'd had his camera out—they already had the individual family mausoleum, the "street" in the "City of the Dead," the supposedly vampire grave, and they were by the brothers who had fought—and reunited—and they were near the devoted dog and his owner, and she was pretty sure, their last assignment.

The zombie.

They needed to finish up. Yep.

Then, yes, get out of there quickly, before their disappearance could be noted. They could head to Frenchman Street to listen to some cool jazz or an up-and-coming local band. Yeah…

"There!" she told Jonah. "You got the brothers, right? Just around here…"

Jonah had stopped. Moonlight was falling on the gravesites, the mausoleums, tombs and markers. As if in on a conspiracy, a fog or a slight night mist had fallen. And the cemetery was beautiful and…

Eerie!

"Okay, we've got everything except for—"

"The zombie!" Jonah said.

"Okay, toward the far wall. He's buried in-ground," Connie said, "by the wall where the tree branches seem to be everywhere, right around this mausoleum."

"You lead the way."

She did.

They had barely reached the area before there was a strange sound in the cemetery in the darkness of the night. It was a plaintive cry in the night at first, and then it turned into something that sounded far more like a growl or a grunt of fury, something that seemed to twist eerily in the mist of the darkness and the strange little rays of light that did nothing but create creeping shadows.

Then it seemed the earth burst open, and a man began to arise from the grave.

Like a zombie.

Back from the dead.

It was almost Halloween. It was Julie's idea of creepy-crawly fun, the party of the season, the year, the decade.

But this was too much. No matter how Connie told herself that it was only a cemetery—it housed the dead—she felt a rash of fear sweeping over her.

Despite herself, she let out a strangled scream. Jonah Jackson grabbed her arm, but Jonah barely choked back a scream himself.

"Something's not right!" he announced.

And it wasn't. But for a few seconds, she was frozen. Rooted to the spot. And after having his head, shoulders, and arms break through the ground, the man went limp.

It was a game, just a game.

One that was proving to be a bit too realistic!

Then the man moved again, laughing with a deep and guttural sound.

"Death is the game!" the corpse cried. "And now death be your name!"

Game. Yeah. That was it, right? It was all a game. Julie had hired people to make her game as real as possible!

Except something about his demeanor, his costume, everything seemed far too real, and she thought about the other "pretend" corpses they had passed in the cemetery, and she wondered...

What the hell was really going on here?

Jonah had her arm. He spoke to her in a whisper. "Run. It's time to get the hell out of here now!"

And he was right because the man had crawled out of the ground. He was covered in dirt, his face, hair, and beard covered with it.

As was the knife in his hand, a weapon that managed to catch a slim shaft of moonlight making its way through the mist.

She knew the cemetery. Knew it well. She twisted around, switching Jonah's hold on her to a hold she had on him.

And she began to run.

She whipped Jonah along with her around the side of a family mausoleum, dragging him around to the front and a pathway between two rows of the ancient stone creations to honor the dead.

But the man's laughter was heard behind them. They wouldn't make it back to Julie's house, to a road, to safety.

Again, she was grateful. So very grateful. Because she did indeed know the history of the place.

And she raced quickly toward one of the mausoleums, one with the family name "Hudson" over the metal fencing that stood before the decaying wooden door.

Jonah didn't protest. He followed along with her into the darkness of the home for the dead.

She pulled the fence back into place and closed the door.

"Call, call, call 911!" she said to Jonah. His phone was in his hand. He could do so quickly.

But they were almost blinded in the small space in the darkness with only a square opening high on the back wall.

Connie desperately wished there was a way she could peek out.

She heard Jonah speaking. He was clear and concise, telling them where they were and what was happening.

Connie wondered if she was crazy, if the corpses were what they had thought, props bought at one of the shops that stocked up insanely when Halloween was on the way. And she wondered if the man after them wasn't a hired actor, one who would laugh at their fear, showing them he carried a plastic, theatrical knife once he'd carried out his performance.

No.

She'd seen the glint of the pale moon on the blade. Plastic couldn't catch a reflection in such a way.

"They'll be here!" Jonah promised, stumbling into the tomb of the family patriarch, Josiah Hudson, where it was positioned in the center of his family's vault.

Connie could hear him clearly, and she reached out, found the tomb herself, and made her way to him.

"You don't think it's a mistake, do you? That I've just ruined Julie's party?" he asked her in a whisper.

"No!" she whispered back. "And if so, it will keep Julie from ever having such a stupid party idea again!" she assured him.

"What about the others?" he murmured.

She wasn't sure which "others" he meant, their friends running around the cemetery trying to get all the required photographs for their scavenger hunt or the others as in the bodies...

"I don't know!" she whispered, speaking so close to him she could feel his body heat, his breathing. "I just...I just hope that *we're* safe in here. We should be—most of the family vaults or mausoleums can't be entered without keys for the padlocks on the gates and for the inner doors." She swallowed hard, listened hard, and took a breath. "Josiah Hudson's great-great-whatever great nephew just died in Virginia. He was a decorated soldier, and they're having a service for him there, but he's being interred here next week. That's why this one has been opened. Family members are supposed to be coming by during the day to...to do whatever they do!"

She felt Jonah move slightly, setting a hand reverently on the tomb. "Thank you, Josiah!" he said softly.

"This one is old, very old! Josiah was in the local government in the 1830s. He loved the city and wanted this place for himself and all those who came after him," she told Jonah. She didn't mention that his was the only tomb. In the darkness, Jonah couldn't see that family members rested in nothing but shrouds on the ledges. In such a working tomb, they were given "a year and a day" in such a position. After that time, their remains, cremated by the intense Louisiana heat, were swept into a little section at the rear of the shelving, family members joining those who came before them in the ashes of death.

"Listen!" Jonah said.

He had fumbled in the darkness, seeking to put a finger against her lips.

Because he'd heard something, she realized. Someone slamming on the different vault doors.

"Weirdo bastards, I'll find you, and you will be dead meat before I run the hell out of here!" The guttural voice of the "zombie" man called out. "Dead meat—right where you should be, along with the rest of the putrefying *dead* meat!"

Then, to Connie's absolute horror, she heard the man touching the gate to the Hudson vault.

How? How could he have possibly known this was the one and only family vault in the cemetery that wasn't securely locked tight? Or had he already tried them all?

She wanted to cry out, to tell him the police were on the way. But this was the outskirts of the big city. How long until...

"No! Down!" Jonah whispered to her.

He pressed her toward the rear of the central tomb of Josiah Hudson.

The gate was slammed open. Their "zombie" laughed with delight.

"Aha! I know you're in there and, well, meat...dead meat! I mean, that's all a cemetery is, right? Meat, food for the worms and the creepy crawlies!"

The wooden door, not so heavy since it was hundreds of years old, opened with a hard slam, a shuddering noise.

Connie felt Jonah's arm around her shoulder. He was trying to assure her, and she knew he was big and strong, but...

The zombie had a knife, and if their fears were correct, he'd already used it. Julie hadn't bought out the prop houses.

The corpses were real.

It was as if the "zombie" read her mind.

"A game, such a game, what a wonderful game! And such a fun game, catching a few druggies out on the street, throwing them over the wall here. See, I know every escape route. But I must admit, I had no idea that this wonderful, wonderful game would be going on, that it would be...oh, so much fun! Hm. It is dark in here, isn't it? Come out, come out, wherever you are! Or don't. Because believe me, I will find you!"

Jonah lifted a hand, warning her to stay still.

She had never realized she was such a coward. She'd always been comfortable in the cemetery.

Comfortable with the dead.

She'd never had to face a living maniac in the shadows, in the darkness of a tomb.

He was moving around, the only benefit being that he was as blinded as they were in the darkness. But he saw the little square window of light at the rear of the tomb and began moving toward it.

She was ready to leap up in terror, to try to run again, out...out, far and fast.

But she felt Jonah's warning touch. She prayed he had an idea of what he was doing.

Closer!

She could hear the man moving slowly, very slowly. She imagined he was throwing his arms out ahead of him, feeling for anything he could find in the darkness.

He was at the central tomb within the vault, where the mortal remains of Josiah Hudson rested in the one area where his flesh and organs would decay, but his skeleton would remain in the tomb, perhaps for eternity.

While the others...

A year and a day.

Connie wondered if any of his descendants had died recently, if their remains still lay shrouded in the catacomb-like shelving on the sides of the little mausoleum.

And what did it matter? She might soon be among the dead herself, rotting flesh and organs, bones going more slowly, ashes to ashes, dust to dust...

Closer. He was moving closer and closer to them.

And Jonah still had his hand upon her back as they hunched behind the remains of Josiah Hudson.

And then...

Another step closer. And another.

He was almost upon them. Connie wondered if he couldn't hear the terrified beat of her heart or smell the fear that had to have been wafting off her.

A step and another step.

"The game is lame, but the game has your name!" the "zombie" said, laughing at his own cleverness. "A game to make you all the same! First! My knife, she'll make you lame, then she'll finish off the game!"

Connie could barely breathe.

Another step...

And then Jonah acted.

He lunged forward, catching the man's ankle, wrenching him up, causing him to fall back with a massive thud on the floor of the vault.

He urged her to her feet, rising, pushing her toward the exit, telling her, "Run!"

But the "zombie" had recovered. He was rising, his knife out.

He lunged at Jonah, but it was dark. Jonah hit him as if he

was a great tackle rather than a quarterback.

They went down together.

"Run, run, run!" Jonah shouted to her again.

She couldn't see! She couldn't see clearly. But she could hear the two of them fighting, fighting viciously, she knew...

Jonah was desperately trying to get his hands on the knife.

It was strange. So strange. Because even in here, in the enclosed darkness, that little window in the rear granted that tiny streak of moonlight.

And it fell on the blade of the knife.

Jonah was on the ground, fighting, fighting hard. And the zombie...

The zombie straddled over him, but he could free his wrist. He was trying to stab the blade into Jonah's heart, or into any point of his body.

She would never know what possessed her, but she couldn't leave him. And she had a bizarre idea.

Floundering around, she swept her hands over the catacomb-like shelving in the tomb. And she damped down the horror of touching a dissolving shroud, feeling human remains beneath her fingers...

But she found what she wanted.

She grabbed the length of bone that her fingers curled around at last.

She stepped back around the central tomb of Josiah Hudson.

She blinked hard, watching for the moonlight to touch the blade.

The zombie still had it, but Jonah's hands were hard around the zombie's wrist.

She knew she had to act, and Connie grasped the long bone with both hands, and then she swung it. Swung it with all her strength.

And her aim was true.

She heard the massive cracking sound as the bone slammed against his skull.

And she waited, barely breathing...

The zombie went down without a sound and crashed to the ground at Jonah's side.

She thought! She hoped! She prayed!

And she was right. Someone began to stand, and she knew it was Jonah. And as he stood, they heard sirens at last.

She jumped when he reached out to touch her.

"We're out of here!" he said.

"We can't run. We must—"

"We're not running anywhere. We're telling the police what happened."

And they did. Julie was, of course, hysterical. As were the others, gathered in Julie's living room to give the police statements before they were allowed to go home.

A nice officer explained to her it wasn't her fault at all. They had been hunting the man—the zombie—in the tomb for weeks. He had killed in Houma before making his way to New Orleans and surrounding towns.

Whether she'd had the party or not, the man had evidently planned to dispose of the remains of those he killed in the cemetery, as he had done in Houma, and possibly other areas before.

"And," the officer said, looking from Jonah to Connie and then back at Julie again, "frankly, thanks to your friends, many lives may be saved in the future."

The killer wasn't dead. An ambulance had arrived with the police, and he was whisked away to the hospital where he would be chained to his bed until he recovered.

Or didn't.

He was still out, but breathing.

As it turned out, because they were the ones who had engaged with the man, Jonah and Connie went to the station with the officers, where they answered questions and signed all the necessary papers.

They learned the man had been Nelson Shoemaker of Monroe, Louisiana. A couple of years earlier, he'd been arrested for assault. He'd served his time in a state facility for the criminally insane.

But—insanely—he'd managed an escape. And local and state and even federal police had been after the man.

"She saved my life!" Jonah told the police.

"After he saved mine," Connie responded. He gasped softly then. "Oh! But I used a bone that...that belonged to a member of the Hudson family. That's so horrible!"

"I don't think so. I don't think so at all," the officer told her. "The Hudson family tend to be very good people. Even a dead Hudson would have been happy to help save your life."

She hoped it was true.

Her parents showed up, and Jonah's dad showed up. They were allowed to go home at last.

Of course, it didn't end that night. There were reporters hounding them, and Julie's father was so angry and apologizing over and over...

And then there was the Hudson funeral and interment for Lieutenant Samuel Hudson.

The funeral service itself was at a functioning church. But then the lieutenant was brought to lie with his family. And they were able to meet some of the family members, the lieutenant's great uncle for one, a man to tell them how proud he was their vault had allowed for them to live—and take down a killer.

And when the service was over...

Jonah, who had attended it as well, spoke softly to Connie.

"I really think it would be okay if we went and saw that jazz now, you know, over on Frenchman Street. I mean, yeah, I know, I'm sorry. I think we were fixed up, and it turned it out not to be such a great night, but..."

She was able to smile at him.

"Seriously. I don't think I could have been set up with such a fine partner for such a night ever!" she told him.

And it was true. He had given her more than she realized.

She would still love the history and beauty of so many cemeteries.

She might still be a coward, but she could act when necessary, even when she was shaking in her bones.

She could easily forgive Julie, even sincerely thank her.

Because Jonah smiled. And she realized they might turn out to be a couple.

Late that night when he brought her home, he vowed, "I'd love to see you again. And again and again. And I promise, I'll never bring you to a cemetery!"

She laughed. "No! I still love our beautiful 'cities of the dead.' There is just one thing!"

"What's that?" he asked.

"Don't you ever, ever, ask me to play a game in a cemetery again!"

Of course, she knew he never would!

FOR SAMMY

Kerry Hammond

I wish I could say I never thought I would be back here again, but it would be a lie. I knew I would be back; I didn't know when. Sometimes when you leave a place, it doesn't leave you. St. Christopher's Home for Boys in New Orleans is one of those places.

Maybe it was because I spent the better part of my youth here, or maybe it was because this place has a way of taking hold of people and not letting go. I know it has always had ahold of me. The fact it was about to be gutted and turned into a country club didn't change the strange pull I felt. Maybe once the renovation was complete, it would no longer have the same effect. Then again, maybe not.

There was talk about closing the place when Jonathan Brightwell was killed, but instead, the state hired a new director and things went on as usual. And by usual, I mean with the usual amount of neglect and disregard.

I was sent to St. Christopher's at a young age. It was April, five days after my tenth birthday, and the weather had started to heat up. I was so excited to hit double digits that year, and I had talked about it for months beforehand. I knew my mom would have to buy two candles for the top of my cake to make the number ten, and for some reason, that excited me. I didn't want a party. I wanted to celebrate with my family. That probably wasn't normal for a ten-year-old, but that was how much I loved my parents.

My mom asked me what I wanted for my birthday, and I knew right away. I wanted the latest Nike tennis shoes. My best friend, Nick, had gotten a pair two months before, also for his birthday, and I had been dreaming of having a pair of my own. I hesitated because I knew they were expensive, but my mom never even blinked an eye when I told her.

Birthdays were a big deal in our house. They were anticipated and celebrated, and they often lasted more than just one day. That year, on the Saturday before my birthday, we took a riverboat ride down the Mississippi River. I had just read *Huck Finn* that year, and I swear I saw his raft in each nook and cranny along the way.

When it happened, I wasn't the only one who arrived at St. Christopher's that warm spring afternoon. My younger brother Sammy was with me. When I left six years later, I was more or less an adult, and Sammy was dead.

My cross-country drive to New Orleans gave me plenty of time to think about the return to my past. I had been living in Denver for the last year, going from job to job, making ends meet. It was a habit to scan online for anything that mentioned St. Christopher's. I had been doing it for years. Last month, I found an article saying that the home had closed down after being in operation for seventy-five years. Some heralded it as a landmark, lamenting the fact that the city was losing such an institution. People can be so dramatic.

I had mixed feelings about going back, but I knew it was necessary. I knew I had to return, just once, before it was too late. Before the home I knew was changed forever, before the walls were torn down and reconfigured into something unrecognizable. Call it exorcizing demons, call it nostalgia. I don't care. Whatever it was, it had to be done.

Since Sammy and I weren't always orphans, we had a hard transition to life at a boys' home. When you come from the streets, moving to a place with shelter, three meals a day, and an education might seem like you cashed in a lottery ticket. When you come from a happy home with two parents who not only loved their kids, but loved each other, well, that's a bit harder to swallow.

It's impossible to get over the death of your parents when you lose them at such a young age. It has taken me years to convince myself that their death wasn't my fault. Much like an addict, I relapse occasionally and blame myself all over again. It's a vicious circle that I doubt I will ever break.

If I hadn't grown so much in my ninth year, the Nike tennis shoes I received as a birthday gift would have fit me. As it turned out, I not only grew three inches that year, I also went up another shoe size. That's what my parents were doing when the semi-truck t-boned their car only three miles from our house. They were going to the mall to exchange the shoes. Sammy and I stayed home because one of our favorite shows was on TV that night. Since the mall was so close, they let us stay home alone. They would only be gone thirty minutes, and we didn't have a babysitter on call.

I would like to be able to convince myself that I noticed their prolonged absence and was worried what might have happened to them, but that wasn't the case. Four hours after they left, Sammy and I were still watching TV, albeit past our bedtime, when a policewoman showed up on our doorstep. She was the one that broke the news that they were gone. Part of my little boy brain felt sorry for her that night. You could tell that she wasn't used to notifying someone of a death, let alone notifying kids they were now orphans.

I stand at the bottom of the massive front steps and stare at the building for a good fifteen minutes. The entrance looks as imposing as it did back when I first laid eyes on it. The stone building, built in 1948, hasn't changed much, but the double doors look aged. Paint is peeling, and the red isn't as vibrant as I remember. I put my hand on the railing and start my ascent. I don't just need the railing for support, though that's part of it. I mainly hold on because it helps me remember. The feel of the cold steel on my hand brings it all back.

To say that we arrived with only the clothes on our backs wasn't that far from the truth. When the police officer whisked us away that night, she told us to each bring along one toy. She also told us we would come back for the rest. I'm not sure if it was a lie or if she actually believed we would return.

Sammy didn't have to think twice. He ran upstairs and grabbed his Disneyland snow globe. It was his prize possession, a souvenir from a trip we took the year before. The globe was made of plastic, glass wouldn't do for children, and the base was shaped like Space Mountain, his favorite roller coaster ride at the park. The base was made of stone and had a bit of heft to it, but Sammy didn't care. He took that thing everywhere with him. The funny part was that he never even rode the ride—he was too short. We spent an hour watching other people ride it. An employee took pity on him and let us inside to watch from the control booth, telling him to come back when he was taller and they would put him at the front of the line.

He stood there, in the room we shared, holding the snow globe to his chest. "What are you gonna take, Simon?" he asked. It was as if we were going away for the weekend, not leaving our house to enter into child custody.

I honestly had no idea what to take, but I didn't want to make too big a deal of it. Sammy was keeping it together, and I didn't want to break the spell. I had read about people who went into shock, but I had no idea how it worked. Did you snap out of it randomly, or was it something that someone said or did that caused reality to break through? Either way, I didn't want that to happen until much later.

I was frozen and didn't know what to choose. My baseball mitt was hanging on a chair in the bedroom. I got the mitt for Christmas that year and was practicing with my Dad in hopes I would make the school team. I absentmindedly grabbed that and put on my best 'it'll be ok' smile. "I think I'll take this," I said. He smiled back at me, a genuine smile, as if to say, 'good choice.' I put my hand on his back and led him out of the room. We would never set foot in that house again.

I know it's clichéd, but kids who grow up in boys' homes tend to be more resourceful than those who grow up in traditional homes. This resourcefulness can include knowing how to break the law without getting caught, something I am proud to say I have mostly avoided. Mostly. I did, however, learn some skills at St. Christopher's that have served me well in my time on this earth. One of those skills was how to pick a lock. I acknowledge the irony that I learned to pick a lock while living at St. Christopher's and I am now picking the lock on the front door of the same place—this time to get inside. It almost makes me smile. Almost.

Some locks are challenging, but the padlock on the large wooden door takes very little time to open. The faint 'click' as it pops is quite satisfying. I pull the chain that is looped through the double doors at the top of the entry steps and drop it on the concrete landing to my left. I take a deep breath and pull open the door.

As I roam the halls of St. Christopher's, memories come flooding back. To be fair, not all of them are bad, and it's the good ones I try to let in first. I had my first kiss with Katie Harrison in the hallway outside the cafeteria. Katie was the daughter of a couple who were there to adopt a son. Her mom nearly died when Katie was born and had to have a hysterectomy, making a second child impossible. They had always wanted a son, something that was way more in fashion when I was a kid. Nowadays the correct answer to 'Do you want a boy or a girl?' is "I just want a healthy baby." We all know that's a lie. Most people still have a preference, but it's not politically correct to voice it.

Katie didn't seem to mind that her parents wanted to adopt a brother for her. She visited St. Christopher's maybe a dozen times. The Harrisons had frequent meetings with the director of the home, Jonathan Brightwell, and had multiple visits with Timmy to make sure adopting him was a good fit. You can't be too careful.

She approached me on her first visit and we sat on the stairs and chatted the entire time her parents were in Brightwell's office. After that, when I knew she was coming, I would hang out where she could find me. We went for walks, jumped rope, and kissed. She was my first love and a fond memory I have of this place.

As I climb the stairs toward the sleeping quarters, I let my memories of Katie go. She has no place here anymore, not with the other memories that are creeping in, and not with what I came here to do.

St. Christopher's closed last year, and it's amazing how much decay has already crept in. I am in awe at how quickly a place can get rundown when there is no one to take care of it. The paint is peeling in the hallway, there is debris on the floor, and some of the ceiling tiles are randomly missing.

The janitorial staff at the home was far better than the professional staff. The cleaners would talk to us and ask how we were. They would joke with us in the hallways and remembered all of our names. The doctors, teachers, and especially the director treated us like lab rats. When they did talk to us, it was to ask us a million questions about how we were feeling or what our mood was like that day. If they had taken the time to have a conversation with us, they would have had their answers.

I only suspected that we were being drugged when I left the home at sixteen. I had always slept like a log at night, not even waking to use the bathroom. I would wake refreshed each morning, but I was always extremely thirsty. The first few nights after leaving, I was awake all night. Memories flooded my head, and I couldn't get my brain to quiet. I had to learn tools to calm my thoughts so that I could get to sleep. If they were willing to drug us to get us to sleep every night, what else were they capable of?

I find the room at the end of the hallway, the room Sammy and I shared. They let us bunk together since we were brothers, and because Sammy had night terrors. Apparently, the drugs couldn't stop those. Losing our parents eventually hit him hard, psychologically. He met with several staff doctors in the two years he lived with me at St. Christopher's. They tried to pull the scary things out of his head and get him to talk about them, thinking that doing so would release the images. It only made him worse. After each session with a doctor, he would wake up every hour on the hour, screaming out for our mother. I tried to explain it to the director, Dr. Jonathan, as we were told to call him, but he clearly had no interest in taking psychiatric advice from a child.

Sammy's treatments continued, and so did his trouble. One evening, after a particularly long session, he curled up on his bed, nearly catatonic. Nothing I did or said drew him out that night. I don't know what they said or did to him, but I knew it was their fault. They were taking a boy who used to love to be tickled and turning him into a zombie. The worst part was that I was powerless to help.

As I stand in our room, I can see it the way it was when we lived here. Two twin beds, not right next to each other, but close enough that if you stood on one, you could jump to the other without touching the floor. We used to pretend we were on pirate ships in the ocean. The floor was the water, and we had to jump from one 'boat' to the other without touching the water. We imagined the water was shark infested and we were traveling the world. Playing pirate was one of the only memories I have of Sammy laughing at St. Christopher's.

It eventually became clear to me that the treatments Sammy got were experimental. Children can be somewhat invisible to adults. They see us, but they also ignore us. I would lurk around the hospital wing before and after Sammy's sessions, listening to the doctors discuss his diagnosis in the hallways.

They discussed his diet, how much exercise he got, what medications he was taking. They named drugs I would be hard pressed to remember. I heard things like, 'not used before on a child,' and 'highly experimental,' and 'dangerous in someone so young.' My small mind assumed that since the things they were discussing were dangerous, they wouldn't even think of trying them on Sammy. But I didn't take into consideration the fact that these doctors wanted to play God with a child that had no family to care about him. I also suspect that the state regulators didn't know what they were up to, or that Dr. Jonathan had friends in high places.

Our old room still has random pieces of furniture in it. The dresser looks new, but the other pieces are pretty much the same. Two chairs, a child-sized table, and two bed frames. This room was always used as a double. After Sammy died, I was moved to another wing with the older children. Since I spent so much time with Sammy the first two years, I never really connected with any of the other boys. Afterwards, they knew what happened to Sammy, so they left me alone. I didn't make any real friends, which was fine by me. I wasn't there to make friends. I was there to serve my time until I could get out.

Our ages ran from twelve, my age at the time, to sixteen, the oldest you could be and still reside at St. Christopher's. At sixteen, you were sent to another state-run facility if they couldn't find a foster home for you until you turned eighteen and aged out of the system. We were the kids who were not going to get adopted. Those kids were younger, cuter, and much more malleable. No one wanted a pre-teen who was gangly and sullen. Their cute young adopted kids would eventually grow into that stage, but they didn't allow themselves to see that far into the future.

St. Christopher's was unique at the time. The state of Louisiana was trying to see if kids would fare better in a group home rather than being farmed out to foster home after foster home.

The idea was they would make friends and be able to grow up with the same kids in a pseudo-family atmosphere. In theory, it was a great idea. In practice, it didn't really work.

Kids who grow up without parents to teach them, discipline them, and love them tend to harden at a young age. This caused territory wars, fights, jealousy, you name it. It was more *Lord of the Flies* than *The Brady Bunch*.

As I grew older, I wondered why neither of my parents had made a will. Neither had siblings and both their parents were dead, something that I suspect bonded them when they met. Maybe since we didn't have extended family, there was no one to take Sammy and me.

Sammy lasted nearly two years at the home. At some point, it was too much for his frail little body. The psychological torture going on in his head, coupled with the meds and 'therapy' he was receiving, took its toll. One day, he didn't wake up.

I knew who I blamed. The doctors were the ones playing with his health, but Dr. Jonathan was the one pulling the strings. He was the puppet master, and they were just his minions.

Even though I didn't need confirmation, I still got it, one beautiful summer day about two months after Sammy's death. I was outside in the courtyard in my favorite spot, next to a large evergreen tree whose roots had grown out of the ground and created a sort of bench next to its trunk. I used to sit there with a notepad and draw. My favorite subjects were the birds that would land nearby. I got used to sitting so still that the birds didn't consider me a danger and many of them got close enough for me to reach out and touch them, although I never tried it. I was content to draw them with their colorful feathers and shiny beaks.

Dr. Jonathan and one of the home's doctors were walking down the path toward my spot next to the tree when they stopped, not more than ten feet away. They were having a hushed conversation, but I could hear every word.

"Bring me the kid's file and I will make the adjustments necessary to remove any appearance of wrongdoing on our part," said Dr. Jonathan.

"I'll bring it over after my two o'clock appointment," said the doctor. "Are you sure that's all we need to do, fix some of the entries?"

"Leave it to me. I'll take care of it. We didn't do anything wrong. Medications don't always work. It's a matter of trial and error most of the time."

My blood boiled. They were talking about Sammy but they didn't even have the decency to use his name. I knew right then what I would do just not how or when. I waited until they both left before I emerged from my spot by the tree.

I push aside the bed frame in my old room and bend down to the cold air return vent underneath the window. I brought my lockpicking tools and a handful of other tools I thought I might need. I pull the backpack off my arm and set it on the floor, reaching inside for my screwdriver.

The screws on the vent are rusted, but they give easily enough. In a few short minutes, the screws are all removed and in a small pile on the floor. I jiggle the vent to loosen it from where it is attached. The years have sealed it to the wall and drywall dust falls as I pull it free. Crouching down I reach my hand into the opening, feeling around gingerly. Not a fan of bugs, but I can only imagine what might be living inside these walls as I find what I am looking for and pull it from its hiding space.

The blue velvet bag is dusty. Loosening the cord around the top and reaching inside I pull out Sammy's Space Mountain snow globe. I give it a shake and watch the snow fall onto Mickey Mouse and feel light-headed, so I sit down on the floor and lean my back up against the wall. Looking down at the globe and turning it around in my hands I see a small crack in the base of the toy, maybe one-half inch long. I rub my finger over the crack, feeling the sharp edge.

I look closely at the crack, somehow expecting to see blood, but deep down knowing I had cleaned it off years ago. Any trace of blood that would still be there would need a forensics team to locate, if all of the television CSI stories can be believed. It's what I was always afraid of.

Dr. Jonathan was a creature of habit, and I learned his routine easily. After dinner, he would go to his office and work until lights out. Then, he would make his rounds to all of the boys' rooms to say goodnight and make sure we were where we were supposed to be. He meant for it to look paternal, but we all took it as it really was: control.

After he made his rounds, he would go out into the back courtyard and smoke a cigar as he stood under the second-floor overhang. The overhang was an unused balcony that you could access from the end of my bedroom wing. He no doubt chose the spot so that, rain or shine, he could smoke his cigar. Like I said, creature of habit.

It was almost too easy to slip out of bed, grab the snow globe, and pick the lock on the door to the balcony. I crept to the edge and looked over the railing. The smoke told me that Dr. Jonathan was underneath, but I couldn't see him from my vantage point. I did the first thing I could think of, I called out—saying my brother's name. "Sammy," I said softly.

I raised the globe over my head, and when I saw him peer up to see where the noise came from, our eyes locked. I thrust the globe down with all my might and as I released it, I repeated, this time a bit louder, "Sammy."

The police were baffled. They found a broken stone planter near where he fell, something I wasn't responsible for, but it worked in my favor. I was only twelve years old. Old enough to commit murder to avenge my brother, but too young to think of the consequences or work out all of the logistics.

I ended up getting lucky when they found that planter. They couldn't quite determine if it was a match for the wound in his head and I remember hearing the word 'inconclusive' thrown around when I eavesdropped on discussions. I also remember hearing, 'too many possible suspects.' The boys did not like Dr. Jonathan much.

I suspected that someone who wanted to hush things up wielded their significant influence to get the case closed. The fact the planter used to sit on the balcony, and that Dr. Jonathan's wound showed he had been looking up when he was hit, was as good an explanation as any. They ended up closing the case and calling it a freak accident, which suited me fine.

I knew I would have to return for the snow globe one day. I couldn't take the risk that they would find it in the remodel and put two and two together. Crime makes you paranoid. Anyone who lived or worked at the home during my stay knew it belonged to Sammy. He took that thing everywhere, like it was a stuffed animal.

In a way, I'm glad I had to come and retrieve the globe. It closes my chapter on St. Christopher's—for good. The next generation of kids won't have to go through what Sammy and I went through. I tell myself that foster care has to be better.

Once I'm outside, I get in the car to leave the home for the last time. I don't even look in my rearview mirror as I pull away and head toward the highway. When I get to the on-ramp, I choose to go east. I think a visit to Space Mountain is just what I need.

BITTERSWEET

Smita Harish Jain

"I think you should break it off with Dr. Sullivan tonight, Sarah. It isn't right," her mother said, not for the first time.

"If it isn't a problem for him, why should it be a problem for me?" Sarah asked, examining herself before a full-length mirror.

"He's your therapist, dear," her mother said.

Sarah shrugged, then undid another button on her cardigan and put her generous cleavage on full display. She took in the final look and, satisfied, turned to face her mother.

"If anyone should break off their relationship with Phillip, it's *her*. Phillip wants to be with me," she said.

"Did he tell you that, dear?" her mother asked, the exasperation in her voice conceding the futility of her efforts.

"He didn't need to," Sarah said. Then, with a flourish, she scooped up a small macrame purse that was sitting on the end of her bed and sailed out of the room.

When Sarah returned home that night, she was still breathless from her session with Dr. Sullivan. She clutched her hands to her chest and danced around the room, deciding then and there that she wanted every night to feel like this one.

***

It was the day after New Year's, and the city of New Orleans was preparing for Carnival. Soon, tourists would flood the Big Easy for the street parties, celebrations, and Mardi Gras, the last day to indulge in some gluttony and debauchery before Lent. Stores stocked up on beads and masks, costumes, and most importantly, the sweets for which the city was famous: pecan pralines, beignets, and king cakes. For Sarah, only one of those would do.

The king cake had come a long way from its traditional coffee cake and cinnamon roll combination. Now, bakeries added fillings made with pralines and savory cream cheeses, pecans and fruits. Sarah had some ingredients of her own in mind.

"What could be more festive than king cake, Mother?" Sarah had been up all night baking.

"Nothing, but that doesn't explain why you're putting pecans in it. King cake only needs cinnamon," her mother reminded her. "No one is going to eat that." Sarah's mother hadn't taken to the change in tradition as well as her daughter had.

Sarah rolled her eyes before answering. "Manny Randazzo puts pecans in his king cakes," she said, invoking the winner of the "King Cake King" distinction to shut her mother up.

"You're messing it up," her mother persisted.

"You can't mess up a king cake, Mom."

This time, it was her mother's turn to roll her eyes. "Our guests aren't going to eat that."

Sarah and her mother ran a bed-and-breakfast in the French Quarter and made the bulk of their annual revenue during Carnival. Her mother was right to be concerned about Sarah's version of the New Orleans treat.

"It's not for our guests, Mother. It's for someone who deserves it," Sarah said.

* * *

The next morning, Sarah drove to the Garden District, the tony area where the Sullivans lived, to call on Anne Sullivan. She knew Phillip would be at work and their children helping build the floats for the Société des Champs-Élysées parade, which would launch the Carnival season in a few days. She wound her way past food trucks and porta johns, parade preparations and gawkers, to get to the Sullivans' home.

"Oh, Sarah," Anne said, moving to the middle of the open doorway to block the entrance to the house. "Dr. Sullivan isn't home."

"I'm not here to see Phil— I mean Dr. Sullivan. I came to give you this," Sarah said, presenting the cake.

Anne stared at the green, purple, and yellow sprinkles scattered haphazardly on the frosted top and then again at Sarah, her look suggesting some combination of confusion and disgust.

Sarah ignored it and pushed past Anne into the living room. By the time Anne closed the door and followed her, Sarah had seated herself on the sofa and placed the king cake on the coffee table in front of her.

"What can I do for you?" Anne asked, remaining standing.

"I wanted to thank you for letting me steal your husband. I know I've been calling on him a lot. He is just so nice to make himself available to his...um, friends, even after hours." Sarah smiled into the horrified face of her hostess.

After a few more pleasantries, which neither woman found especially pleasant, Sarah slid the cake towards Anne.

"Why don't we have some of this delicious king cake? I got it at Bender's Bakery," she lied.

Anne realized she was not going to get rid of her pesky visitor until she had some cake with her. She took the container into the kitchen and returned a minute later with two small pieces on dessert plates. She placed one in front of Sarah and took her own to an occasional chair on the other side of the coffee table, across from the young woman.

"These pieces are so small, Anne. We'll never find the baby

in these," Sarah said, referencing the king cake tradition started in the 1940s, that promised the person who found a plastic baby in their slice luck and prosperity and the responsibility of providing the next king cake and accompanying celebration.

Anne vowed to herself that she would swallow the plastic baby if she found it, rather than host this lunatic again. She ate quickly, working her way through various bits of creamy and crunchy miscellany—pecans, fruit filling, even chicory, which gave every sweet bite a smack of bitterness.

"How is it?" Sarah asked, her piece still untouched.

Anne looked up from her plate. "It's fine."

"Let me get you another piece then," Sarah offered quickly. "It's impossible to eat just one slice of king cake."

"No, this is enough," Anne said and shoved the last piece from her plate into her mouth. "I couldn't eat another bite. King cakes can be so heavy." She used her tongue to dislodge bits of food stuck in her teeth.

Just then, the phone at the Sullivan house rang. Anne jumped up to get it, hoping it was someone she could engage in a long conversation and not just a wrong number or a sales call. Even still, she could always pretend, she thought.

"Phillip! Sweetheart!" she said, then placed one hand over the phone's mouthpiece and whispered to Sarah, "I have to take this. It could be awhile." She returned to the call and carried on loudly with her husband, laughing and flirting, using pet names that were filled with innuendo, until Sarah grew tired of listening to it all and saw herself out.

Anne made no mention of her visitor to her husband during that phone call. In fact, she made no mention of her for a few days, while she fought unexpected flu symptoms: vomiting, diarrhea, stomach pains, and something she hadn't experienced with past colds and flus, a numbness in her legs. She knew then that she did not have the flu, and with her symptoms getting worse, she also had no choice—she would have to tell Phillip about Sarah's visit.

Somewhere in the back of her mind, she had known about their affair but had thought it harmless, nothing to lose her marriage over. It wasn't like she had any other prospects, and she did not want to be alone.

When Anne told Phillip her suspicions about Sarah's king cake, he reacted exactly as she had hoped he would.

"She did what?" he said, slamming his hands on his desk.

Anne bit back her smile. Even though he was angry, he was angry at *her*.

"I'm afraid of what she might do next," Anne said. "I think she's crazy. Isn't there something you can do?"

"Oh, there's something I can do, all right," he said. "Where's that king cake now?"

"She took the rest of it with her," Anne said.

"Why did you let her do that? How am I supposed to confront her without any proof?" he asked, irritated.

"I didn't know at the time there was any reason to keep the cake. I was happy to see it, and her, gone," Anne said.

Phillip grumbled and paced the floor. If Sarah was willing to go to these lengths to get Anne out of the way, what else was she capable of? Would she tell people about them? Would she tell Anne's parents? They would remove him as trustee of the sizable accounts they had created for their grandchildren—money he could "invest" as he pleased until the kids turned twenty-one. If they got the slightest wind of Phillip's affair with Sarah, they might even implicate him in a conspiracy to kill their daughter, and he would lose everything—his children, his wife, and, especially, his wife's money. He had to take care of things before they came down for Mardi Gras, and Sarah did something even worse.

He told Anne he was going for a walk to figure things out and headed straight to Sarah's bed-and-breakfast. He found her in her bedroom, folding the guest linens.

"What the hell did you do?" he shouted, slamming the door shut behind him.

Sarah startled and dropped the sheet she was holding. She turned around and, when she saw it was Phillip, ran to him. He grabbed her wrists and kept her at arm's length.

"Aa-aah!" she cried. "What are you doing?"

He tightened his grip to keep from shaking her.

"Phillip! You're hurting me. Please stop," she said.

He held onto her for another few seconds, then, as if snapping out of a trance, let her go.

She wrapped her freed hands around his head and ran her fingers through his hair.

"What's wrong, darling?" she asked, as if he hadn't threatened her.

Phillip pushed her hands from his face.

"What the hell were you doing? My wife told me about the king cake. Have you lost your mind?" he asked, without stopping to take a breath between questions.

"King cake?" she asked, her eyes wide.

For a moment, he believed she didn't know what he was talking about. Then he saw the smallest trace of a smirk flickering at the corners of her mouth.

"You bitch! What did you put in there?" he demanded.

"It was nothing. Why don't we forget about that silly cake and..." She started towards him again.

"Tell me, damn you! I can't do anything unless I know what you gave her!"

"You're a doctor. Why don't you just run some tests," she said, dismissing his question.

"I can't just run tests. I would have to take her to a hospital, and how would I explain that?"

Sarah shrugged, as if to say, "Who cares?"

"If people find out about us, it's over for me!" he said. "Anne's been throwing up for two days. Now, tell me, what was in the king cake?"

"I have no idea, Phillip, but I've been throwing up ever since I ate that cake, too. Did you ever think that maybe it was Anne who put something in there just to make me look bad? After all, she was alone with the cake in the kitchen. She could have done something to it," Sarah said.

"Anne didn't put anything in the cake," Phillip said between clenched teeth. He stared at Sarah, still hoping for an answer to his question. When he saw he was getting nowhere, he let out a final exasperated breath and turned to leave.

"Where are you going, Phillip?" Sarah asked.

"Goodbye, Sarah. Don't call me again."

"Wait!" she called out behind him. "Please don't go."

Phillip stared at her but said nothing. Sarah knew that was her last chance to answer his question.

"I didn't poison her," she said again. "I got sick from that cake, too." She looked at him for any sign that he believed her.

Phillip turned and left the room. He took the long way home, to give him enough time to figure out what he should do next. He had no idea what Sarah had put in the king cake, and having Anne tested would raise too many eyebrows. The worst that could happen was that Anne might die or, at the very least, be confined to bed. Either way, he would be in the clear, and her parents would let him keep control of the money.

He decided to leave his wife to her symptoms and see where they led. He would treat the ones he could—so Anne felt like he was doing something—and not worry about the rest.

This might all work out, after all, he thought.

Sarah stood alone in her room, spouting plausible theories about the king cake for several minutes after Phillip left.

"It was Mr. Bender. I bought the king cake at his bakery. I know Old Man Bender is crazy. He's the one who must have poisoned the cake. He's mad because everyone buys their sweets at Sucré and Haydel's and only come to him when the other two bakeries are sold out, which they are all the time now that Carnival has started." She stopped, then repeated, "Everyone does buy their king cakes at Bender's when they have no other choice."

A smile spread slowly across her face.

The next day, Sarah strolled down to Sweet Saint, where she knew the usual assortment of junior high school boys would be hanging out, sharing sorbets. For some minor compensation, three of them agreed to go into Bender's Bakery and purchase several king cakes for her and say that they were running an errand for their mothers.

Sarah took the cakes home and prepared them like she had the one she brought to Anne Sullivan. A few hours later, she returned the entire batch to the bakery—the original packaging restored to make the boxes look unopened—and told the baker she and her mother had ordered too many for the few guests they had at the B&B. The cakes got resold to various families who lived in and around the French Quarter, and then it started.

Within days, reports came in about a flu epidemic that had hit neighborhoods from Bywater to Tulane-Gravier. People were complaining of aches and pains, lethargy, and vomiting, but no one thought to get tests run to see what was making them sick. After all, it was the time of year for such things. Most people were happy just to treat the symptoms for a few days, until they went away.

"This isn't what's supposed to happen," Sarah grumbled, pacing around her bedroom.

Her plan wouldn't work if people so easily accepted their illnesses as being the result of a virus. She would have to raise the possibility of a mad poisoner in the French Quarter herself, knowing that the police would jump through every hoop to apprehend the perpetrator, before the hordes of tourists who funded the area economy for the year descended upon the city for Mardi Gras.

The Krewe of Chewbacchus Parade was starting at 7 p.m. Soon, hundreds of people dressed like Trekkies, Whovians, and every other manner of sci-fi enthusiast would march in the streets to celebrate Carnival. Sarah made her way through the masses gathered at Franklin and St. Claude to Elysian Fields Avenue, the center of the parade route, listening to people's conversations along the way.

"I heard one of the floats is in the shape of a spaceship!" a spectator dressed like the krewe's namesake itself said through a furry mask.

"May the force be with them," a Luke Skywalker-lookalike said.

The group broke out into uproarious laughter, and Sarah realized the only thing they were into were the other nerds who would soon float before them.

She moved to another group, this time a family not in costume, thinking they might talk about more normal things while they waited for the parade to arrive.

"Chelsea, stop it!" a harried looking woman yelled at a preteen girl who was pulling a little boy's hair.

"Mo-ooo-om!" the boy wailed until the woman untangled Chelsea's fingers from the boy's hair and directed a man—Sarah assumed their dad—to hold onto the girl while she tended to the boy.

Sarah didn't see this conversation giving her anything she could use and moved on. It took her several more tries, but she finally hit pay dirt.

"He's been throwing up for days. His wife hasn't been to work, because she's afraid to leave him alone," someone near Sarah said.

She pivoted in the direction of the voice and saw a group of young couples huddled in conversation.

"I heard there's something going around," another one of the group members said.

"I heard he's a big drinker, and that's why he's throwing up."

This is it, Sarah thought, and inserted herself into their conversation.

"Has he eaten any king cake from Bender's Bakery?" she asked.

The group broke its huddle and turned to Sarah.

"I wouldn't eat one of Harry Bender's king cakes if you paid me," she informed them. "My mother and I run the Crescent Bed and Breakfast and had to take all the king cakes we bought from Bender's back, when our guests started getting sick."

She told them about the suspicions she had always had about Harry Bender and his grudge against the people of New Orleans, assuming tourists wouldn't bother to check on her story.

The couples looked at each other, then craned their necks to find an escape route. Before they could leave, several other parade watchers drifted over to listen.

Sarah explained the symptoms Bender's king cakes produced. "I remember biting into small bits of something crunchy, but I assumed they were just pecans, so I swallowed them. Well, that was my mistake, because a few hours later, I had blurred vision, jaw tightness, muscle pain and soreness, vomiting, and spasms." She stared up at the sky as she ticked off the symptoms on her fingers.

"Good God, did she swallow a medical textbook?" a young woman in the crowd whispered to the person standing next to her.

"So, all these people who think they have the flu are wrong; they were poisoned...by Harry Bender." Sarah said the last three words with deliberate emphasis on each syllable and a continuous nodding of her head, as if that would generate instant agreement from her audience.

"My biggest regret is that I gave a king cake from Bender's Bakery to my dear friend, Anne Sullivan, before I realized it would make her very sick. I don't know if I will ever be able to forgive myself for that. But Phillip, I mean, Dr. Sullivan has been simply wonderful," she said, drawing out the "won."

She looked up at exactly the moment she had rehearsed, to gauge her effect on the crowd that had gathered. She couldn't decide if their gaping mouths indicated approval and sympathy, or something else. In either case, she couldn't help being pleased by her own performance. She was on center stage, and she was milking it.

A young woman in the crowd responded. "I bought a king cake from Harry Bender last week. My husband has been complaining of stomach pains for days. I thought he was trying to get out of hosting my family for Carnival. You don't think..." Amy Miller couldn't finish her thought. She pushed her way through the parade watchers and raced to her car, hoping she wasn't too late.

Sarah seized on the opportunity. "See? This is exactly what I'm talking about," she said, feeling triumphant. "We have to tell everyone about Harry Bender and his dangerous king cakes."

Before anyone else could respond, the captain of the first subkrewe appeared on Elysian Fields, and the cheering of the crowd became too loud for the conversation to continue. It was fine, Sarah thought. Soon, word of the town's outrage against the baker would get back to Phillip, and she would be vindicated. She and Phillip could pick up where they had left off.

Sarah's jubilation over the impact she thought she had made on the tourists and the townspeople dwindled over the next few days as Amy Miller's husband recovered.

"Pecans sit around for years. The oil probably got rancid,

and some people didn't know they bought a tainted cake," one resident said.

"I've been eating Bender's cakes for decades and never gotten sick," another said.

"That sweet old man wouldn't hurt a fly," a third agreed.

"Damn it! Damn it! Damn it!" Sarah cursed her bad luck.

She needed a new plan.

"Look what Sammy the Butcher sent us!" Sarah's mother came into her bedroom holding the biggest gift basket she had ever seen. "The card says, 'Thank you for your business this year!' Isn't that nice?" She placed the basket on Sarah's bed and removed the cellophane wrapping.

Sarah watched as her mother pulled out a bottle of Asti Spumanti, a can of Café du Monde coffee, a box of beignet mix, and bags of Aunt Sally's Creamy Pralines, Cajun Pop, jambalaya seasoning, dipping pretzels, a small king cake, a Mardi Gras feather mask, a handful of Mardi Gras beads, and a tiara that said, "Queen of the Krewe."

While her mother tore into the bags of snacks and sweets, an idea formed in Sarah's mind. She ran to the kitchen and pulled several piping bags and tips, cake tins, pie plates, and enough butter, flour, cinnamon, cream cheese, chicory, pralines, baking chocolate, and fruit filling to make twenty baskets worth of cakes, cookies, and pies. This time, she wouldn't skimp on her special ingredient.

Several hours later, the B&B's kitchen counters were covered in cooling pies, frosted king cakes, and plates piled with cookies. Sarah looked at the apple and lemon filling oozing out of one of her king cakes and squealed. "No one will be able to resist these!"

She arranged rows of baskets along the kitchen counters and filled each one with a sampling of her baked goods. She added trinkets she found in the attic to each of the baskets and wove a thick ribbon around the handles. In each one, she included a handwritten card with something pleasant like, "All the season's best from Bender's Bakery." The rest of the card read, "From our family to yours." Eventually, those who got a basket would thank Harry Bender for his gift, but with the busyness of Carnival season, Sarah hoped that wouldn't happen until she had gotten what she wanted.

A few days later, Sarah caught a break. Old Lady Bannon died in her home, somewhere in Marigny. Sarah was elated. Her plan was finally working, and all it took was a few boxes of jagged orange-red pellets, which crunched like nuts. The autopsy on the eighty-seven-year-old reported toxic levels of strychnine, commonly found in rat poison.

Now Phillip would have to believe her. She ran to his office to tell him the good news.

"Did you hear?" she asked when she got there, still catching her breath.

Phillip looked up from the patient record he had been reviewing. When he didn't respond right away, Sarah elaborated.

"Mrs. Bannon died. The coroner said it was rat poison, found in a Bender's Bakery king cake Harry sent her daughter." Sarah broke into a crazed, breathy laugh.

Phillip sat back in his leather chair and opened his mouth to speak.

"Don't you see?" She cut him off before he could say anything. "This means that Anne's king cake must have been poisoned by Harry, too."

"Why would he do that, Sarah?" Phillip asked, perversely curious about what she would say.

"Well, he must be crazy. I've always thought so. That 'sweet old man' routine is, well, I've never bought it. Anyway, now that you know it wasn't me, we can be together again," she said hopefully.

Phillip Sullivan shook his head, half in answer to her offer and half in disbelief at her words.

"Just go," he said and returned to his file.

Sarah sputtered a few perfunctory challenges and reasons why things could return to the way they used to be, but Phillip gave her no way to get there and no option but to leave.

No other deaths were reported for several days until Anne Sullivan's. On the morning she died, Anne found a specially prepared Carnival surprise on her front porch, from one of her favorite stores. The card on Anne's bread pudding read simply, "For your Mardi Gras celebration from Bread and Circuses, your source for festival feasting." She did not realize that the handwriting was different than on the other cards.

When Anne was found dead, the obvious suspect was Sarah. No one in town knew, or particularly cared, what had led the police to make her their prime suspect—her tirades against the sweet, elderly baker, Harry Bender; her obvious feelings for the dead woman's husband; or the insanity believed to run through generations of her family. They were anxious to have their lives return to normal.

Two officers from the eighth district arrived at the Sullivan home to collect the uneaten portion of the bourbon-covered sugary treat. They offered their condolences to Phillip and left with the evidence.

When the sheriff's car had driven out of sight, Phillip checked his outside trash bin to make sure the empty box of rat poison he had discarded there earlier in the week was still properly hidden. He shifted some things around until he found it, then threw some more newspapers and trash on top of it.

He stepped back into his house and went upstairs to get dressed for his dinner with Old Lady Bannon's daughter. After all, they could both use some comforting.

DON'T BE SCARED

Jon Land and Jeff Ayers

Everything was fine until the drug dealers showed up.

"Get your ass gone, son!" a dude with big arms layered with tattoos, ordered.

Sitting cross-legged on the sidewalk, T-Bone, all a hundred and twelve pounds of him, held his ground, and didn't budge. "This is my corner."

"Nah," said the second and bigger one, his arms, exposed by a tank top, rippling with veins and sinewy muscle, "it used to be your corner, dawg. You wanna get yourself gone before the boss man shows."

Seated atop a cracked black milk crate, T-Bone went back to pounding the bottom of the upturned plastic bucket with drumsticks provided by a local music store owner after T-Bone had pleaded his case. This had been his corner after school and on weekends for a couple of months, and it was the most profitable of the three he'd staked out by far. T-Bone would play pretty much nonstop. Some strolling by dropped bills into a plastic candy jar he'd found protruding from a trash can outside the subsidized apartment building he shared with his grandmother, who had to quit her job because diabetes had chewed up her legs. The largest bill ever deposited was a twenty, and he'd learned to always start the day with a few bills already tucked inside, most notably a matching twenty to plant that figure in the minds of passersby to stoke their generosity.

The corner of Bourbon and Bienville had been treating him well, great even, including the overhang that offered cover from the summer sun and occasional thunderstorm. T-Bone didn't mind getting his long, braided hair and clothes wet, because it increased sympathy and led to a steady stream of bills being dropped through the top of his plastic candy jar once the storm cleared. It felt like he was on stage, his audience changing by the moment based on the whims of street traffic. No two days were the same, and no two people either. And T-Bone found himself in love with performing for them, the smiles and claps cast by those who hung before him for seconds or minutes almost as fulfilling as the cash they plucked from their pockets.

Almost.

His drumming yielded enough to make up the difference for the diabetes drugs his grandmother needed, but Medicaid only paid a portion of it. There were six of them, four of which T-Bone had given up trying to pronounce. His grandma's consumption of sugar had gotten so bad he didn't like leaving her alone. As soon as he got home, he'd apply antiseptic and bandages to the sores on her feet that had left her housebound. She'd gotten him this far when nobody else had bothered, so it suited T-Bone just fine to be returning the favor. His father was some white guy who was one of his mom's regulars before she died of a drug overdose. According to his grandmother, his mom liked to call T-Bone a gift from God when it had more to do with a torn condom. He wasn't even three when she'd OD'd, and his last memories of her faded a year back. The best he could do now was his grandmother's pictures of his mom smiling in better times. His grandma was all he had, but her sores were getting worse no matter how much he treated them, and they had started to smell like she was rotting from the inside out, something like spoiled fish fouling the fridge.

A big SUV pulled up to the corner. The back door flung open, and an average-sized guy dropped out, his metallic front teeth glistening as he exchanged bro hugs with the two guys trying to evict T-Bone from his corner.

The boss man, no doubt.

He chuckled as the bigger of the two dudes explained the situation to him, then rode his shadow when he approached T-Bone, who stopped his drumming to listen to what he had to say.

"This ain't your corner no more."

T-Bone gave his plastic tub a rhythmic pounding that finished with a *rat-tat-TAT*. "Says who?"

"You know who I am, son?"

"I asked because I don't."

"Ever heard the name Shakes?"

The confident smile slipped from T-Bone's expression. "Heard he runs the French Quarter. Like a mayor or something."

A fresh smile flashed. "Mayor…I like that. *Mayor* Shakes." He looked toward the dudes standing on either side of him. "From now on, dawgs, that's what you call me. Mayor Shakes." His gaze shifted back to T-Bone. "I'm gonna let you keep your cash for giving me the name. But come back here again and I'll shove those drumsticks so far up your ass they'll come out your nostrils. We clear?"

T-Bone nodded.

He tried other corners over the next week, staying clear of Shakes, but that whole week didn't put as much cash in his candy jar as a single day at the corner of Bourbon and Bienville Streets. Not even enough to keep his grandmother's meds up to date. T-Bone saw only one solution: his old corner, where he'd raked in cash from even cops who pulled over in their cruisers to drop some bills into his jar.

There was his answer!

That night, T-Bone flagged down a cop car from the next block down, still in clear view of his former corner.

"Watcha say, squirt," greeted a smiling cop whose ID plate

read JAMISON.

"I got something to tell you." He gestured down the street, gazing at the corner Shakes had stolen from him. "Those guys are dealing drugs out of their asses. I saw them do it while I was drumming. All kinds of drugs, lots of drugs."

Jamison flashed a big, broad smile. "Is that a fact?"

"Yes, sir."

"Bad for the neighborhood, then," said his partner from the shadows of the passenger seat, WEEKS, according to the ID plate over his badge.

"Bad as it gets, putting people in the hospital and shit. In the grave too, thanks to fentanyl."

Jamison turned his massive head toward Weeks. T-Bone realized just how big he was.

"Kid's got a point," Jamison said. "Let's see about dispensing some justice."

T-Bone watched the police cruiser approach the corner slowly. It angled into a no-parking zone with its ass-end sticking out into the street. Jamison and Weeks climbed out. Shakes and his big dudes paid them no heed until the cops approached. T-Bone was waiting for the handcuffs to come out when the big cop Jamison half-swallowed Shakes in a bro hug instead, while one of his dudes casually sucked on a vape and another guzzled beer from a forty. Then Jamison pointed down the street.

Straight toward T. Bone.

Holding his finger on him like he was aiming a gun until Shakes and his boys started beating tracks straight toward him.

Oh, shit...

T-Bone turned and ran down the sidewalk. He jetted past Café Beignet and weaved off the sidewalk onto the street when he passed the Hard Rock. T-Bone was fast and could run forever. Back when he played youth football, nobody could touch him, and he scored a whole bunch of touchdowns. He thought Shakes would have given up by the time he reached Toulouse Street near the Sheraton, but a glance back showed three shapes barreling on, maybe not making up ground but not losing much either.

T-Bone had messed this up badly, committing the cardinal sin of the streets by ratting the dealers out to reclaim his corner. What had he been thinking? Of course, the cops were on the take, padding their pockets to let Shakes conduct business as usual. It took a fool not to see that.

A couple of blocks down Toulouse, T-Bone started gasping, fear having sucked up all his wind. He could hear the whine of his wheezing, and his heart had ratcheted up to a beat even faster than the sticks twirling agilely in his grasp when he pounded his plastic tub for the gathered crowd. His beat-up Nikes were no match for the pavement, allowing Shakes and his dudes to close the gap further. He needed to find a place to hide while they passed right on by, after which T-Bone would hightail it home and maybe never leave the apartment again.

He thought about steering toward New Orleans police headquarters dead ahead but opted against it, given how Jamison and Weeks were so chummy with these drug dealers. Then T-Bone spotted St. Louis Cemetery No. 1 directly across the street, the angular tops of the crypts and tips of the statues poking at the thick New Orleans night. This was the city's oldest cemetery, with so many dead squeezed in over two-and-a-half centuries that the crypts, vaults, tombs, and larger mausoleums made it the perfect place to find refuge in the dark.

His chest was on fire and he was gasping for breath when he leaped up to mount the wrought-iron fence with pointy tips that rimmed the cemetery on the Basin Street side. T-Bone couldn't dunk, but he could touch the rim, and that athletic prowess served him well, until he spilled to a patch of grass after hurdling over the fence. His ankle twisted, and fiery pain erupted, but he limped on, scanning for a dark patch he could disappear into.

T-Bone believed Shakes had every intention of killing him for being a rat, and all he could think of was tomorrow morning when he wouldn't be there to rub the circulation back into his grandma's feet. Most days, the neuropathy was so bad she could barely feel them, and she'd be the only person who'd miss him.

He limped along, clinging to the patches of earth untouched by light. His ankle had given him about all it could when he came upon a small above-ground crypt surrounded by a waist-high iron fence that looked like a smaller version of the one enclosing the cemetery. All the graves were above ground because the city's water level was known to leave coffins floating in the streets even in moderate storms.

T-Bone took the last his ankle would give him and catapulted himself over the fence, taking cover with his back pressed against the rear of the crypt. The night gave up no sounds of Shakes and his dudes. T-Bone's breathing had settled, and he thought he may have lost them when a hand that smelled like it had been used to wipe its owner's ass yanked him to his feet like he was a rag doll.

That hand, belonging to the bigger of Shakes's two dudes, drew him up to his toes, almost eye-to-eye with the mayor himself, his metal front teeth looking like black tar stuck in his mouth. His other dude was doubled over, puking from the sprint here.

"I ain't killed no kid since I was a kid myself. Wonder if it's gonna feel as good now as it did then."

That's when T-Bone glimpsed the knife in Shakes's grasp, as dull in the black of the night as his metal teeth. He was pretty sure those teeth flashed a smile, but he was too scared to record anything besides the blade about to shred his guts. He thought of his grandma and started to cry.

"Keep crying, son. It'll make this hurt even more."

Shakes drew the knife back and started it forward. T-Bone's world was lost to a bright flash, and he figured dying hadn't been as bad as he had thought, not even close. Then the flash was gone, and he saw the knife sticking out of Shakes's throat.

He was gurgling out a fountain of blood and gasping for breath at the same time, his eyes bulging so wide they looked like pool balls wedged into his face.

More flashes erupted like somebody was moving so fast they couldn't be seen. T-Bone pulled at the hand still clutching his hair and came away with an arm severed at the wrist. He angled his gaze left and saw the face of the big dude it belonged to pressed into the vault as if the granite had hardened around it. The head of the man who was doubled over puking, meanwhile, was pressed into a thin scrape of grass, looking like the rest of him had sprouted from the ground.

He remembered Shakes and turned to see he had sunk to his knees, not gasping anymore. Just sitting there with his face pitched downward and throat still dripping blood.

T-Bone sank to the ground and wrapped his arms around his knees, reminding himself to breathe as he rocked back and forth.

"Hello."

It didn't sound like a real voice, but T-Bone was certain he'd heard it. And when he looked up, he saw a figure that looked conjured by special effects. An ethereal, translucent figure wrapped in a shroud of flickering light, a girl about his age T-Bone figured from the white dress she was wearing.

"Don't be scared," the soft voice that wasn't a voice resumed.

He awoke with the first light of dawn, his first thought being to wonder if it had all been a dream. That was quickly overpowered by the sight of the three bodies, which looked much worse in the burgeoning light and smelled as bad as bad got. They didn't look real. More special effects in a movie, while the blood that had dried on the concrete looked black under the first of the sun's rays.

Dazed, T-Bone struggled to his feet, forgetting all about his twisted ankle, which exploded in pain as soon as he put weight on it. He almost fell back down but managed to right himself by leaning back against the vault next to the man whose face was embedded in the granite.

Then he remembered the ghost.

Don't be scared.

A soft female voice had said that. T-Bone remembered the hazy glow of her apparition silhouetted by light. She had blond hair and blue eyes so bright they were like headlights cutting through the night. T-Bone couldn't recall if she was floating before him or standing on the concrete surrounding her vault.

T-Bone shuffled around to the front because it must have been her vault. He backed off gingerly enough to make out the gravestone itself.

ANNA DESIREE
JULY 1, 1885-OCTOBER 10,1898
BELOVED DAUGHTER AND SISTER

Thirteen, same age as him. That was what the life of the ghost girl who'd saved his life had been reduced to through time, BELOVED DAUGHTER AND SISTER, because she hadn't lived long enough to be much more than that. Just like T-Bone wouldn't have if she hadn't intervened the night before.

A ghost saved my life....

Thinking that made it feel more like a dream again, except a dream didn't save his life by killing three dudes to save a punk kid's life.

Don't be scared.

But he was.

He found the notice tacked to the apartment door when he got home to his grandmother.

He'd dragged his foot to keep the pressure off his ankle through much of the walk to the apartment building on

Decatur. It had swelled up to the size of a golf ball on the outside of his foot. Could have been broken, too, though T-Bone didn't think so.

The building where he lived with his grandmother wasn't much to look at on the outside or, certainly, on the inside. The color of the brick exterior had washed out, still pretty much intact in the places the sun didn't reach, but bleached almost white where it took a pounding all day.

There were sixty apartments, all pretty much the same, except some were one-bedroom and some were two. His grandmother had been living in a one-bedroom since before T-Bone was born. His room was the den adjoining the galley kitchen that had been renovated when he was five. The couch was a pull-out, but he didn't bother pulling it out most nights. He drifted off atop its soft cushions, preferring that because the tighter fit made him feel more secure. It really was like his own room because his grandmother spent almost all her time in the bedroom, though this morning found them seated next to each other on the couch with her squinting through her glasses to read the notice's tiny print.

"Eviction notice," she repeated.

T-Bone swallowed hard and nodded.

"Not a good thing, Tommy," she said, calling him by his real name like she always did, "not a good thing at all."

Apparently, some bullshit had revoked the low income, rent control status of the building, and all tenants living there on subsidized housing were being forced to leave—no ifs, ands, or buts.

"Where's my phone? I'm gonna call that number there and raise holy hell, I am."

His grandma did just that, six times. All six times her call went to voice mail, and all six times she left messages that got increasingly sharp and angry until the last one left her out of breath.

"That'll teach these fools," she said.

She got the cell phone for free, along with three hundred minutes a month between them, from a city subsidy program. It was a used Samsung that worked well enough. Their building came with free wi-fi that helped with the signal, only the wi-fi was pretty shitty, so it didn't help much.

"I need to go back out for a while."

The notice's address was near the corner of Rampart and Canal Streets. It turned out to be a one-room office in a nice building. The sign on the door read FLEISCHMAN REAL ESTATE. It was locked, and nobody answered when he knocked. T-Bone sat down on the floor and waited a bit, listening to a phone ringing inside and nobody answering it. It must have rung twenty times while he sat, and more angry voicemails were being left for sure.

While he sat there, he thought about Anna Desiree, beloved daughter and sister, convinced less and less last night had happened. Everybody knew ghosts weren't real, and if they were real, they didn't kill people. Then again, something made Anna Desiree different.

A branch of the New Orleans Public Library was located between Fleischman Real Estate and his apartment building on Decatur, so T-Bone stopped there on his way home. It was an old building, so the air conditioning didn't work great, but anything was better than the hundred-degree temperature outside. T-Bone liked the smell of the stacks and enjoyed hiding away in one of the cramped carrels, going to the different worlds portrayed in books, which was the only way he would ever see them.

He found an unoccupied computer and Googled the ghost's name, drawing a blank. There were plenty of Anna Desirees, but none that had been born in 1885 and died in 1898. He tried some other things without success, then gave up when it was time to go home to massage his grandma's feet, anyway. But he ended up stopping at the front desk.

"Excuse me," T-Bone said to the woman wearing thick glasses behind the counter.

He explained what he was looking for, and much to his surprise, the woman nodded.

"We got back issues of the *Times-Picayune* on microfiche in the basement."

"On *what*?"

That night, when his grandmother was asleep, T-Bone soundlessly skulked out of the house and walked back to St. Louis Cemetery No. 1 on an ankle that only hurt a little now. He took a long route along dark side streets where the soldiers of Shakes's street dude army were least likely to spot him. He'd been scared all day of a knock at the door or, more likely, a big work boot-clad foot kicking it in, but so far, so good.

The first thing he noticed when he reached Anna Desiree's grave was the bodies were gone, and so was the blood. But there was a crack in the vault's granite and a depression in the ground where the faces of Shakes's dudes had been planted, the only evidence anything had transpired here at all. T-Bone would have expected to see crime scene tape strung everywhere. At the library, he'd checked the latest news on the internet and found no mention of a notorious drug dealer being found there either. So maybe it really hadn't happened at all, and perhaps that crack in the granite had another entirely different explanation.

T-Bone didn't think so. He'd balled his braided hair into a tight bun before heading over, largely to disguise himself in case anyone was looking since people knew him by his braids on the streets. The gate to the rusted fence enclosing Anna Desiree's final resting place didn't open all the way, so he slithered through it.

"Hey, Anna," he said softly. "You there, Anna? It's me, T-Bone. You know, the kid whose life you saved last night. I just came to say thank you."

When there was no response, he sat down with his back against the vault, exactly where he'd been sitting the night before when the ghost appeared.

"I went to the library today," T-Bone told the empty night, "and they got this thing called microfiche which lets you look at old newspapers, and I found your obituary. I'm sorry you died the way you did. That sucks. I hope the bastard who did it is rotting in hell."

T-Bone swallowed hard, sitting here in the dark talking to no one.

"You're welcome," he heard.

T-Bone's body lurched, literally a few inches off the ground. The breath bottlenecked in his throat.

"Don't be scared."

Gooseflesh prickled his skin and he could feel his arm hairs standing up. "Is that you, Anna?"

"Uh-huh."

"I can't see you."

"I'm right here."

The bright light from last night appeared before him again, only softer so he could more clearly see the white dress and the girl wearing it, though her features kept fading in and out.

"T-Bone's a funny name."

He swallowed hard. "My real name's Thomas, and when I was little, I was so skinny that my mama said she could see my bones. So, I became T-Bone."

She kept fading in and out. "Those men last night were going to hurt you, so I had to hurt them. Like somebody hurt me."

Anna faded out altogether, and then T-Bone heard her voice again from right beside him, where she was sitting now. She looked more like a hazy projection, like a movie spilling off the screen.

"I've been here for a long time."

"More than a hundred and thirty years."

"It doesn't feel like that. It doesn't feel like anything. I'm glad I could help you. I wish somebody had helped me."

A thought struck T-Bone. Before he could change his mind, he told Anna about Fleischman, who was evicting him and his grandma from their apartment, forcing them out onto the streets.

"Bring him here, T-Bone. Bring him to me."

T-Bone used to hang with friends who broke into places to steal stuff, so he knew his way around breaking into a second-rate office like that of Fleischman Real Estate. Doors could be tough, but windows were easy-peasy, as his grandma always said. He headed back to the corner of Rampart and Canal Streets that night after she was asleep in her chair in the bedroom watching reruns of *The Price is Right,* which she liked to play along with.

Fleischman Real Estate had an interior office, which boasted a single twin set of windows in the back, looking out over an alley that formed a gap between that and another matching office building across the block. T-Bone broke one by smacking it with a rock, then used the same rock to knock enough of the glass away to clear a safe path for his hand to reach in to twist open the lock. No alarm sounded then or when he raised the window and tumbled inside, careful to put the least weight possible on his still aching ankle. He wasn't sure what he would steal to lure Fleischman to St. Louis Cemetery No. 1, but a big seventeen-inch Dell laptop glistened in the thin light atop a big, fancy desk cluttered with papers and files. Pictures plastering the walls gave T-Bone his first look at Fleishman, a short, unimpressive, overweight man who fancied what were clearly expensive suits. A plaque on the wall pronounced him Real Estate Man of the Year for 2020, a joke since Covid ruled the day then, with no one buying or selling anything.

The first thing T-Bone noticed was that there was no computer lock chaining the Dell to the desk. The second thing was the business card scotch taped to the lower right corner. Wasting no further time, he gathered up the laptop and lowered it to the ground before gingerly following through the window and closing it behind him. He tucked the Dell into the backpack he'd brought along, slung it over his shoulders, and made his way back to St. Louis Cemetery No. 1.

Leaning against Anna's vault, T-Bone eased the Samsung he'd lifted from his grandma's lap from his back pocket. He hated leaving her without it on the chance an emergency surfaced, but getting the asshole Fleischman out of the picture was an emergency too, and he needed the phone to do that.

"Hey, I found your laptop," he said, leaving a voice mail at the office number he'd already committed to memory but was also on the business card taped to the Dell. "Hit me back at the number in your Caller ID and I'll tell you where I'm at so you can come get it."

The Samsung rang almost immediately, Fleischman's number lighting up on the screen.

"Who is this?" a nasally voice demanded after T-Bone answered.

"T-Bone. I got your laptop. Found it in the cemetery where I work cleaning things up. St. Louis Cemetery No. 1. You lose it here?"

"Somebody broke into my office and stole it."

"Your lucky day then, dude."

After an hour, he thought Fleischman might have gotten suspicious and maybe it would be the cops who came instead. Then again, he also figured there might be plenty on that laptop Fleischman wouldn't want the cops to see.

"You don't have to do this, Anna," he said out loud, a small part of him hoping Fleischman didn't show. "I don't want to make you do this."

T-Bone could feel her presence, like static dancing in the air.

Then he heard heavy, awkward footsteps clacking down the concrete walkway toward Anna's grave. T-Bone bounced up to his feet and waved his arms when he recognized Fleischman from the pictures on his wall. Except he was heavier in the gut now and lighter in the hairline. The gate was open so he could enter Anna's world.

"Thanks for the call," he said in his nasally voice from the other side of the fence.

"No problem, man. With all the passwords and shit, it's not going to do me any good."

Fleischman gazed about as if sizing the place up. "So, what do you do here, kid?"

"Clean up shit, like I told you on the phone. People leave wrappers and all these dead flowers that need to be tossed."

"You ever want a real job, come see me."

"No shit?"

"No shit."

"I got mad skills, man." T-Bone gestured for Fleischman to join him inside the gate. "Let's get you reunited with your laptop."

The bell-shaped man hesitated for a moment, then twisted his features into a frown and squeezed through the narrow opening.

"Got it right here." T-Bone crouched and pulled the Dell from his backpack. "Here you go, man."

He handed it over, and Fleischman ran his eyes over the machine as if to convince himself it was his. He tucked it under his arm and reached into a front pocket with his free hand.

"How much I owe you, kid?"

"How about you let my grandma and me stay in our apartment on Decatur, and we'll call it even."

T-Bone could see Fleischman's spine stiffen, his stomach sticking out further over his waist. He stared at T-Bone for a long moment, trying to assess what was really going down here through eyes narrowed into slits. Then he smirked.

"Little boy like you shouldn't be out alone at night."

That's when T-Bone felt the static electricity again, like a hundred crickets buzzing in the air, plenty stronger than last night.

She's coming....

"It's a done deal, son," Fleischman continued. "Live with it."

"'Least I get to live."

A bright flash settled over Fleischman and swallowed him. T-Bone saw smaller flashes erupting in the sphere of blinding white light, seeming to coincide with the screams and cries that followed. And there was blood, lots of blood, splashing everywhere, its coppery scent filling his nostrils. Then the bright light dimmed, revealing Anna's shape standing there over what was left of Fleischman. She must have taken on a more physical nature tonight because T-Bone realized he couldn't see through her like he could yesterday. She wasn't fading in and out of reality—she had become that reality standing five feet from T-Bone.

"Thank you, Anna," he said to her. He didn't feel any guilt or remorse, and maybe he should have. "I owe you big time for this."

"I'm glad I could help, T-Bone, but I wish I could stop."

"So why don't you?"

"I can't. Not yet."

"When?"

She looked at him differently than she had before, sad. *"Soon, I think."* Her expression changed. *"You need to get home."*

"I want to stay here with you for a while."

"You need to get home. Hurry."

***

T-Bone ran most of the way back to Decatur Street, ankle screaming all the way, but it was too late. The cops and the ambulance were outside in force as well as inside, tending to his grandma's body.

She must have woken up from watching her *Price is Right* reruns, realizing her blood sugar was high from all the candy she'd eaten, based on the wrappers he saw on the floor. She'd either slipped or passed out on the way over to the kitchen to give herself the shot that was his job. By the look of things, she'd banged her head hard, and either bled out or died from an aneurysm or something.

"You must be the grandson," T-Bone heard a familiar voice say.

He turned to find the cop Jamison standing there, the cop Weeks riding his shadow. Their expressions tightened, narrowed. They exchanged a glance.

"We better talk to you down at the station," Jamison resumed.

"Why?"

"Let's go, kid," Weeks said, and reached for T-Bone's arm.

T-Bone backed away from the grasp. "What do we have to go to the station for?"

Jamison stepped forward, towering over him. "We got some questions for you about Shakes. Seems he's disappeared. Last we saw, he was chasing you. You come with us, we can help you make this right."

T-Bone nodded meekly, pretending to be cooperating and already planning and plotting. He'd be toast if he went with the cops. They'd never get to any station. He could link them to Shakes and the shit storm that must have sprung up when he vanished.

Outside, as Weeks steered him toward the nearest squad car, T-Bone pulled free of his grasp and shoved him into Jamison, then took off running the fastest he ever had, ignoring the fiery pain in his ankle that got hotter and hotter with each stride.

Anna, I'm coming, Anna! I need you!

Firecrackers going off drowned out his next thoughts. No,

not firecrackers.

Gunshots...Jamison and Weeks were shooting at him!

T-Bone dipped, darted, and dashed, making the familiar streets his friend, weaving in and out of alleyways, clinging to the dark, and widening the gap between him and the cops giving chase. Fiery pain cramped up his back and circled to his side, from pushing the bad leg on that side too hard. The cramp made him slow his pace, the pounding steps of the cops finding his ears again.

Then he was back in St. Louis Cemetery No. 1, rushing to Anna so she could save him.

"Anna!" he screamed, definitely out loud this time. *"Annnnaaaaaaaaaaaaa!"*

He pushed through the gate and collapsed out of breath against the front of her vault. T-Bone recorded the fact that Fleischman's body had disappeared, just as the bodies of Shakes and his two dudes had the night before. He closed his eyes, and when he opened them, Jamison and Weeks stood there. Doubled over, huffing for breath, steadying their shiny Glocks, ready to shoot.

Anna took Jamison first and immediately swept him away into a blinding white light. The screams made T-Bone's ears flutter. Panicking, Weeks started firing into the light and kept shooting until his empty Glock's slide locked open. Then the light swept over him, and the screams returned, only worse. T-Bone felt something splash against him and realized it was blood, its sharp metallic smell making him sick.

He wanted to stand up, but couldn't find the strength. Then Anna was sitting next to him—just her, with no shroud of light holding her like a blanket anymore. She leaned against him and lay her head on his shoulder, and in that moment, she was real. T-Bone could feel her. She was there, more than just a ghost.

"You saved me, Anna," T-Bone said, still unable to steady his breath.

She looked sad. "You saved me, T-Bone."

He followed her eyes to the stitch in his side where he felt the cramp. There was blood, lots of it. And not the cops' blood either: his, from the bullet that must have found him.

"It hurts, Anna."

"Not for much longer. I can go now."

T-Bone reached out for her, feeling something soft and spongy in his grasp. "Don't leave me. Please."

"I have to. My parents and brother are waiting for me. They've been waiting a long time."

"It doesn't hurt anymore, Anna."

"I know. I love you, T-Bone. Don't be scared."

T-Bone tried to speak, but the words caught in his throat because his breath was gone, and he couldn't get it back. There was a light, warm and soft, settling over him.

Then the light was gone, and there was nothing.

She couldn't run anymore. They'd chased her and they'd caught up, and now she was going to die. Three men, each reeking of body odor. They'd gotten her drunk, drugged her, but she'd gotten away. Briefly.

"You're in a world of hurt, bitch!"

She backed up against a freshly milled vault in St. Louis Cemetery No. 1, wishing she could transport herself inside where she'd be safe and these bad men couldn't get her the way her daddy had on plenty of nights. Instead, she was blinded by a flashbulb that didn't flash but lingered. The light swallowed the three men, but not their screams, which gave way to grunts, groans, and finally, a watery sound combined with something like air escaping a balloon. When the light dimmed, she saw all three men had been impaled on the spikes of the low fence.

She sank to the ground, back resting against the newly minted vault, hearing a boy's voice coming from the radiant light that wavered before her.

"Don't be scared."

THE UNRELIABLE NARRATOR

Robert Lopresti

"I can't believe this is happening," I said.

"I'm sorry for your loss," Detective Franklin said. She didn't look sorry. Or sound it. Her voice was nearly monotone, as if she had spoken those words so often they had lost all meaning.

Or maybe I was wasting too much energy interpreting her voice. Call that an occupational hazard.

"Could you explain what Mr. March's role was at your company?"

I took a deep breath. "Baronne Audio produces audio books. Dan March is—was—one of the actors we hire to narrate them. He—"

"Actors?" Franklin frowned. She was a middle-aged woman with a severe haircut and a look of intense concentration, as if she were perpetually afraid she might miss something. "Why do you need an actor to read a book? Is it like a play?"

"No. Oh, sometimes we do dramatizations, but not usually. Look, narrating a book is more than just reading out loud. Especially fiction. A good narrator *performs* the characters, using slightly different voices and intonations. If you listen to two different actors reading the same text, you will see—or hear—what I mean."

"And that's what Mr. March did?"

"Yes. He was excellent at it. Made most of his living as a

narrator, although I know he did some voice-over work in commercials."

Dan had a great voice, one that women swooned over. Unfortunately, his ordinary physical appearance meant that when he left his native New Orleans for a year-long invasion of Los Angeles, his screen appearances had been limited to parts like "Lab Tech," or "Third Juror."

"You say he was excellent," Franklin said. "Did everyone who worked here agree?"

"Oh, absolutely." I felt myself coloring. I'm a terrible liar.

Franklin raised an eyebrow and waited.

I shrugged. "We all admired his work. The problem was getting him to do it."

"Please explain."

"Dan was undependable. He would show up late at least once a week. I mean, *hours* late. Some days, he never appeared at all. Not only did it throw off our production schedule, but it wasted our engineer's time and left the studio empty."

"Why put up with it? Couldn't you fire him?"

"Sure. But other companies would have been happy to snap him up."

I pointed at my office wall. "See those three plaques? Awards for best narrated books. He was the voice on all of them. So, we tolerated his lack of reliability, the way you do with a great artist, or musician."

"But someone stopped tolerating him today."

I shuddered.

"Let's go over again how you found him."

I rubbed my face, trying to block out the memory.

"Emilia, that's our chief engineer, went out to the studio with me when lunch was almost over."

Our company was crammed into a creole townhouse in Faubourg Marigny. The actual studio was in the former slave-quarters at the rear of the property. We had spent a lot of money soundproofing it and improving the wiring, but, for better or worse, we had outgrown the place now.

"And why did you do that?"

"Oh. We were supposed to be recording a new book about Ukraine. I wanted to make sure everything was set up."

"Was Mr. March going to be the reader?"

"No. That was Vickie Justice, another of our best readers. She was still at the luncheon."

"All right. Go on. You went out to the studio."

"We went upstairs. You've seen the building."

She nodded.

The first floor was basically a storeroom for recording equipment. The upstairs was divided into two rooms.

"We found Dan lying on the floor of the control room. He had managed to struggle in from the actual studio. I mean, the recording room."

"How did you know that's where he came from?"

Was she kidding? "The trail of blood. Besides, I didn't think he could have come up the stairs in his condition."

"All right. And then what did you do?"

"I told Emilia to call an ambulance. There's no landline in there, and neither of us had our phones with us. She ran off. I bent down to see if he was dead. I could see the knife in his chest—"

"Ms. Serrano says she couldn't see the knife."

Lucky her, I thought, and shuddered again.

"That's 'cause Dan fell on his side. You saw that. His back was to the door. And his sweatshirt..." I closed my eyes, as if I could make the image vanish. On cooler days, Dan usually wore a Loyola hoodie like a cape with the sleeves wrapped around his neck, but when I found him it lay crumpled in front of him, and soaked with blood.

Franklin nodded. "Tell me about that knife. You said you were familiar with it?"

"It's part of the equipment in our kitchen, but when Dan's recording, he insists—insisted—on a pitcher of water with fresh lemons. He would cut the lemons himself, right there in the studio. And that was the knife he always used. The knife and a plate were there because he was supposed to be recording this morning."

"There were no lemons in the studio."

"He always brought his own. He demanded organic ones and didn't trust us to buy ones that were good enough."

Franklin's expression suggested she began to see what a pleasure the man had been to work with.

"So why didn't he bring any today?"

"I don't know."

"When was he supposed to arrive?"

"Ten a.m." I frowned. "He had called in sick with a headache. Dan had headaches whenever he didn't feel like coming in. But it wasn't like him to skip a free meal."

"Let's talk about that lunch. I understand you had a big catered meal in the conference room."

"That's right."

"And Mr. March was invited?"

"Of course."

"What were you celebrating?"

I sighed. This wasn't going to sound good.

"We just signed a lease for a new headquarters." It was a warehouse on Chartres Street in Bywater. Bigger than we needed right now, but we had hopes to keep growing.

"I heard there was an argument about it."

"An argument? I don't know if I'd call it that."

"What would you call it?"

"Disappointing news. Bill Theno was a guest at the luncheon. He's the head of Lake Arthur Press, one of the biggest publishers in Louisiana." I swallowed. "One of our biggest customers."

Franklin nodded. "They publish romances, right?"

Was she a fan? Better not to ask.

"Mostly."

"So, Dan March was their favorite narrator?"

"Yes and no. Most romances are narrated by women but, well, their readers love Dan's voice. Plus, his accent work."

The cop frowned. "Foreign accents?"

"Not usually. Most of Lake Arthur's books are set in the south. But you don't want a Baton Rouge bureaucrat to sound the same as a Dallas oil man."

From the look on her face, I guess Franklin had never thought about different accents, which made me wonder just how sharp a detective she could be.

"So, Mr. Theno admired his work."

"Bill had a real love-hate relationship with him. Because, like I said, Dan was great at his job, but you couldn't rely on him to show up and do it."

"I understand they came to an agreement."

This was the bad part. I mean the *worst*.

"Yes. Bill announced at our luncheon that Lake Arthur was going to start their own audiobook wing, and he was hiring Dan as division president. I told him he was crazy to put so much responsibility in the man's hands."

"And Mr. Rice had some complaints as well, didn't he?"

Sonny Rice was my co-owner. He handled the business end while I was creative director, meaning I produced the recordings and herded the talent. Including the maddening Dan March.

"Sonny was upset because Bill Theno deliberately waited until we signed the lease on the new building before he told us he was pulling his work."

"And that was a bad thing."

"A disaster. Losing Lake Arthur any time would cut us deep. But when we're trying to move to bigger, more expensive quarters? It might kill us."

Franklin nodded. "I understand Mr. Rice thought that was the point."

"Well, sure. It seemed pretty obvious that Bill was hoping to drive us out of business. Then his new division could fill the gap for audio books in this part of the country."

"The man had a right to change his business plans."

"Of course. But we had told him about our expansion before we made any commitments. He had promised that our relationship was secure."

I remember Bill smirking as he finished one of the muffulettas we had brought in from his favorite restaurant.

"I know what I said, Hector. But the problem is, you asked the wrong question. You asked if I was happy with Dan's work and I said I was. You never asked whether I planned to steal him away."

The Germans have a word that means "a face that needs to be punched." I never really grasped the concept until that moment.

But Sonny was the one who had screamed at him.

"Mr. Rice lost his temper," Franklin said.

"He did," I admitted. "But Bill isn't the one who died."

"No, but Mr. March was part of the, well, plot, correct? And he didn't attend the luncheon."

"That's right."

"Tell me about Emilia Serrano. What was her relationship with the victim?"

I bristled. "We found the body together. She couldn't have killed him."

"Unlike you, she left the conference room during lunch. To visit the restroom, she says. But she could have gone out to check the studio, just like she did with you later. So please answer the question."

I took a deep breath. "She thought Dan was a pain in the ass, which he was. Emilia worked with him more closely than anyone else. If he botched a line or didn't like the way something came out on the recording, it was never his fault. Oh, no. Clearly she had screwed up somehow."

I didn't bother to mention that Dan deserting us for Lake Arthur Press endangered her job as well.

Franklin nodded. "Did she ever threaten him?"

"What? Of course not. We wouldn't keep anyone on the staff who threatened someone."

She looked at her notes. "Does that include Chuck Greaves?"

I swallowed. "Oh, that. He wasn't serious."

Our marketing director stood just under five foot tall. Dan had once called him "the mighty midget." Chuck had suggested they step outside and settle it. Dan just laughed at him.

I thought of something that might be helpful.

"Chuck is an expert on martial arts. If he wanted to kill Dan, he wouldn't have used a knife."

"You're assuming the killer made a logical choice. That's not the way murder works, Mr. Harper." She scratched her nose. "The only other person at your luncheon who isn't alibied is Vickie Justice. Tell me about her."

It was bizarre seeing my co-workers through the eyes of a police officer, as if they were all possible murderers.

"Vickie is one of our narrators."

"Were she and March rivals? You said most romances were narrated by women..."

"They weren't rivals. Not really. Vickie's specialty is nonfiction. We get a lot of books about Southern history, naturally." I tried a smile. "She speaks, I don't know, half a dozen languages, so she is brilliant at books full of French, Spanish, and Creole words that are tricky to pronounce. Oh, Russian as well. In fact, she was supposed to narrate that book on Ukraine this afternoon."

"So, you're saying she got along with Mr. March."

"Oh, I'd say they were just..." I could feel myself coloring. And from the look on Franklin's face, she could see it, too. Like I said, I'm a terrible liar. I changed gears.

"They used to quarrel because of Dan's unreliability. Vickie would come to work and find Dan still in the studio, because he started late. That's hardly a reason to kill someone!"

Franklin offered no opinion on that. “Did they have any more personal issues? You mention him mocking Mr. Greaves for his appearance...”

She was sharp, all right. Vickie was butch, her word, and proud of it.

“Dan was sometimes rude to her. But he always stayed on this side of the harassment rules.” I didn’t sound convincing, even to myself.

Franklin nodded. “And if Mr. March left, and the company failed, I would assume she would be out of work, too.”

“That’s not true.” I was happy to be taking the heat off someone, even though it meant putting more on the other suspects. “Vickie did plenty of voice work for radio stations and other companies in town.”

“So, if you had to—”

“Detective?”

A uniformed cop was standing in the door of my office. “You’d better come.”

Franklin walked out. I followed her as far as the conference room where my co-workers and the other lunch guests were standing, not looking happy. Half of the po-boys, finger sandwiches, soft drinks, and other treats we had had brought in were scattered on the table, like leftovers from some battle.

Sonny walked over to me. “You okay, Hector?”

“Hell, no. How’s everyone coping?”

“Not great.” My partner glanced around the room. “Do you think someone broke in and killed him?”

I shook my head. It would be great if the cops thought that, but I didn’t believe for a minute that they did.

I looked at Bill Theno, who, in a very real sense, was the cause of it all. The publisher who set out to destroy our business was on his phone in a corner, apparently in furious conversation. I suppose Dan’s death had upset his plans just as much as Bill’s plans had ruined ours.

Emilia was crying in Chuck Greaves’ arms. I don’t think she

had stopped weeping since we found Dan in the control room.

And Vickie, our other top narrator, was standing against the wall with an Abita in one hand. She was watching us all in turn, as if she wouldn't permit anyone to get behind her.

I can't say I blamed her.

The others, the rest of our staff, looked frightened, angry, and miserable.

"Should we say something to them?" I asked Sonny.

He raised his eyebrows. "Like what? We don't *know* anything."

Before I could answer, Detective Franklin walked into the lobby. Her expression said she had big news. She looked around for Emilia.

"Ms. Serrano, would you come with me, please?"

Our engineer shrank back. "Why? Where?"

"I need you in the control room."

"No! I'm never going back in there again."

Franklin took a breath. I had a feeling patience wasn't her strong suit. "The body—Mr. March has been removed. I need your help with an engineering problem."

Emilia folded her arms. "You'll have to drag me."

The cop looked ready to say something that might lead to a disciplinary hearing.

I jumped in. "Detective, can I help? I know how all the machinery works."

Franklin considered. "Fine. Come with me."

She nodded to two patrolmen who took up stations at the door.

I followed her out back to the grassy patio lined with azalea bushes. A moan from a ship's horn made me jump. We reached the slave-quarters and went upstairs to the control room. The evidence technicians had not cleaned up the blood trail, and I was glad Emilia wouldn't have to see it again.

Franklin pointed to the soundboard. "One of my techs finally noticed these lights are on. I think we may have figured out why Mr. March came to the studio today while the rest of you were having lunch."

I frowned. "What do you mean?"

"He came to record something, but not a book. That's why he didn't bother to bring lemons. Zimmerman, come over here."

A short, tough-looking man with a crewcut came over.

"Mr. Hoskin here is going to play back whatever was recorded this afternoon. You're going to get out your phone and video everything he does."

She gave me a phony smile. "Just in case you accidentally erase anything."

I swallowed. "So, no pressure, in other words."

"Exactly."

Now I saw what I had missed under the shock of finding Dan bleeding on the floor: lights were on, indicating that the system was recording. Assuming a microphone was live in the studio, there should be a complete audio recording of everything that happened in there.

"Okay," I said to Zimmerman. "Watch my hands. I'll describe exactly what I'm doing."

I turned off the recording, reset to the beginning, and hit play.

We heard a few moments of silence and then footsteps growing louder. No doubt Dan March had started the recording and then walked from the control room into the studio.

"Hello? Is this on?"

Franklin's eyes widened, and I knew she was reacting to his voice. It's a smooth baritone rumble that startles you the first time you hear it.

"Hello to all my friends at Baronne Audio, worthless cretins that you are." He chuckled, ending with a hiccup. Not the first time he had come in drunk.

"You're all feeding your faces in there. By now, Bill has probably given you the good news that he and I are going to conquer the pathetic little world of audiobooks and drive you couyons out of business. Not so much a drive as a putt, as the old joke goes."

He snickered at his own wit.

Franklin, standing behind me, made an irritated noise.

"Bill wanted me to be there for the big reveal, but I didn't think I'd get much satisfaction watching Sonny and Hector's hearts break, no matter how badly and unfairly they've treated me. I just thought I'd—"

"What the hell are you doing here?"

I winced, recognizing the new voice.

My business partner.

"Well, hello Sonny. So nice to see you. Had a good lunch?"

"You bastard! I can't believe you betrayed us like this."

"Me betray you? How about all the times you and Hector promised to make me a partner?"

"We never did that, Dan. That was just your pipe dream."

"Was it? Well, I must have been smoking something pretty strong because Bill got a whiff of it and decided to make my dream come true. Now, if you'll get out of the way, I'll leave you to plan your bankruptcy. Best of luck."

"Where do you think you're taking that book?"

"This? It's Bill's. It'll be the first title for Lake Arthur's audio line."

"Not that copy. It has Hector's notes. That's our property. Give it to me."

"You get the hell away from—"

There was the sound of a struggle. Detective Franklin and the other cops were standing rigid, all of us mesmerized. Then we heard the sound of a body falling to the floor. Dan March gasped.

"You bastard."

"Oh, my God. Oh, my..."

We heard Sonny running out of the room.

I won't describe the sounds of Dan struggling to his feet.

Once he left the studio for the control room, there was nothing else to hear.

Franklin put a hand on my shoulder, making me jump. "Move away from the panel, Mr. Hoskin. Don't touch anything."

I obeyed.

She turned to a patrolman. "Take him back to his office. Make sure he doesn't talk to anyone, or make any calls."

She ordered another man to summon an officer who knew about recording equipment. "Meanwhile, nobody gets near this sound board. Got it?"

Then she headed down the stairs. Off to arrest poor Sonny.

I followed, much more slowly, with a cop trailing right behind.

In my office, I sat at my desk, wondering how a day that had begun with such promise had tumbled straight down to hell. My business partner was going to prison. Could the company survive? Maybe Bill Theno would change his plans, now that Dan was dead.

I shook my head. It was too early to think about that.

Then I started thinking about what Bill had said at the luncheon, about being sure to ask the right questions. And I was glad Detective Franklin had failed to do so, because I am a terrible liar.

I told her I sent Emilia to call the police while I checked that Dan was really dead.

Franklin should have asked: *And was he dead?*

But she didn't.

As I was trying to find a pulse, Dan's eyes came open, and I fell back in shock.

When I recovered my wits I said: "Take it easy, Dan. Help is on the way."

He gasped. His words came out with bubbles of blood. "Sonny did this to me. That bastard."

"Just stay still."

He gave me a grim smile. “I’ll sue you creeps for everything...I’ll own this company. I’ll own *you.*”

And then he died.

What’s that? You think the right question to ask now is: Did he die right away? Or did you wrap his bloody sweatshirt around the knife and give it one more twist?

My answer is: I did no such thing.

Would I lie to you?

TRILOGY

DP Lyle

This was a bad idea. Wasn't it? After two years of silence, did she want him back in her life? Like an echo from the past, he had called yesterday, saying that he had a new deal in the works. One that would be perfect for her. "No," formed in her head, along with an explanation that she was out of the business and had no intention of returning, but it came out as, "When?"

She wrestled with her decision all night, and again today, and almost didn't show. Even now, sitting here, second thoughts raced through her mind. She should leave. Like he had done two years ago. Yet she remained glued to her seat. Why? The only answer that came was curiosity. About him. About why he ghosted her. About what this new project could be. Wasn't it curiosity that did in the cat?

She sat at a window-side table in Lafitte's Blacksmith Shop Bar, reputed to be the oldest structure to house a bar in the US and believed to have been a storage area for pirate Jean Lafitte's smuggling operations. True or not, it was an intriguing story and added to the mystique of the place.

Rustic with dark, well-worn wooden tables and a substantial stone fireplace. On Bourbon Street, but in a quieter area, a couple of blocks removed from the unrestrained action along the iconic "party street." A lean, black, long-fingered piano player with a slanted fedora tapped out subdued jazz.

Cool night air drifted through the open window. Welcome after another hot, humid New Orleans day. Outside, the street, still wet from the earlier rain, reflected the glow of the street lamps. A young couple, holding hands, laughing, enjoying the night, strolled by.

Life should be that simple.

She had no illusions why Kirk had chosen this place. Their first "date." At least the first time they saw each other socially, not on the set. He could manipulate, if nothing else, and this was exactly that. A sales job. She shouldn't be here. Didn't want or need this. She had left the business. Firm in her decision. Yet, a month ago, a producer had called, dangling a lucrative film in front of her. She had declined, but the idea of returning wouldn't leave her head. Besides, she could use the money.

Hadn't she promised herself she'd never return to that world?

Decision made, she unhooked her purse from the back of her chair.

Then movement near the doorway. He entered and scanned the half-empty bar. His gaze found her, and he flashed that smile. The one that lit up his eyes and crinkled their corners. And made him so damn irresistible. He snaked through the tables and sat across from her.

"You look great," Kirk said.

"So do you," Rose replied.

He did. The same unruly blonde hair, crystal blue eyes, and quiet, laconic manner. All the things she had fallen for.

"I wasn't sure you'd show," he said.

"I wasn't either." She gave a half smile. "I'm still not sure it's a good idea."

"Relax. Worse case, we have a drink, a few laughs, and you go on your way."

"And the best case?"

"You make some money. Maybe lots of money."

A waitress appeared. She took their orders. Margaritas.

A car slowly rolled by. Its headlamps cast his face into a light/dark Chiaroscuro mask. In two years, he had changed little.

"You were always special," Kirk said. "We had a bunch of good times. Both on set and off."

"We did indeed." She shrugged. "Then you disappeared. Poof." She snapped her fingers.

"I'm sorry. I wanted to see you again, but—"

"But what? Found a better deal?"

"No," he said. "Not even close."

"Right."

"The truth? You scared me. I developed feelings. Feelings that lead to attachments. In this business, those can be trouble."

Wasn't that the truth? She had wandered into that shit storm before. Some guy you work with. Go out a few times. He becomes all clingy, possessive, and gets himself kicked to the curb. Then the stalking begins. One, nearly two years ago now, resulted in six months of hell. Until he got tagged for an armed robbery. Clay Watson. Hooking up with him had been a Kirk rebound thing. Fortunately, the judge locked down dear old Clay for a dozen years.

She could really pick the winners.

With Kirk, she, too, had developed feelings. She fought them, but they were there. And growing. Enough to create tension during the last film they co-starred together. Then he was gone. That's when "Clay the Stalker" showed up.

The waitress returned with their margaritas. Said she'd check back shortly.

"I was having the same doubts," Rose said. "About us seeing each other off set." Using her right hand, she forked her blonde hair back from her forehead. "Still, a call would've been nice."

"I was in Paris. Doing a shoot."

"They don't have phones in France?" She smiled to soften

her scolding.

"I didn't want things to get messy. I figured a clean cut was best."

"With a sharp knife."

He sighed. "I'm sorry."

"Don't be. It's life. As you said, entanglements in our business only stir the pond." A sip of her margarita. "Always the case when sex is involved."

He nodded. "Even performance sex."

That was another thing about him. Even when on the set, scripted, well-lit, and surrounded by a crew, sex had been great. Behind closed doors, even more so. She felt heat expand in her chest, rise into her face. Did she appear flushed? Did he sense what she felt? She quickly took another sip of her drink.

"You've done well," Rose said. "I've kept tabs on your movies. Congrats on the AVN award."

"A welcome surprise." He leaned forward, propped his elbows on the table. "I've followed your career as well. Not a bad resume."

"I've done nothing for six months." She stared at the tabletop for a beat. "Thinking about leaving the business."

"Really?"

She smiled. "I'm getting long in the tooth. Twenty-five is old in this world."

"Not for you. You have that Swedish blood. You still look eighteen."

"Ah, flattery."

"It's not flattery if it's true."

"So? What's this project you wanted to talk about?"

"It's tailor made for you," Kirk said.

"So you said." She ran a finger around the rim of her glass. "I thought maybe it was a ploy to get me into bed."

"It is." He smiled. "With the cameras rolling, of course."

"Why me? You have dozens of actresses at your disposal."

"Like I said, you're special. So is this project. It could be big for both of us. Could make us famous."

"You already are."

He shrugged. "To a point. This will kick us to a different level. Believe me, you're perfect. In fact, it's made for you."

"Now I'm intrigued."

"Good."

"What is it? Gang bang? Orgy? B and D?"

"A little light bondage."

"Cool."

She liked B and D. Ropes and handcuffs and ball gags. Sort of her niche in the industry. That and groups. She and Kirk had made eight movies together. Six involved bondage. Then he disappeared and moved behind the camera. Where the money was. Where he kept his clothes on.

"Remember the video we did in that old house? The Gothic theme?"

"Maybe the best film we ever made."

"No doubt. I want to expand on that concept."

"How?"

"This will be a trilogy. A Gothic porn trilogy."

She laughed. "I love the concept. So, you want to make three films?"

"Only one. I've done the other two. I want you for the finale. The centerpiece story."

"I see."

"Rose, we had great chemistry." He reached across the table and clasped her hand. "I hope to recapture that."

"Who would I be working with?" She tilted her head. "Not that I've agreed yet, but that could make a difference."

"Me."

"Really? Aren't you out of the on-camera stuff? Being a big producer and all."

"That's one of the many things that'll make this project successful. Me coming out of retirement for one last video series."

"Not that I wouldn't like to work with you again, but I am seriously considering walking away from all this."

"Which will add to the marketability. Both of us saying adieu."

"Intriguing. I'll have to think about it."

"It pays well with a significant back-end potential."

She brushed a wayward strand of hair from her cheek. "What are we talking?"

"Ten thousand up front and ten percent of the gross going forward."

"Not exactly scale. Why so generous?"

That smile again. "I believe in this project. And you. It will be huge."

"I could use the money. And I know that if this is like your other recent projects, the potential residuals are real."

"Jump on board. We'll have fun and make bank."

She glanced out the window. A light drizzle smeared the streetlamp reflections. "I'll consider it."

"Tell you what. Let me take you to the set. Give you a better feel for everything. I think you'll like it."

"Where?"

"A nearby warehouse. It's the perfect backdrop."

The location was nearby. A couple of blocks up Tchoupitoulas Street, past Canal, in the older working part of the warehouse district. Just beyond the upscale area were high-end restaurants, such as Emeril's, held court and a stone's throw from the National WWII Museum. Here, Mercedes and BMWs became pickups and box trucks. Tired and mostly derelict buildings lined Tchoupitoulas as it slid beneath Highway 90, near where the busy highway bounced over the Mississippi River into Algiers. Most were brick, concrete block, or metal, with large front bay doors, dark and locked down for the night. Several displayed "For Sale" signs.

Kirk swung into a pocked, trash strewn asphalt lot next to a long, narrow brick building. The drizzle had dissipated.

Rose climbed from the car and scanned the area. "Not exactly the French Quarter."

"Which makes it perfect."

He led her to a metal side door, its black paint cracked, chipped, and carved with names, dates, and crude messages. He keyed the pad lock, scraped the door open, and flicked on the overhead fluorescent lights. Rose shielded her eyes from the sudden glare. Debris cluttered the concrete floor, the air musty. As her eyes adjusted, she saw bare walls, a network of metal beams, and toward the far reaches a collection of shapes. Too dark for her to make out any details. She followed him that way.

A large four-poster dark-wooden bed sat against the wall, which was covered by heavy golden-tasseled, maroon drapes. Four light stands, a microphone boom, and a camera nestled on a tripod surrounded the bed, as if waiting to jump to life.

"This is officially creepy," Rose said.

"Don't you love it?"

"I don't hate it." She approached the bed, running a hand over its black satin sheets. "I see your vision here."

"I knew you would."

She smiled. "What does that say about me?"

"That you're perfect for the grand finale."

She now noticed the ropes. Black, connected to each of the posts. She lifted one. "So, it is a bondage set up."

"It is."

She turned and faced him. "What's the script?"

"The usual, with a few twists. Damsel in distress, bound to the bed, a mysterious lover appears." He opened his palms, gave a half shrug. "A very hot sex scene."

"Which you do so well."

He approached her. His hand cupped her face. "As do you." He leaned in, kissed her. She didn't resist. "God, I've missed you."

The kiss intensified. She wrapped her arms around his neck, pressed against him. She felt his excitement. Their lips separated.

"Like old times," Rose said.

"I should never have let you go."

Was that true? Was he trying to seduce her? Is that what she wanted? Needed? She had to admit that rekindling their relationship here on black satin was enticing.

"You've been working out," Kirk said. "Your body's even firmer and tighter than I remembered."

"Running, yoga, even some kick boxing."

"It shows."

She laughed. "Good. I'd hate to have done all that for nothing."

"Hop on. Check it out." He patted the bed. "It's actually quite comfortable."

"Why, kind sir, are you trying to take advantage of a poor damsel?"

"Of course."

Their eyes locked. The heat in her chest descended. She kissed him. With even more passion. She broke the kiss, her lips now near his ear. "I could get into that."

He lifted her and laid her on the cool sheets. She stretched her arms above her head.

"Here." He wrapped a rope around her left wrist and secured it. "That too tight?"

"No."

Moving to the other side of the bed, he did the same with her right wrist. Then her ankles.

"This brings back a few memories," Rose said.

"It does."

He splayed her blonde hair around her head. "Perfect." He leaned over and kissed her again. His hand slid down over her breasts. She had worn a short black dress, no bra. Her nipples hardened. He pinched one and then the other.

She moaned. "This is so hot."

"Merely the beginning."

His hand crept down her body, beneath the hem until he touched her.

"Somebody's ready to play."

"If you only knew." She writhed beneath his touch, her hips rising to meet him. "I've never been so turned on in my life."

"Then let's begin."

He removed his hand. He unbuttoned his shirt and shed it. Next came his jeans. He stood over her, naked.

"Looks like someone else is ready."

"I've waited a long time for this."

He moved away. One of the lights snapped to life.

"What are you doing?" she asked.

"Making a movie."

"Right now?"

"Why not?"

Like a flash fire, the old excitement of being under the lights and having sex on camera rekindled.Walking away from the business seemed silly. Not a good business decision, as her father would have said. Not about this business, of course. She was still young enough to have a few years left. She had made good money with her videos, and this promised to be huge. Maybe generate enough to sustain her for many years after she finally called it quits.

She smiled. "I can't think of a reason we shouldn't."

The other three lights snapped to life, creating a shadowless scene. He positioned the mic boom high over her head, out of the shot, but close enough to capture their voices. Finally, he settled the camera near the foot of the bed, adjusting its angle and setting the focus. He stepped back and examined the arrangement.

"Ready?" he asked.

An understatement. The heat inside her peaked. Her heart raced, her breathing now raspy pants. She couldn't believe how quickly everything unfolded. How her need for him blossomed and how her thoughts of leaving all this behind evaporated.

"More than ready."

He walked to a dark corner where he rummaged inside a cardboard box. He extracted a couple of items and returned. A black jumpsuit and a rubber mask. He stepped into the jumpsuit and zippered it to his neck. He snugged the mask into place. Only his mouth, nose, and eyes visible.

"No one is going to recognize you in that," Rose said.

"I know."

"But, I thought..."

"You were wrong."

He activated the camera. "Show time."

A knife appeared. Its long, thick blade reflected shards of light. He held it near her face.

"What the hell?" she asked.

"The final act of thc trilogy."

He slid the blade beneath the hem of her dress and ran it upward, slicing through the material.

"What are you doing?"

"Preparing you."

The blade parted the dress, then the short sleeves, one side and then the other. He tugged the dress remnants from beneath her.

"Are you crazy? What am I going to wear home?"

"You won't need it."

The heat inside her crashed, followed by frigid waves. What the hell was going on? She struggled against her restraints.

"You're scaring me," she said.

"I see that."

The knife snapped each side of her black thong and this too he tugged free. She was now completed naked.

"Come on, Kirk. That's enough."

"Merely the prologue." He snatched his jeans from the floor where he had shed them. He extracted his phone from one pocket. "Let me show you something."

"Cut me loose," Rose said.

A soft, cold laugh. "Let's go to the movies instead."

He worked his phone, tapping and swiping, until he found what he searched for. Rose heard moaning, sharp cries, screams. He held the screen before her face. At first, she couldn't make sense of what she saw. Then, she did. She screamed, her back arched, she flailed and yanked against the ropes.

"What the hell?" she said.

"Act one."

Her eyes refocused. The horror she saw was unimaginable. Was this real? No one could do this. Then she realized she knew the girl in the video. "That's Marla."

"Yes, she was a worthy beginning."

"Oh God, why?"

"It's art," he said. "My masterpiece."

He tapped the screen again. The screams and moans died, then restarted. A different voice. "Act two," he said and again placed the phone before her.

No, no, no. She knew this girl, too. Charlaine. They had worked together several times, became good friends. She couldn't breathe. Her heart hammered. Cold sweat erupted. The warm night was now frigid.

He placed the knife point against her abdomen. It dug in. A shock of pain ripped through her. She raised her head and saw a trickle of blood. Another prick. Another.

The assault continued. Slow and methodical. The knife point marched across her legs, abdomen, chest, neck, leaving a trail of bloody punctures. Dozens and dozens. Worse was yet to come.

The horrific images of her former co-stars' destruction—no other word fit—that he so proudly displayed left no doubt.

Her instinct was to scream, but she knew no one would hear her. Just like no one heard Marla or Charlaine. Better to bargain.

"You don't have to do this," she said.

"Actually, I do. It's a trilogy." He smiled. "Two movies just won't do."

"I won't say a word. I swear."

Another puncture, and another. "I know."

The rope that bound her right wrist scraped and burned her flesh as she twisted and pulled. Slowly, to avoid him noticing. She sensed forgiveness in the coarse binding. Or was that her wishful imagination?

Keep him talking. Distracted. Slow things down.

"I can help you. I'll find other girls for you. We can be a team."

He leaned toward her, bringing his masked face close. His breath, warm against her cheek. His eyes narrowed, his lips lifted into a slight smile. He tapped the knife blade against her chest, between her breasts. "Amazing. Charlaine said the same thing. You know, she suggested you."

Another stick. This one with a slight twist of the blade, the cut deeper.

She recoiled.

"But you were on my radar from the start," he said. "The jewel in the crown, so to speak."

The knot loosened.

"I know lots of young girls. Ones that would be perfect for you. Not to mention the great sex we would have as partners."

"Oh, we will have sex again." He leaned closer, his mouth near her ear, and whispered. "At least I will."

Jesus. How sick was he?

Think. Do something.

"Then kiss me goodbye," Rose said.

His back stiffened and straightened. His eyes revealed confusion. Not what he expected her to say.

"Please," Rose continued. "One last kiss."

"Good idea. That will play well for the finale."

He leaned down. His lips touched hers.

She yanked her right hand free and immediately went for his left eye. Her thumbnail dug in. His eyeball collapsed.

He screamed, recoiled, dropped to the floor. She heard the knife clatter against the concrete. His wails echoed against the walls.

She twisted and untied her left wrist. Sitting up, she clawed at the ropes that bound her ankles. The left one came free. She worked on the other.

Back on his feet, he ripped off the mask. His damaged eye now a bloody socket. He reached for her.

She slammed her left heel into the center of his face. His nose caved with an audible crunch. Blood erupted.

He screamed, staggered, tripped over a light stand, and fell. The light crashed against the concrete floor. Its bulb flashed brightly, then died.

She untied her other ankle and rolled from the bed.

Now what?

She ran for the side door and yanked the handle. No give. Two deadbolts. She didn't remember him locking them. She twisted open the first one, but before she could work the second lock, she heard him rushing toward her.

As her kick boxing instructor had hammered into her and her classmates, she relaxed, let a calm come over her. She crouched, coiled, ready to attack. He loomed over her, arms extended, hands like claws. She spun and landed a perfect heel kick to the side of his head. He staggered but did not fall. She slammed her other foot into his gut. He bent forward, retching.

Run or fight.

Finish this.

Scurrying around him, she scooped up the knife.

He charged toward her, swinging wildly.

She ducked, his fist whistling past her head, and drove the knife into his abdomen. He stumbled back a step. She followed, stabbed again. And again.

He collapsed.

He wasn't dead. Why wasn't he dead?

He lay in a tight ball, moaning, clutching his belly. Blood flowed between his fingers and fanned on the floor.

Time to run.

She ripped open the second dead bolt and raced into the night. The gravel and debris that littered the asphalt dug into her feet.

She stopped and looked back, expecting him to burst through the door. Nothing.

Why hadn't she grabbed her phone, her purse?

Should she risk going back? No. Keep moving.

She heard a car approaching. Headlights washed over the street, and the buildings that lined its far side. She ran toward the lot's exit on unsteady legs, reaching the sidewalk as the car rolled by.

"Help." Her voice raspy and weak. "Help me." This time with more force.

Brake lights. The car chirped to a stop.

She staggered that way.

The driver's window slid down, revealing a young couple. Hispanic. Both wide-eyed.

"Help me," Rose said.

The young man stared, looked her up and down. She realized she was completely naked. And covered with blood.

He jumped from the car. "Are you okay?"

"He's in there." She pointed toward the warehouse. "He tried to kill me."

The young woman, out of the car now, rushed to her side.

"I stabbed him, but he's alive.

The woman tugged her phone from the back pocket of her jeans and dialed.

Rose heard the voice on the other end.

"Nine-one-one. What's your emergency?"

"We need an ambulance. And the police."

"What's happening?"

"Hurry. A woman's been attacked. She's bleeding. We're on Tchoupitoulas. Near Highway Ninety."

Two hours later, Rose lay on a hard, uncomfortable emergency room bed, an IV tube in her left arm. Her three-dozen wounds, now cleaned and dressed, were minor, only one requiring stitches, a few needing Steri-Strips.

A female detective, who introduced herself as Kate Linden, stood beside her, pen and pad in hand. She wanted the story. Could Rose tell it? Did she have the strength? She had to. She owed it to Marla and Charlaine.

Detective Linden scribbled notes as Rose unfolded the events. The detective asked a few questions, jotted down Rose's answers, occasionally raising an eyebrow.

Did she believe her? Even as the words tumbled out, Rose felt her story came off as crazy. She had lived every horrible minute of it, and yet even to her, it sounded freakish. Like the ramblings of a madwoman.

"Anything else?" Detective Linden asked.

Rose considered it. She gave a headshake. "I think that's it But, right now my brain's doing flips."

Linden smiled. "Understandable." She closed her pad and stuffed it in her pocket. "I told you Kirk didn't make it. You did a number on him."

"I didn't want to. I was scared."

"Trust me, no one's blaming you. You did the impossible. I'm impressed."

Rose had no response. She nodded.

"I saw the videos," Linden said. "Disturbing and then some. Not only you, but the other two girls. They were much more gruesome."

"Marla and Charlaine."

Linden gave her a puzzled look. "You knew them?"

"We worked together. In the business."

"I see."

"I'm not proud of everything in my past, but I guess it's too late to change that."

"You have nothing to apologize for or to feel ashamed of." Linden squeezed her hand, glanced back over her shoulder to make sure no one was nearby, then leaned close, her voice low. "Before I was a cop, I danced in a topless club." She smiled. "But don't tell anyone."

Rose smiled. A weight lifted from her.

She was going to be all right.

THE SKINNY OLD MAN ON FRENCHMAN STREET

Jonathan Maberry

"Waste no more time arguing
about what a good man should be.
Be one."
—Marcus Aurelius

-1-

They pushed the little girl down.

Three of them. Teens, sure, but old enough to know better. Seventeen or eighteen.

Old enough to own their actions.

The kind who wanted to grow up to be wiseguys, made men, players. Like their uncles and fathers. Thinking they understood what it meant to live that life. Punching down, though. Running their clumsy version of protection games in their own neighborhood, on their own street.

The skinny old man who lived over Bongo Billy's Blues Bar saw it all.

-2-

He saw everything that happened on the street.

The things that happened at night, and the things that happened during the day. Different games for different times of day. That's how New Orleans was. It's how it always had been—not at all the same town when the sun went down as it was when it came up.

The guys who threw their weight around at night were serious players, the old man knew that firsthand. Some were remnants of the old Mafia families that ran things in the eighties and nineties. Some were 21st century players who belonged to any of the newer blood—the Cubans, Jamaicans, Vietnamese, Russians, and a mixed bag of others. They were mean and rough, but there were some lines in the sand for them. They rarely put their hands on kids.

The young Turks, though...that was different. They were trying to earn their way up the ladder and doing it wrong. Doing it badly. They made store owners give them beers even though the store could lose its license. They stole stuff from back yards and dared anyone to say a goddamn word. They worked hard at being stupid enough to think the neighbors were afraid of them instead of who they were *related* to.

The old man saw this from his window, and sometimes from a chair he set by the alley. An old folding chair that was one of the few pieces of furniture he owned. Not that he couldn't afford more, but he didn't need more. A chair, a bed, a couch, a bureau, and not much else. A few pictures on the wall of a woman he still loved, even though he'd buried her thirty years ago. Now it was just him and his dog. The dog's name was Dog. The old man liked things simple.

Dog watched them, too. Sometimes he was at the window for more hours than his master. Watching the street and the players and the games.

Dog was getting on now. Just like his owner. The skinny old man did not like to think about what would happen when he died. The dog, not himself. He didn't much care about his own death. To him, that was more inevitable than the death of his dog. He figured he was way past his own sell-by date. Someone should have punched his ticket by now, but he'd outlived everyone who tried. Now, there was nobody who even knew his dog was still alive. Nobody who knew *he* was alive. Even if they saw him, they probably wouldn't equate the white-haired, wrinkle-faced old scarecrow in the oversized clothes with who he had been back in the day. Who and *what* he had been. But life was a trickster like that. At first, his age was a good cover story; now it was a cosmic joke.

Once upon a time, his name had meant something. It meant a lot of things to different kinds of people. To the guys in the life. To some old guys stacking time in Angola or the State pen. To a lot of cops who looked everywhere but at him. To the press who hung that stupid-ass nickname on him.

The Good Neighbor.

A joke name. Or that's how it started. Something he's painted on a wall once on a whim. Painted it in hot red to make a joke, but only he knew the punch line to it. The reporters wanted a cool name, something that would jump out of headlines. The Good Neighbor had all the richness, the implications, the irony, and the readability. That was back before social media and trending and all that shit. It was who he was to the cops and crooks, the press and the public once upon a time.

The Good Neighbor.

Past tense.

Now he was just an old man with an old dog who lived in an old apartment above an old bar that played old blues to old drinkers. Even the guy who owned the place didn't know his real name. The one on the lease was fake, a last remnant of a good set of phony papers. His real name was gone, erased by time. His family was long gone, mostly consumed by a fire when he'd been a boy. He never had any real friends. There were people he liked and people who liked him, but he was always on the fringes of community life, never a key player in it.

Not in the way people thought. There were far more people who were afraid of him, and most of them had never met him. They knew him from the news stories, the History Channel docudramas, the two cable movies, and the film with that actor with the mustache who always played cowboys. He even sat through the movie when it was in the theater, quietly amused at all of the assumptions the filmmakers made. Some were even close to the mark, though they couldn't know it. The film, the TV stuff, the documentaries and at least a dozen books all had theories about The Good Neighbor. None were even close to the mark. They got the crime scene stuff right, but missed the clues. They looked at—and right through—the stage management of those *moments* and drew the wrong inferences. He thought it was funny that the screenwriter was nominated for an Oscar for a script that was mostly made-up bullshit.

His nickname mattered, but no one actually knew him. Not then, and far less so now. Everyone assumed The Good Neighbor had died, or was maybe in prison for some other crimes that the system hadn't connected. He wondered if there were frustrated cold case dicks still leafing through their files in hopes of finding a clue. He knew they never would. He had always been careful. That was how he stayed free and stayed alive.

Now he was a ghost in almost every way that counted.

Sitting and watching life but not participating in it.

-3-

He sat outside the blues club in old jeans faded from use rather than style, and a cotton work-shirt buttoned to cuffs and throat. Shoes with arch supports. His cane leaned wearily against the painted brick wall. The place wouldn't open until sundown, which meant he could relax. Dog lay in a patch of sunlight, dreaming doggy dreams, his tail twitching now and then. The old man wondered if Dog was dreaming of his own past, his own days as a dog nobody ever messed with.

There was a bottle of spring water on the step beside him, and the old man took occasional sips. His mouth was always dry these days. An old man thing, he reckoned—his body drying up in a slow-motion process of him turning to dust. He could feel the slow, small, vicious bites of cancer, too. It was there in his chest, and he didn't do much about it. No surgeries, no colostomy bags, no chemo drugs, no radiation. The pain was worse every day, and he studied it. There were lessons to learn, even this late in life, and he wanted his mind clear so he could study his own death.

He came outside to smoke because he wasn't allowed to do it inside. Rules. Quitting had no real play because his chest X-Rays told him that card game was lost. So, now he fed the cancer and watched the kids and the cars and the pigeons and counted the minutes in each day. They seemed longer now. Slower.

As if time was winding down, too.

-4-

He saw the little girl every day. Teresa.

She was nine, the old man thought. He'd remembered when her mother brought her home in an Uber. No husband, no boyfriend, no one at all there at home. Just another twenty-year-old with a kid. Welfare until the girl started school, and then working at the McDonalds nineteen blocks over.

Teresa.

Latch-key kid at nine.

Her mom thinking it was only three blocks home from school, and the neighborhood was like a village, that there were eyes watching out all the time.

The old man shook his head.

That kind of thinking was what had made his life so easy

back in the day. People thinking that watchful eyes were open and alert. The problem there was that all kinds of people were watching. He watched. Others did.

Those teenage boys were sure watching.

He watched them watch the girl. Trying to see what they saw. What they wanted to see. Making comments to her most days. Pretending to grab her and laughing. Slapping her book bag out of her hands, and laughing. Once shaking a beer and shooting the frenzied foam at her. And laughing. Always laughing. Hyena laughs that bruised the air.

The old man saw all of this. Day after day.

Today was different, though.

For a couple of reasons.

The first was personal. He'd been to the clinic that morning, and instead of the doctor talking about months, now they were talking weeks.

Was it weird that it made his cigarettes taste better on the way home?

The other reason was that even someone like him had a limit. A lot of people wouldn't think so. The FBI sure as fuck never thought so. The people who wrote those books and made those shows about him did.

The Good Neighbor.

He'd hated that name for years because it never really reflected his vision. All those things he did, all of the lives, the blood, the screams...it had nothing to do with that name. The whole thing was a coincidence because his first three kills—well, *known* kills—had been in the same neighborhood. A wife-beater, a child molester, and a rapist. They mythologized that he was a vigilante, targeting only the dregs of society. The scum.

Not true at all.

But, as the saying went, when the legend becomes fact, print the legend. Despite the inherent misunderstandings, The Good Neighbor he'd become. No matter who he selected, or why, the press kept using that name. So did the cops. So did everyone.

The nickname would die with him, too. The old man thought about that and was okay with it. That time had passed. His mission, however self-imposed, had ended. His calling no longer called to him.

The nickname was all the police and the press would ever know about him. They had nothing else. Not a shred of DNA, not a CCTV photo, not even a vague description. It belonged to a version of him who had been fully alive in the 20th century. But that ship sailed, hit an iceberg, caught fire, and sank, taking any real truths with it. Now, all these years later, he was just a neighbor. An old guy who lived over a blues bar on Frenchman Street. Passive, smiling, quiet, uninvolved.

Until today.

Until now.

-5-

It was the way they knocked her down. A shove that sent her into an elbow-abrading sprawl, her Catholic school uniform skirt flipping up to reveal skinny legs and child's underwear.

That did something to the old man.

The humiliation he witnessed was part of it.

The high-pitched shriek of pain was another part.

But there was a bigger part, and even from where he sat he could see it. It was a little girl—and likely for the first time in her life—understanding she was *female* in a world of male savages. That she was something that could be taken. That there was something to lose that was more important than the skin of her elbows or even a bruise from a punch. In that moment, the little girl became a woman-to-be. Equal to every other woman, in any culture, anywhere in the fucking world. No matter what happened now, she would never forget this moment because it was the moment that the cancer of vulnerability began to metastasize in her heart and mind. It was a scar that no makeup or clothing could conceal. She knew these boys could take her and hurt her and own her. Even if she grew up and got strong, they would own whatever happened next.

The old man looked at the cigarette between his fingers. He took a last, long, delicious drag, held the smoke in his dying lungs, and blew it out with a satisfied smile.

Then he got up, clicked his tongue for Dog, and went upstairs to get ready.

-6-

It had been a long time since he felt the old hunger.

The rage that he managed the way a surgeon handles a scalpel. Cold rage, not hot. Not reckless. And for all that, there was a fire in his heart. Righteous and cruel and unflinching. Unforgiving, like God used to be before Jesus turned him into a sentimental old dotard.

The god of vengeance.

He glanced out of the window and saw the drama playing out. The three teens towered over the little girl. Leering at her, making jokes.

Scaring her.

Scarring her.

He tilted his bureau over, then got down on his knees—accepting the pain; listening to the creaks and pops—and removed the false bottom. That's where his real possessions were. It was where the beauty was.

The knives. The wires and hooks. The scalpels and bone saws. Glittering and sweet with their silver magic. He closed his eyes for a moment, listening to their song of red potential.

Through the open window he heard the crude sexual jokes, the taunts, the promises. They echoed through the dusty shadows of his memory, recalling what his parents had said. And done. And what the foster parents had said. And done.

He remembered with the clarity of the very old and the assuredly dying how those monsters tried to justify what they did because of their own scars. He had silenced them with the truth of sharpened steel and righteous purpose. He freed them by opening them up so their evil could spill out and wash away, leaving the world a better place. Safer for kids like he had been. Safer for the people who lived down the street or around the corner from such monsters. Making the neighborhood safer.

Safe enough for him to live in it. Safe for kids who had been *like* him to live in it.

Downstairs, the girl was screaming for someone to help her.

The old man looked over at his dog. "Fade away or burn out?" he asked.

Dog thumped his tail on the bare wooden floor.

"What I thought," agreed the old man. He made his selection and left the dresser on its side. He doubted he'd return to set it aright.

"Come on, boy," he said as he, and the dog, got slowly and painfully to their feet. They went downstairs together.

The teenagers never heard or saw him coming until his shadow fell across them. One, the oldest and biggest of the three, turned and grinned up at him.

"Who the fuck are you, old man?"

"No one," he said truthfully. "Just being a good neighbor."

The three boys grinned at that. At him. At the old man and the old dog. They began to laugh.

Began.

Until they couldn't.

LUCKY HEART: A NEW ORLEANS STORY

Tim Maleeny

The foot was severed at the ankle.

A jagged cut made with a serrated blade. The exposed cartilage was splintered, a consequence of a rushed job. Drawing a blade back and forth until tendons snapped, and the foot separated from the leg was a tedious task.

Carter had seen chicken feet before coming to Louisiana, mostly on live chickens as they hopped and pecked their way around a farm. Since arriving in New Orleans, he'd lost count of the disembodied feet he'd spotted on doors, shelves, or worn around someone's neck. His appetite for poultry was severely diminished.

No more chicken sandwiches or hot wings at the local sports bar. Something about four talons on a disembodied leg conjured an image of a tiny velociraptor, and Carter had a policy to never eat any animal capable of eating him.

Shark, snake, and baby dinosaurs were permanently off the menu.

This particular foot was nailed to the doorpost at eye level, a voodoo mezuzah to ward away evil spirits before they could enter. Carter assumed this didn't apply to him and knocked on the door. It swung open to reveal a room filled with dust motes drunk on the cloying scent of incense, tiny dancers caught in beams of sunlight bleeding through wooden blinds.

Madame Marie stood behind a long bar, its entire surface covered with dead bats.

Carter counted eight of the flying rodents. The first four were pale gray and small enough to fit in your hand. The next two were silver and almost a foot wide, followed by a dark brown bat with a broken right wing. The last was a monster, eighteen inches across, with long brown fur and round ears.

Carter would never claim to be a chiropterologist but was secretly pleased with himself for remembering the word from an old episode of *Jeopardy*. Beyond that, he knew fuck-all about bats.

"Want to come closer?" Madame Marie gave Carter a playful smile.

Her dark hair was wrapped in a scarf the color of blood, caramel skin exposed from her neckline past the shoulders of a black dress, down to long nails panted red to match her scarf. Her left eye was the color of honey, the right a smoky brown, and both regarded Carter with equal helpings of mockery and seduction.

This woman didn't need Tarot cards to read your fortune. She could see right through someone the minute they walked through her door. Carter took a tentative step towards the bar.

"Don't they carry diseases?"

Marie shrugged. "The dead ones, not so much."

"How long have these been dead?"

"Long enough to get cold."

Carter closed the distance to rest his hands on the bar without touching the bats.

He noticed a filleting knife on the bar next to the brown bat. The blade was about eight inches long and sat within easy reach. On the wall behind Marie were glass shelves crowded with the usual assortment of rum, tequila, vodka, bourbon, and other whiskeys. Squeezed between the bottles was a strange assortment of talismans, amulets, dolls, and religious paraphernalia more familiar to Carter, including a wooden cross and small alabaster statue of Mary holding a baby Jesus.

Carter had bought a guidebook at the airport and read it cover-to-cover on his first night in the French Quarter, when the neon sign across from the hotel invited insomnia into his bed. The book explained how voodoo became intertwined with the Catholic faith when slaves arrived in New Orleans from West Africa and embraced the local religion. Marie Laveau, the most famous voodoo priestess of the nineteenth century, attended daily mass at St. Louis Cathedral in the French Quarter, only four blocks from this bar.

The woman standing in front of him claimed to be Marie Laveau's direct descendant. Carter didn't know if that was true or merely good marketing. He didn't care, as long as she was willing to help.

"Why bats?" he asked.

"When you first came to visit, you said this man is a gambler."

This man sounded like *dis mon*. Marie's voice was a blend of Creole consonants and elongated vowels that turned every sentence into a melody. Carter didn't want to interrupt for fear of ruining the song. He nodded but didn't say anything.

Marie gestured at the corpses. "Bats are for games of chance."

"Never heard that before."

"And where you from again?"

"Milwaukee."

Marie's smile lit the space between them. "How you like it here?"

"It's nice..." Carter glanced at the bats. "...and strange."

"You been here how long now?"

"Almost a week."

"And you couldn't find this man?" asked Marie. "Isn't that what you do, find folks?"

"He was easy enough to follow," said Carter. "Milwaukee to Chicago to New Orleans. Everybody, and I mean *everybody*, leaves a trail. Digital footprints like cash withdrawals, roaming SIM cards. Even pros who jump to a new identity leave a bread crumb or two." His voice trailed off as his eyes roamed the shelves, looking for clues among the knick-knacks and charms. "But once he landed in the French Quarter, he just..."

"*...vanished.*" Marie's tone suggested that people went missing on a daily basis in New Orleans. "So, you found me instead."

"He's a compulsive gambler," said Carter. "Finds an underground game wherever he goes. Bets big, loses more than he wins, cheats if he can. Always looking for an edge."

"The heart brings you luck," said Marie. "That's the edge he wants." She extended a manicured hand. "And when he called me today, I called you, didn't I?"

Carter pulled a thick envelope from his jacket and laid it across her open palm. Marie riffled the bills like playing cards, making the presidents' faces shift and shimmy as if they were laughing. She finished counting and set the envelope down next to the knife.

Carter turned his attention back to the specimens on the bar. "Only the bat's heart?"

"Other night creatures are good for different kinds of luck." Marie ticked off the fingers on her right hand. "Bat, owl, wild boar, and..." The index finger was still extended as she pointed a sharp nail at Carter's chest. "...man."

"But just the heart," said Carter. "Not the foot or—"

"—the heart holds the power." Marie touched the breastbone of the brown bat. "You bury the rest when you're done."

Carter thought of the busy nightlife, all the bars and restaurants, crowds of locals and tourists, and the cobblestone alley behind the bar. "Where do bodies get buried around here?"

"These poor fellas will go back to the bayou." Marie tugged at the wing of the nearest bat. "Only a couple miles away, and they'll have lots of company there."

"And what exactly does someone do with a heart?" asked

Carter.

"You cut it out, dry it, and carry it with you."

"In my pocket?"

"In a pouch, in a bag." Marie shrugged. "Make no matter either way."

"So, if I carry a heart around, then I feel lucky."

"Then you *are* lucky."

"For how long?"

"Everybody's luck runs out." Marie tilted her head. "Trick is knowing when."

Carter gestured at the bat with the broken wing. "He wasn't so lucky."

"Metal trees in the swamp," said Marie.

"The wind turbines along the highway?"

"Spinning wheels of death." Marie looked at the bat with an expression of deep sadness. "Kills birds in the daytime, bats at nighttime."

"Too bad the bat's heart couldn't help the bat."

"Our own hearts betray us all the time," said Marie. "Man like you must know that."

Carter let that slide. "Does it matter what type of bat?"

Marie shook her head. "Long as you got the heart, your odds get better."

"So why not display a jar of hearts?" asked Carter. "Instead of all this?"

The corners of Marie's mouth twitched. "You squeamish?"

"Curious."

"People come to me," said Marie. "Worry, worry, worry...been to other queens, shamans, *houngan*, witch doctors." Her lips curled into a sneer. "*Tricksters.*"

"And?"

"Selling people *hokum*, bunch of nonsense," said Marie. "Or worse."

"Worse?"

"Might sell somebody a chicken heart, tell 'em it came from

a bat." Marie scowled. "You don't want no chicken heart."

Carter thought about the doorpost. "A chicken's no good?"

"Chicken's good for lots of things," said Marie. "Blood from a live chicken works all sorts of spells. You can put the foot on the door when you're done, keep the bad *loa* away."

"Loa?"

"Spirits." Marie waved a hand dismissively. "But you want to win at cards, better make sure it's a bat."

"So, you let them pick the bat, then cut the heart out in front of them."

"That's why they come to Madame Marie."

"No hokum."

Marie chuckled. "I like you, Carter."

"I intend to stay on your good side," he replied, "so I don't wind up on your bar."

"You have a good aura."

Carter raised his eyebrows. "No one's ever said that before."

Marie's one amber eye glowed in the dim light as she laid her right hand on top of his, then drew her fingers across his scarred knuckles before breaking the connection.

"You hurt people who hurt people," said Marie.

Carter caught himself before he said anything, then decided it didn't matter. He held Marie's gaze until the corners of her mouth curled, stopping short of a smile.

"No shame in that, Carter."

"No honor, either," he said. "It's a job."

"Oh, I think it's *much* more than that," she said. "So, what you want from Marie? You don't need my permission to follow a man after he leaves my bar."

"What if I wanted to be behind the bar?" asked Carter. "When he arrives."

"You did say you wanted to stay close." Marie gave a short laugh. "And now you want to borrow my bar."

"You said you'd consider my little problem."

"Man kills another man. That's a big problem, not little."

"Figure of speech."

Marie glanced over her shoulder at the Virgin Mary before turning back to Carter.

"Tell me, what's this man to you?"

"Nothing." Carter bit the word in half. "Nothing at all."

Marie shook her head, her hypnotic eyes moving like a metronome. "Not the man you hunting, the man he killed."

This was her final test and Carter knew he couldn't cheat on the exam. "My nephew."

Marie stroked the nearest bat but didn't say anything.

"My sister's kid," said Carter. "Only nineteen, but this guy stabs him over a card game." Despite his feeling that Marie already knew what he was about to say, Carter added, "Right through the heart."

Neither spoke for a long time until Marie broke the silence.

"Now *that's* a good reason," she said.

Carter took his hands off the bar. "Reason for what?"

Marie smiled ruefully, a teacher being patient with a slow student.

"For what you're gonna do, of course."

"And what's that, Marie?"

"Honey, I don't need to know."

Carter reclined in his seat and wondered if the flight was going to be delayed for much longer. He was anxious to leave New Orleans behind, but summer thunderstorms trapped them on the tarmac, away from the gate but not yet cleared for takeoff.

No escape, just waiting in purgatory until a higher authority decided they could fly.

Carter didn't realize he'd dozed off until a hand touched his shoulder. He blinked himself awake to find the flight attendant looking at him with a worried expression.

"Sorry to bother you, sir, but we need the overhead space." She smiled apologetically. "Another passenger's suitcase doesn't fit safely under her seat. Do you mind if I move yours?"

Carter started to stand, but the attendant reached into the open bin before he could move. She removed a cloth bag and held it aloft.

"Is this the right one?" she asked. "It's so light."

It was an unstructured beige duffle that appeared almost empty, sagging in the middle like a plastic grocery bag holding a single apple or orange. Looking up from his seat at the bottom of the bag, Carter noticed a small stain the color of rust.

"That's mine." Carter took the bag and set it on his lap. "I should probably be holding it, anyway."

The flight attendant placed the other passenger's suitcase overhead and closed the bin, then looked down at Carter. "Thanks for being so flexible. We should be in the air soon. And sorry I woke you." She smiled. "You feeling okay?"

"Oh, yeah," said Carter, cradling the bag in his lap with both hands. "I feel lucky."

THE CURIOUS CASE OF THE SAD TROMBONE

J. M. Redmann

"Baby girl, baby girl, baby girl!"

My head was deep in my trunk, reaching for a lemon that had suicidally slipped out of the grocery bag. I could not see the person who dared call me 'baby girl.' I am not even close. On the dried up, old side of forty, salt overtaking the pepper in my hair, queerer than a dyed purple three-dollar bill. A licensed PI and I carry.

I was considering reaching for my gun. In that kind of mood. Nobody calls me 'baby girl' and doesn't learn to reconsider their life choices.

Well, except for Rodney, my across the street neighbor. He was the mayor of the block. We had met shortly after I'd moved here, both of us out in the street to clean the storm drains for an upcoming hurricane—luckily a minor one. Rodney had lived here about forever; the kind of guy who painted his house a bright violet because his wife liked that color. His little bar down the corner was where all the second lines stopped. I owned him many a pleasant afternoon sitting on my stoop listening to the music. As far as I could tell, he called most women, no matter their age, height, sexual orientation, etc., 'baby girl'. As much a feminist as I am, I'm not about to rock the neighborhood traditions.

I grabbed the lemon, then stood up.

"What's up?" I asked, as he trotted across the street.

"Claude's trombone got stolen!"

"Uh, trombone?"

"You know," Rodney continued. "You hear him sometimes in the evening."

"Oh, the sad trombone." I live in Tremé, a block and a half out of the French Quarter. A lot of musicians live around here and it's not unusual to hear a tuba on a walk home, or trumpet practice, or the somber tones of the trombone.

"Yeah, him. His trombone was stolen!"

Rodney is a laid-back guy, and he was not being laid back about the missing instrument.

"Have you contacted the police?" I said.

"'Course. They took a report, said it might show up in a pawnshop or sale online. But that takes too long. You do detective work, right?"

"I'm a private investigator," I said slowly, seeing where this was leading. I do a lot of missing persons, had on one occasion tracked down a stolen Mardi Gras float (rival upstart krewe bribed the tractor driver), a few pets for friends. But never a trombone.

"Can you help get it back? Battle of the bands is coming up, and we need our trombone. Can't pay much, but you get free catfish dinner any Friday you want." They did a fish fry every week, and it's pretty good. "And watch your parking space when you're out." Also, not bad. When I moved here, it was considered a bad neighborhood and we had it to ourselves. Now, we were the free parking lot for the French Quarter. Four bags of groceries and two blocks away leads me to thoughts of car vandalism. I did, accidentally of course, once drop a carton of eggs on a badly parked, way too expensive SUV.

"Okay," I relented. "Tell me what happened."

I glanced in my trunk for any more wayward lemons, then carried my three bags to my steps, indicated we could sit on the stoop while he told me the tale.

"Let me text Claude, see if he's around," he said as he sat. "They did their practice at that bar over on St. Claude, in the cabaret. Left their instruments and went to the bar to have a beer. Half an hour, went back, Claude's trombone was gone, along with Willy's trumpet and Joe's sax. Trumpet and sax they got at a pawn shop and were trying them out. But it was Claude's special silver trombone and he is right down sad about it."

"When was this?"

"Yesterday, 'bout six in the evening."

I got all the information I could from Rodney, then said, "I'll do what I can, but can't make any promises. They might be out of town by now and selling them in Atlanta."

"Yeah, baby girl, I know. It's just we got the battle coming up and Claude without a trombone is going to hurt. Gotta try the best we can."

I'd hit the Robert's over on Elysian Fields, leaving my office down in the Bywater area a little early. The advantages of being my own boss. The week had been busy, three missing persons cases, two with happy endings of a sort. I'd found the people and they were alive. One was an elderly uncle, left for Canada to avoid the Vietnam war and the family lost touch. His niece and nephew hired me. He was still around, happy to hear from the estranged family and they were planning a visit. One was a husband who had disappeared to the casinos in Biloxi and into the arms of a showgirl. Which was not great news to his wife, but it gave her ample evidence for the divorce. And one led to a grave. A teenager who ran away over a decade ago. His mother kept hoping he was alive and would come back. His sister hired me. Not a happy ending, but at least they could grieve and say good-bye.

The good news for Rodney was I had wrapped those up, had nothing pressing, and had enough money in the bank that taking a case for fried catfish wouldn't break me.

"Okay, I'll ask around and see what I can find out," I told

him.

Just as I was finishing with Rodney, Claude of the sad trombone arrived.

I motioned Claude to get comfortable on my steps and excused myself to put my groceries inside, claiming I had ice cream. I really needed to go to the bathroom, but ice cream sounded like a better excuse.

Once back on the steps, I asked Claude to tell me what happened.

"So weird, man, I mean, woman. Did our rehearsal like we always do. Then a quick beer at the bar to wind down, like half an hour. Left our stuff on the stage. Come back and it's gone. Just gone." He shook his head sadly.

"Did you see anyone go in or out during that half-hour?"

"Busy bar, so lots of people, but wasn't really paying attention. I think I know who did it, though. My kid sister thinks girls can play the horn, so she and her friends started a band. She's always got to outdo me, so if she stole the horns, we can't compete."

"Did you see her in the bar?"

He hesitated. "Maybe, but she might've got someone else to do it."

"Like who?"

"I don't know. Some friend."

"Anyone else?" I wasn't quite buying his sister; he was too quick to blame her. Families can be messy and the blame might be about something that happened in third grade.

"Anyone else?" he repeated. "I told you who done it. No way to prove it but most likely."

"How about other bands? Garden variety thieves?"

"I don't know. Got neighbors two doors down. They got pissed when they had to get to the airport and we had a second line coming down the street. They said music ought to be banned in residential areas."

"They just moved here, right?"

"Yeah, 'bout six months ago."

Ah, Brooklyn, we love you, but the housing code in Tremé requires every home to have a musical instrument, with extra points for trumpets and drums. There are schedules for the parades (not strictly honored, mind you) and if you live in this 'hood, you need to check them before making plans to drive anywhere. It's walk or enjoy the show.

I got Claude to send me a photo of his trombone, got the names and numbers of the other band members, gave him my card and said to call me if anything came up.

After I ate supper—getting groceries and preparing food in the same day is a bridge too far—I'd picked up a muffaletta (half, I can't do that whole thing) to eat. Working this case gave me an excuse to go to their practice bar

It was a nice night, so I hiked, about a ten-minute walk, just the other side of Elysian Fields from here. The street, not paradise, although there are some po'boy places around there that come close.

It was early evening slow. The bar was gay and neighborhood, with an even mix of both. Like most bars in New Orleans, I've been here a few times. I sat at the bar and ordered a draft.

When she handed it to me, I asked, "You heard about Claude's trombone being stolen?"

She eyed me warily. I pulled out my license and showed it to her. "A friend of the band is my neighbor and he asked me to see if I could find it."

"You're a real private detective?" she said, staring at my license.

"Yep," I answered, taking my license back, hoping to forestall hearing the tired joke about being a dyke dick. "Were you working yesterday?"

"Yeah, I usually do the afternoon shift, works with my class schedule."

"What did you see?"

"Not much. Heard the practice. We usually turn the music down to listen. They stopped, came in here to get a drink, then went back to get their horns and saw they were gone."

A back and forth of questions told me that it wasn't one beer, but three and closer to two hours at the bar. Also, the back area, which was large enough for shows, was locked from the outside, but the door between it and the bar had been open since it led to the bathrooms that served both areas.

"Could the thieves have come in, then gone out the outside door?" I asked.

"No, it's a deadbolt and alarmed."

"So, they would have had to come back through the bar with the instruments?" I asked.

"Yeah, I guess so," then before I could ask, "but I didn't see anything. I mean, I was busy, so might have been at the other end of the bar."

I asked if I could look at the cabaret area. She glanced around to make sure no one needed a refill, then took me there. A corridor from the bar led to the space. It was set up as a small cabaret theater. I've been to drag shows here a few times.

An empty theater always seems expectant, somber and silent without the performers and audience, a bare face waiting for makeup. It would fit about a hundred people with tables in the front and raked seats in the back. There were two entrances, the one through the corridor from the bar and one directly from the street. It was booked several times a week, from music groups, to drag shows to karaoke. I asked for the schedule for the last few weeks and she directed me to their web site. I keep forgetting the world of paper has passed.

She was glancing back to the bar the whole time I was in there, since she was technically AOL from her paying job. I snapped a few photos from my phone—yes, I do have that technical skill—and we headed back to the bar.

I decided since I was walking and not driving, I could have a second beer, while I studied the pictures. If I had more questions, I would be here to ask them.

The pictures didn't tell me anything that my review of it in person had. At least the beer was a decent local draft.

Just as I was contemplating having a third or being good and going home, a group came in, carrying musical cases. They got the key from the bartender and headed to the backstage area.

"Who are they?" I asked as I returned my beer glass.

"Oh, another group practicing here. The Brass Broads, I think they're called."

I followed them back into their rehearsal space.

"Ya got to buy us all a beer, if you want to listen in," said a tall woman, taking a clarinet out of a case.

I smiled and said, "Sure, but I just want to ask a few questions." I pulled out my license and showed it to them. All five passed it around. We're exotic, women playing a trombone and women being private detectives.

"You here about Claude's trombone?" a short woman asked, taking a beat-up old trombone out of her case.

"Let me guess. You're Claude's sister," I said.

"Yep, Claudette," she introduced herself. "He hates we share a name and that a girl can play as well as him."

"He thinks you stole it," I said, keeping my voice neutral, not believing, not disbelieving.

"'Course he does. Hates to think it was him being stupid, leaving everything sitting out while they're in here drinking for hours."

"Did you?" I asked.

"No, I did not. He got Uncle Thurgood's old 'bone. Fancy, silver and all that. That's fine. He's older. I got this one." She lifted the trombone, showing its dented bell and tarnished finish.

"Ms. C. did not steal it," the clarinetist said.

"We're not going to cheat like that," the drummer said, backed up by the trumpet and tuba players.

"Nice to win, but we're new, only jamming for a year, if we

don't come in last, we're good," Claudette added, then a cacophony of tuning and they started playing.

After the first song, a young man joined us. They seemed to know him. He looked at me, then sat as far away as possible. Not the chatty type.

I stayed for a few minutes. They sounded pretty good, but I'm not the one judging. I gave them a nod of thanks, then let myself out of the theater area.

Two beers required a stop at the bathroom. Once done with the necessities, I noticed a window opposite the door. It was high and not easily accessible, but a small person might get through. I stood on my tiptoes, then retrieved a rickety wooden chair from the corridor.

Carefully balancing on it, I examined the window. Layers of dust, and the latch was stuck, painted over several times. Nothing had come in or out of this window since Edwin Edwards was governor. (Famous for his election slogan—Vote for the Crook, It's Important—he was running against the white nationalist David Duke.)

Back in the corridor, I waited a few minutes, giving anyone in the gents' room time to exit. Then I ducked in, carrying the chair. Same routine with the window.

This one had been recently opened. Dust brushed away, the latch barely caught, instead of firmly in place, like someone was in a hurry.

Of course, two men came in, not sure if they wanted to pee or to have privacy, but a tall woman perched on a wobbly chair, made them change their minds about both options.

"Rats. Gotta keep the rats from getting in," I said to their retreating shapes.

I hurriedly exited, replacing the chair, then stopped at the bar long enough to leave two twenties with the bartender to cover beers for the Brass Broads.

I headed out, then made my way around the building to the garbage alley on the other side of the windows, threading my way through the trash cans to get under the windows.

With the handy light of my phone, I examined the ground. I'm tall, my feet aren't small delicate ones and the footprint here was larger. Someone with big feet.

There was also a gouge in the dirt, like something heavy had hit. The corner of an instrument case? It would be tight for a person to wiggle through, but easy to drop objects, like a trombone.

Big foot print and using the men's room. Probably not the fairer sex.

Could be random thieves, but they'd have had to go through a crowded bar, know the layout of the bathrooms and know the band was practicing then.

I scrutinized the garbage area. No security cameras, not that I expected any. I did security consulting, mostly for the gay bars, because they preferred working with an out queer woman than homophobic men from the 'burbs. This little back alley was used by the bar and a pizza place next to it.

But across the street was a new complex with several stores, including an upscale coffee shop with big plate glass windows. Yep, a couple of cameras covering their entrance and parking lot.

I scrolled my security contacts and three phone calls later, I lucked on someone I knew who had worked on them. Even luckier, he was on the premises. He trotted out to meet me.

"Micky Knight! What are you doing back here?"

"Nick, trying to rob a bank. This is the right alley, isn't it?" Nick Gauthier was an old friend. I'd known him back before he became Nick.

"Not even close. What are you looking for? Maybe I can help?"

I give him a quick rundown. Nick and I overlapped and often worked together. He was better at scrambling about laying cables and I was better at writing contracts and talking to bar owners about what they might need.

"Of course we have cameras; why I'm here. Training the night staff," he told me.

"Where's the camera?"

He pointed to several of them, two up front, and one back where the alley met the street. "Not all the way back, but can see if anyone comes in or out."

"Got anything from last night?" I gave him the time frame.

"Give me a bit to see what I can dig up."

He had to get back to work. I went to the garbage area for one last look. Not sure why I opened the lids of the large trash cans. Habit—we will know you by your garbage.

Under a pile of rubbish, all bagged thankfully, I could see the corner of what looked like an instrument case. Usually, I carry a PI bag with things like latex gloves, but not tonight. I gingerly moved the garbage bag, thanked my parents for making me tall and reached in to grab the case. I thought about calling the police, but this was a minor robbery and it could be hours that I didn't have to wait before they showed up.

I managed to get the case out, then saw a second one under it. Ensuring I would be doing laundry and dry cleaning, I reached it as well. I poked and pried as much as I could, but these were the only two. A trumpet and a saxophone.

No trombone.

One in each hand, so it wasn't too bad a walk home.

It was a little after 8 p.m. when I got there, not too late to call the other band members. Voice mail. Voice mail. Ah, luck, Willie, the trumpet player, picked up. He was a little more honest about how long they had been in the bar. "At least three beers; work hard, play hard." Like Claude, he said he didn't see anyone. "Alley cat versus alley cat," was how he described Claude and Claudette, but he was skeptical she stole them. "She's upfront tough, not sneaky tough."

I didn't mention I'd found a trumpet. That could wait.

I also reached Steve, the drummer. He was talkative. "Real mess and bad timing. Claude was sweating the contest since we won the last two years. Sounds good, right? But it's a small thing, 'bout five bands, march down a block and the crowd cheers. Loudest cheer is the winner. Claude was real right pissed that his baby sister and her friends had pulled together a band. Ella, the clarinetist went to the Manhattan School of Music. Said she heard Delores and her band playing outside the grocery in the Quarter and decided she had to come down here. Damn, she can wail that thing. I think the more music, the better, but Claude ain't that way. He worries, then he worries about his worrying, so he worries when he should be practicing."

When he took a breath, I asked him if he's seen anything in the bar.

"Oh, yeah, lots of things. A group of Midwestern tourists who didn't realize they were in a mostly gay bar. The looks on their faces when they saw the pictures of naked men on the wall was priceless. Not my jam, but the place is cool and they let us rehearse in the stage area dirt cheap."

He'd seen a lot, but couldn't remember anyone save for the regulars going back to the bathrooms.

"Oh, also, the pissy people from around the block were getting pizza at the pizza place when we left and they hassled us."

I didn't even need to ask what happened; he went right ahead. "Told us we needed to give them a week's notice if we were going to 'obstruct the roadway' and how much they paid for off street parking, so they had the right to use it. 'Course we laughed. Dude, you moved to Tremé, paid too much and think the road should be reserved for you. Wound too tight for the 'burbs, let alone down below Canal Street."

He didn't know their names, but told me the house they lived in.

I thanked him for his time. He invited me to their next show. And then it was bed time for this old baby girl.

The next day I headed for my office in Bywater. I'd first rented it when it was cheap enough for me to afford, then made the jump and bought when I realized the area was gentrifying and I could either buy it or pay an ever-increasing rent. It was three floors. I was on top and rented out the other two.

Time for a computer search. Decent web page for Claude's band. Brand new rudimentary one for Claudette's. (What were their parents thinking with those names?) Also, a search for recent thefts in the area, especially musical instruments. A slow week for crooks in general and no instruments stolen.

Knowing the house let me look up the address, which gave me the names of the people who owned it. Brent Westerly and his wife, Deborah. Both accountants, both worked in the CBD, both moved here six months ago from, nope, not Brooklyn, but the DC area. They lived two doors down from where the double Claude/Claudette shared, each on one side. If you don't like trombones, living close to them can be a circle of hell. Me? I like trombones.

They were in the vicinity and they had motive.

I called her work number. I was on hold for over ten minutes.

"Deborah Westerly. How can I help you?" came from my phone as I was debating whether I would be on hold on long enough for a bathroom run and be done before she picked up.

"I'm calling about the noise complaint," I used as the bait for my fishing expedition.

"We love music, of course, but not at all hours. Last week at nine p.m., a drum line went by our house. That's outrageous. I want to choose to go to concerts, not have them thrust on me."

"We have a report of musical instruments being stolen and you and your husband were named as suspects."

"What? That's outrageous! Who's accusing us?"

"There are security tapes from behind the pizza place you were at two nights ago, near where they were stolen," I said. "Showed the person who stole them. Was your husband with you the entire time?"

"What? We wouldn't do such a thing!" Then, "I need to talk

to my husband." The line was dead.

Too much protesting. I had stirred up something, just not sure what.

After another cup of coffee, I got an email from Nick, with the footage attached.

Helpful, not helpful. A medium height person coming from back in the garbage area carrying a trombone. Hoodie pulled low and not great light. Male, more from the shoe size than the height. But no way to tell which one.

I sighed and decided it was time to let my brain think. Save for catfish dinners, this wasn't a paying case.

Threw out the trumpet and sax, but kept the trombone. Who would do that?

That afternoon, I caught up with Claude's band. They were practicing at the same space. The others were playing and he was sitting, bereft of a trombone.

"Hey, Claude," I said as I sat beside him.

He looked at me, nodded at my presence. "Find anything?" he asked, then looked away as if he didn't want an answer.

"It's hard when people expect you to be something you're not. I was supposed to be straight and marry the quarterback, but my road in life took me a different direction. Some people didn't approve. I found out who my friends were. The ones who wanted me to be happy, not the ones who wanted me to do what they wanted."

"Yeah, so?" He acted bored.

"Security tape from the coffee shop. Shows who comes in and out of the alley."

"Yeah, so?" He wasn't acting bored now.

"Easy way to get out of doing something you don't want to do. Trombone is stolen and you can't play."

He looked down. Didn't say anything.

"You were going to throw them all away, but kept Uncle Thurgood's special trombone. Keep it hidden for a while, go do what you want to do and then maybe it shows up for someone else to play."

"Damn it, I told Rodney not to get involved." He shook his head.

"I found the trumpet and sax. We can return them."

"You gonna rat me out?"

"Only if I have to. Your sister likes to play, right? You, not so much?"

"Yeah, no. I like math and stuff, want to do sports numbers. Maybe work for the Saints. But...the 'bone takes so much time."

"Your life, Claude. Get the math classes and learn to be a sports dork nerd. Give your sister the trombone and cheer her on like she's your favorite team. In exchange, I'll say I suspected the obnoxious people who hate music, and found all the instruments in a dumpster near where they live. No proof they did it, so nothing we can do. That work?"

It took a moment, but he said, "Yeah, that works."

I put out my hand to shake on the deal. He nodded and we shook.

"Hey, thanks," he said as I turned to leave.

We met the next day at Claude's house, me with the sax and trumpet and him with the trombone. We told Rodney and the other band members our made-up story.

Then Claude said, "Y'all have been great and all, but this got me thinking 'bout what I want to do. I want to do sports, the guy that does all the numbers and stats. The trombone goes to Claudette, keep it playing in the family. She's into it way more than I am and she deserves it."

He handed the trombone case to Claudette, who was sitting on her step. She was first shocked, then a wide smile spread across her face.

She took it out of its case and started playing, first a soulful wail, then into a hot jam, working the slide so fast it blurred.

The music hating neighbors came out. "How long is this going to go on?"

"Seen the ghosts yet?" I called out to them. "Y'all know you moved into the murder house, right?"

They didn't, so I made up a really gruesome tale. "Yep, boiled her head to get the flesh off. They found two left hands in the backyard. Never did find the right ones. Yet." They were green when I finished. They got in their car and left, hopefully to look for other places to live.

Joe and Willy got their horns out, then Rodney got his trumpet, and the music played.

Claude sat and watched, a big smile on his face.

No, not everyone was happy, but if we let everyone else decide our happy endings, we never find them.

READING BETWEEN THE LIES

Liese Sherwood-Fabre

Seraphine Babineaux, *traiteuse* and owner of *The Little Shop of Blessings*, sat at the tarot table, laying out the cards for a reading. The healer did this every morning as she sipped her café au lait. Always good to get some insight into the day ahead. A mixture of believers and the curious would make their way to her shop on St. Philip Street in New Orleans' Treme district. Which would there be more of today?

Her hand hovered over the first card, preparing to turn it over, when Madison Laurent rapped on the glass door. While her store wasn't technically open, the girl, a secretary in a big law firm in the business district, was a regular customer, and if she arrived this early—before going to work—it had to be important. Seraphine gave her coffee one last sip, reached for her cane, and pushed herself from the table. She didn't need the cane, but her clients seemed to expect an old, crippled woman to treat them for their ailments—both physical and psychic.

By the time she made it to the door, Madison was pounding on the glass.

"Good Lord, girl, you're going to break it down," she said as she slid back the deadbolt to let her in.

Before the bolt had finished its travels, the girl pushed open the door, trailing a cloud of too-sweet perfume in her wake. Her entrance had sent the older woman reeling backward, and now she wailed at the store's display of herbs, candles, and religious figurines. "I'm losing him. I can feel it. You must help me."

"Sit," the older woman said. "Take a deep breath and tell me what's going on."

She would brew her a soothing tea, but there was no time. Madison needed to be at work by nine. On her first visit more than a year ago, Seraphine had known her story before she spoke a word. She'd heard it from countless others over the years. A pretty, young thing (and Madison, with her golden, coppery skin, her wavy black hair, and high cheekbones, fit the bill perfectly) attracts the eye of some older, well-to-do libertine. He brings her into his world, takes what he wants, and gives little more than empty promises in return.

Madison had visited her shop too late for any warning. She had already succumbed to the man's promises. All that Seraphine could do then was help her control the situation, providing stronger potions and fetishes on each visit to stir the passions of the old lech.

Taking her place at the table across from the girl, she gathered the cards into a stack. "Let's see what the cards say first."

After shuffling the deck, she placed them in Madison's outstretched hands. The girl held them for a breath, her lips forming words of a silent prayer. Receiving the cards back, Seraphine placed them in the familiar pattern and turned them over, one at a time.

The first, at the center of the spread, showed a man and woman in the Garden of Eden.

"There," Madison said, tapping the card, "see, we're in love."

The older woman raised a finger. "It is at the center. That means you are at a crossroads. The question is, where is your relationship going?"

"That's my question. I need to know the problem and how to fix it." The girl flopped back in her chair, arms crossed. "This reading is worthless."

Seraphine pressed her lips together. The impatience of this younger generation!

Following a calming breath, she reached for the next card. "We've just begun. Let's see the next cards."

Methodically, she turned the others: the Empress, the Devil, the Knight of Wands, and the Two Cups. Once all was revealed, she waved her hand, fingers spread wide, over the reading. "Taken all together, I see true affection exists between you, but it must be nurtured. Go beyond the physical, make an emotional bond, and don't come from a place of weakness but from security. You have something he wants. But he has something for you as well. Make sure he provides it."

"But he'll just leave me if I push too hard."

"Have you gotten that promotion he promised you?"

"No," she said, drawing out the vowel. "But it's not just up to him. There are rules—"

"Is that what *he* tells you? Is he so powerless in his own firm that he can't make such a decision? You have power here. Use it. I'll give you some items for the next time he comes to you. They will increase his desire for you. But make him pay. Do not give in to him on hollow vows."

Seraphine moved back from the table and reached for her cane. Madison put a hand over hers to stop her. "You know what it is. His witch of a wife. She has her claws in him so far he can't free himself. I know you are a powerful *traiteuse*. That's why I came to you. I've been told you can create stronger brews. Something that eliminates obstacles."

The woman yanked back her hand. "Stop. You do not ask for such things. It is a sin. Ask me again, and I will not help you anymore. I will refuse you in my shop, and you will be on your own."

Madison's calculating eyes widened in shock, and she stammered out a hasty response. "I'm sorry, Mama Sera. I didn't mean—I only thought—of course, I'll never mention such a thing again."

She met the girl's gaze, and the lines on her face softened. Laying a hand on the side of her face, she said, "I can't condone such thoughts. You are hinting at a cardinal sin. I'm going to include a rosary for you. Stop at the church on the way to work. Say the rosary for the next three days in penance."

The girl dropped her head. "Of course, Mama Sera. It was evil of me to even think it."

With a pat on her cheek, the *traiteuse* stepped to the shelves lining the walls. She gathered a candle, a few sachets, and several packets of tea into a bag.

Returning to Madison, she held out the collection to her. "Light the candle and serve him the tea at his next visit. The herbs you put in under the pillow and on the stand next to the bed. It should not only strengthen his desire for you but also the bonds between you."

The girl gathered the bag to her chest and pressed some bills into the woman's hand. "Thank you, Mama Sera. Thank you."

Only after the door swung shut did she check the donation the girl had left. She made more when she sold the items to the tourists who wanted to take home a "genuine" souvenir of their visit to a *traiteuse*, but between her true practice and that from tourists, it kept her in café au laits.

She sighed. Now, that coffee was cold, and she must open the shop. Time to put on her act for the tourists.

The morning passed slowly, with tourists drifting in and out, buying one or two cheap trinkets. Slightly before noon, a young couple from Wisconsin entered. Two fresh-faced youths who held hands and, with shy giggles, asked for a tea reading. The girl was expecting, and they wanted to know the sex of their child. She hesitated. These days, with all the medical equipment, her readings didn't always coincide with what a specialist would say. Seraphine agreed to the reading when she learned they were only in town for a few days, and they had confirmed the pregnancy only that morning. They would be back among the cows before any sonogram could show otherwise. Both the swinging pendulum over the girl's abdomen and the image in the tea leaves showed the same—a boy. They left happy and with a generous donation to her practice.

She was about to step into the back to heat her lunch when the woman stepped to the shop's entrance. She reached for the knob but didn't turn it. Even through the door's glass, she could see the woman was too well-dressed for the tourist. More importantly, the dark circles under her eyes were visible even from a distance, and she glanced to each side of the street as if checking for spies. For a woman such as her to come to her shop at midday and risk being seen, her situation was serious.

When she stepped in, Seraphine smiled at her. "Hello, Linda."

At that simple greeting, the woman burst into tears. Forgetting her cane, the *traiteuse* darted to her side, led her to a chair at the tarot table, returned to the door to flip the "Open" sign to "Out to Lunch," and pulled the shades over the door and windows. In the darkened room, Seraphine placed a candle on the table to make the reading easier. The woman continued to weep silently as Seraphine poured the rest of the tea she'd made for the couple into a cup.

Linda Guidry had been coming to her for several years. Her story was as old as the Bible. Philandering husbands were as old as marriage, and the men never learned. Neither did their wives. They'd believe the lies about how he only loved his wife, it would never happen again, and they would be faithful if only she would take him back. Things might be good for a while, but then...A shudder passed down Seraphine's back. She knew the story because it had been hers as well.

"Things are no better between you?" she asked, placing the tea in front of her.

Linda raised the cup to her lips, her hands shaking so badly that the liquid sloshed against the sides and threatened to spill over. Placing the cup back onto its saucer, she shook her head. "He doesn't even try to hide it this time. He comes home smelling of her, a smirk on his face. He's been opening new bank accounts and moving funds, saying it's for the kids, but I know better. My friend Janine, her husband did the same thing before he left her. She had to move in with her parents. Her, the three kids, and her parents all in an old three-bedroom. I don't even have that safety net."

She shifted in her chair, her nostrils flaring. "Do you know I put him through law school? I worked as a secretary those three years to keep us fed in a one-room walkup. Saved every penny I could to pay as much of his tuition as possible. The promise was that once he got his job, I'd get to finish my own degree. But then, the kids came and..." The flames that had sparked in her eyes sputtered and died with a sigh, releasing all the pain, anger, and disappointment she had locked away deep within herself. "My life is over if he leaves me."

The *traiteuse* knew that sigh. Seraphine's father may have taught her the ways of their profession, but it was her mother who had taught her that even a man as powerful as he could not resist the pull of other women. And she herself had known the heartbreak of love lost. But she'd saved both her and her mother, and she could do the same for Linda—if warranted. But she needed to confirm it was ordained.

She patted the woman's hand. "It may not be as bad as all that. Let's see what the cards say."

While she placed the cards in the same pattern as she had for Madison, the faces could not be more different. The first: The Tower. Seraphine's brows drew together. Not a good omen to start with. "There is to be great upheaval in your life."

The woman bit her lip and watched as Seraphine slowly turned over each card. The healer's heart beat faster with each revelation, dread rising as she exposed The Three of Swords, The Five of Cups, and The Moon. With The Justice card, her hand trembled ever so slightly as she pulled away.

"What is it? What do you see?" Linda asked.

"Nothing. The other cards, together, only tell us what you

already know. Your relationship is in peril, and he is having an affair. This one," she tapped the newly revealed card, "says that all is not lost. You will resolve this soon. And equitably."

"And the last card?"

Seraphine took a deep breath and turned it over, already guessing its face.

The Death Card.

The skeleton in the middle seemed to smile at her as if reading her thoughts.

"Death?" her client asked. "Does that mean someone's going to die?"

Without hesitating, she said, "No. In this case, it means the death of a relationship. I think divorce is inevitable. But as I said, it will be equitable."

"No, no, no," she said, shaking her head. She pushed back from the table. "I told you. I can't survive a divorce. I'll lose everything. And he'll give it all to that slip of a girl who's done nothing but throw herself at him since he hired her."

Seraphine said nothing, staring dumbly at the cards as their true meaning became clear. This reading wasn't for Linda. It was speaking to her. She'd been playing the two—Madison and Linda—off each other for months after the girl had let slip her boss's name. Her counsel and love potions had unbalanced the natural course of his affair, keeping it enflamed instead of it dying out. Now, she saw the destruction she'd created. The cards carried a warning: end the charade and make things right.

But to make it right...

The *traiteuse* shook her head. Surely the cards weren't suggesting that? She pushed the thought aside until Linda's whimpering recurred. Once again, she saw her mother's tears and heard the quiet prayers as she said the rosary over and over at night. She recalled her own husband's clothes carrying the scent of other women and the pain in her chest as her heart cracked in two. She still had the root she'd used before.

Madison was young and pretty—a catch for any man—and

with her help, could find a suitable one. Linda, however, had sacrificed for her husband, only to be kicked aside like an old tin can.

She pushed herself up from the table.

"What are you doing?" the woman asked, a quiver in her voice.

Seraphine patted her shoulder. "I know what to do." She pointed to the Justice card. "I can help you ensure justice for yourself and your children. But I need to know. Are you willing to accept this time he will not change?"

Linda's gaze dropped to her hands, and a tear dripped onto her thumb. Without a word, she nodded.

"To take this next step," Seraphine said, "means no going back. He will be out of your life. No more of his lies."

The woman seated across from her raised her gaze and blinked. A heartbeat later, her eyes rounded in understanding. "I'm ready, Mama Sera."

Using her cane, the *traiteuse* hobbled to the back of the store, passing through the bead curtain that marked the front from the back. While the beads clacked against each other behind her, she passed the shelves holding the jars and bottles used in her healing practice. These weren't for the tourists. They were for the believers. The ones who knew she could cure their ills and mend their bodies—including broken hearts. At the back of the room, she stopped at a locked cabinet holding the most serious herbs. She unlocked the cabinet and pulled out the dried root that still bore the cut from the last time she'd used it. After measuring off a piece, she pounded it into a powder and put it in a small glass vial.

As she passed toward the front room, she selected a candle and a vial of oil from a backroom shelf.

Returning to stand in front of Linda, she placed both on the table. Linda followed her actions with dry eyes.

"Are there times you know when he goes to her?" she asked.

A nod.

"On the day before he goes to her, light the candle. Dab the oil on your wrists and neck. It will make him desire you." She then held up the vial with the powder. "This, you put in his morning coffee on the day he will visit her."

A slight smile turned up the corners of Linda's lips. "Yes." She took the vial from the older woman's hand. "Thank you, Mama Sera."

With that, she gathered the items and placed some bills in the *traiteuse*'s hand.

After the woman left, Seraphine lowered herself into her chair and stared at the reading on the table. She knew what would happen next. After the night with his wife, the man would waver in his desire for Madison, and the girl would return for a stronger potion. When she did, Seraphine would give her the other half of the powdered root.

Everyone would think he died of a heart attack.

THE HANGING ON DUMAINE STREET

Clay Stafford

The French Quarter. Dumaine Street. Art galleries, antique stores, clothing boutiques, jewelry shops, music outlets, bookstores, voodoo and occult vendors. And one dead jazz singer hanging by her neck.

"Bill Walton, MLI, Medicolegal Death Investigator," I said. I ducked under the crime tape and pointed to the laminated badge with my name, title, and photo that looked worse than my Tennessee driver's license. I was now a guy on loan, a locum tenens of sorts. I knew Barry Rosenberg, a New Orleans medical examiner, from our Board membership. After what happened with my wife, with me, my career, my soul, I couldn't stand it in Tennessee wallowing in what used to be, and Barry needed the warm body. It was a pay cut, but it was peace of mind.

NOPD Homicide detective Clémence Thibodeaux was on the scene. Good. No introductions, no vague explanations needed. It was easy to spot Wynona Rich hanging from the second floor and dangling over the foyer. I knew of her before her death.

"Suicide?" Clémence pondered.

One might think that a stupid question, but it wasn't. "The drop from the second floor. Or maybe something more sinister. That's up to the Medical Examiner."

"But you used to be an ME."

I looked at her. Clémence had been doing her homework. There was a time when a person could leave their troubles behind, start over, begin a new life, turn a page, but with the internet, you were stuck with both who you were and who you used to be and all the baggage that went between. Clémence asked me several more logical questions about my past, except the one she wanted to know, but I didn't answer. I'd left Baltimore because of this sort of personal inquiry. Frankly, it made me feel like a failure. "Barry Rosenberg is my ME. We'll follow what he says. I'm here to take pictures. I'm Rhymin' Simon with a Nikon full of Kodachrome."

I knew of Wynona Rich. She was a legend that everybody had forgotten. She'd made it in vinyl, 8-tracks, cassettes, but never CDs. By then, the magic was gone. Alcohol and drugs took their toll. You could hear her soulful tunes on Apple Music if you wanted to search, but you'd have to know what to search for. Type in her name, and if you weren't selective, you'd get Wynonna Judd, Winona Ryder, Drake, or Jelly Roll. You wouldn't get a jazz singer who sang her heart out like Janis Joplin. I once saw Wynona in performance when I visited one February with my wife for Mardi Gras. We came to New Orleans every few years. We traveled a lot, my wife and I. There was hardly a state, city, or even many countries that didn't hold a piece of her and took a little piece of my heart. That was my wife. She left a part of her soul wherever she went, an essence, a palpable love of life. She left that on me.

"They said Wynona was making a comeback," Clémence said.

"They're always making a comeback. Or a farewell tour." Wynona was hanging alright, but, looking closely, I wasn't sure that was how she died. "She left a suicide note? That's what dispatch said. Two hours ago?"

"She sent it to her husband, Harry Rich, on his cellphone."

"And he called the police immediately?"

"As soon as he got home and saw the body. He's outside

rocking and crying."

"Poor man," I said. "It won't help."

Wynona's head was about two feet above mine. What bothered me was that while the neck was elongated—snapped and the skin and muscles stretched so she indisputably had a broken neck from the drop from the second floor—there were no ligature marks, only slight abrasions. There were no petechial hemorrhages, no pale face with congestion, no Tardieu spots, no swollen face or tongue. Wynona had been noosed and dropped from the second floor. She didn't do it herself. I'd bet money that Barry would say she was already dead when she dropped.

I give everybody dignity because, in death, there is not a lot of it. I asked everyone to leave while I did my routine: I took pictures, cut her down, wrote notes, examined her, took the ambient temperature and hers. Algor mortis puzzled me. The house was 71 degrees. Wynona Rich's body was 91.4. She'd been dead for about four hours. That was strange because she'd texted her husband two hours ago to say she was going to kill herself. I'd leave that to Barry to run the math. Because of my suspicions, I bagged her hands and feet. After we got Wynona in a body bag and loaded in the mortuary van, I told Clémence, "We probably need to talk to the husband," as I watched the Orleans Parish Coroner's Office logo grow smaller on the side of the vehicle as it drove away.

It was evening. Harry Rich was sitting in a white wicker chair on the front porch with a uniformed officer beside him to keep him from talking to anyone. Several neighbors were outside watching. We'd become Dumaine's momentary sideshow. New Orleans loved sideshows, spectacles, and pomp. I've always liked Dumaine Street. Unlike boisterous Bourbon Street one block south, Dumaine had a subdued mix of mystery, history, and quiet charm. The soft glow of the gas lamps already cast long shadows on the street and sidewalks. As if offering a eulogy for one of its own, smooth haunting notes of jazz wafted north from Bourbon Street. One could feel the history of ghosts, voodoo, and supernatural lore for which Dumaine was famous. The ambiance was perfect for a hanging woman whose best years had long been buried to the point she had become a ghost herself.

"You know Wynona was on bail for the murder of her former manager Stanley Kleminsky?" Clémence whispered. "Case has been dragging on."

"That was before I got here." I'd only been in town a few months.

"She stabbed him with a blunt letter opener. Allegedly. Twenty-two times."

"What was their beef?"

"She wanted to make a comeback. Kleminsky agreed to manage her again, though his connections had faded. Both lived in a dream of the old days. She never would say what was discussed, but according to the charges, something didn't fit her fancy. She was drunk when they arrested her—passed out in the office with Kleminsky. Detective Henley had the case. She's been out on bail, claims, in the end, it was self-defense. From what, not sure. Kleminsky required a walker to get around. Not clear what kind of a threat he exhibited. There were no firearms or any other traditional weapons found. Just the blunt letter opener sticking out between his ribs. She had a court case coming up."

"She was a strong woman."

"I've heard she's used to getting her way."

We walked across the veranda to where Harry Rich sat, his eyes red.

"Why'd she do it?" Harry asked pitifully.

"That's what we're hoping to learn," Clémence said. "Her text to you was rather vague." All it said was that she could not go on.

"Such a beautiful woman, but haunted. Stanley Kleminsky was a rat. She never hurt that man."

"You called the police today the minute you got the text?"

"I called the minute I saw her."

"Where were you before you saw her?"

"I was eating at Antoine's."

"Alone?"

"Wynona said she felt ill."

"The rope?"

Harry flinched.

"I have to ask," Clémence said. "Do you know where she got it?"

"Garage. We bought it to build a tree swing for the grand-kids, and I...I hadn't put it up yet. I should have put it up. Kleminsky, her former manager, was too old. He piddled. Pretended to be involved to make himself feel useful. Wynona, in her condition, wasn't making a comeback either. They were both in La-La Land. I told them both. Wynona was insulted."

"Why?"

"Her age. She never liked growing old. I wonder if my saying that, that it pushed her over."

"She had had an affair with Kleminsky..."

"I don't know how. Stanley used a walker. He couldn't get anything up, not even himself. Two old people."

"I'm sure we'll have questions later."

"I don't want questions," Harry said. "I want answers. If you can tell me why."

Clémence turned. I followed. When she got to the street, Clémence opened her phone and googled Wynona Rich, then her husband. There was a recent picture of Harry online. Considering her obscurity now, I wouldn't have thought there would be anything recent on Wynona or her husband, but the internet allowed no secrets, though it didn't tell the truth either. "I'm going to visit Antoine's."

"We walking?" Antoine's was only about ten minutes away by foot. My twelve-hour shift was coming to an end.

"Let's drive," she said. We got into her unmarked, black

Tahoe. "For a man his age, he's spry. I don't think it impossible he threw her over the stairwell after putting a noose around her neck."

I'd never been to Antoine's, but I knew it well. Antoine Alciatore, a French immigrant, founded the restaurant in 1840. It's the oldest family-run restaurant in the United States. A black and gold sign hung above the entrance. Sometime before the turn of the century, Antoine invented Oysters Rockefeller. You can get the dish in about any better restaurant serving fresh seafood, but I've heard Antoine's is unique. Like Coke, they have a secretly-guarded recipe.

Clémence parked, and we walked beneath the green awning leading to the doorway. White curtains adorned the windows. The whole effect was classic, Old World, a quality I felt was becoming an endangered species in many parts of gentrified New Orleans.

I took in the place as Clémence asked for the manager. I'd heard it had fourteen different dining rooms, each decorated with a specific personality. The manager was prompt.

Clémence showed him the picture. He knew Harry on sight. He also knew Wynona. He asked about Wynona's health. Clémence said she'd had better days, then asked if Harry had been there for dinner about two hours ago.

"What's this about? Nothing wrong with Harry?"

"No," Clémence said. "Looking into something."

"I didn't see Harry," the manager said, "let me ask." He checked the guest registry, remarking that Harry always made reservations. Nothing listed. He excused himself. He was gone maybe five minutes. "Mr. and Mrs. Rich don't seem to have dined here tonight. Is there anything..."

"All's good," Clémence said. "You've been helpful. Thank you." Clémence wished him a good evening, and we returned to her SUV.

"Story's starting to fall apart," Clémence said, driving back. She suspected the husband. About twenty-five percent of murders in the United States are committed by family members against other family members. Murder appears easier to some than getting a divorce or simply moving out.

My shift had ended. My apartment in Tulane-Gravier was too lonely. I only liked to go there when ready to crash. I walked to my company van. I drove my unmarked Ford Transit to what felt more like my apartment than my apartment, the Orleans Parish Coroner's Office in Mid-City.

Part of my MLI job was to help Barry with autopsy preparation. This time of night, the office was dead. It was violating protocol a bit, but I was an ME before I came upon that personal case I couldn't solve and decided to change professions and locations, the event that destroyed my life and sent me on the road as a wandering desperado. Kind of like the guy in the Eagle's song. I knew I'd never find another woman who loved me like she did. The rest of my life would be spent mending fences. I doubted I'd ever come to my senses. Not until her murderer was found. Love makes you do crazy things.

I went to the body cooler and found Wynona's tray. I slid her onto a gurney and took her into the autopsy suite, where I shifted the body tray onto the stainless-steel table. I scrubbed and gloved up.

You can't do anything to a human body or mind that doesn't leave evidence. Kids are messed up from psychological trauma. Husbands are forever altered mentally and emotionally because of the unfairness of losing their wives. Even a cut on your finger while chopping onions leaves a trace scar. Whatever happened to Wynona Rich would be there waiting for me to discover it.

I unzipped the body bag. For what I wanted, there was no need to take her out. Her body had started to change. Livor mortis was setting in. The blood had left her face and was pooling towards her back. Carefully, I inspected the white rope around her neck. It wasn't tight, so it was easy to adjust it so I could get a better look. Her neck was broken, consistent with the drop from the second floor. I could feel the separation in her spine with my fingers. I prodded gently, not wanting to mess with anything that Barry needed to do tomorrow. Defense attorneys were sticklers about improper procedures. The court system loved to throw things out because someone forgot to knock before they opened a door. I knew what I needed to do and how to do it so no one, not even Barry, knew I'd already conducted an exam.

There were abrasions on the neck, as I'd seen when I first cut Wynona down, but that's precisely what they were: abrasions. There were no deep ligature marks usually associated with a hanging. Considering my calculation—which can be iffy, but I had faith in it—Wynona was dead two hours before she ever texted the suicide note to her husband. The hanging broke her neck, but that's not what killed her.

I wanted to run a toxicology report, but that would have to wait until Barry ordered it. I didn't have a license to practice in Louisiana, but that didn't stop my curiosity. What were they going to charge me with? Tampering with a dead body? Maybe, but I doubted it. The worst they'd do is probably ask me to leave town, which I was already contemplating. Summer was coming to New Orleans. I'd been figuring that I might want to go and travel north. I'd already contacted an ME friend in Minnesota. Land of ten thousand lakes and millions of walleye. I thought that might be an excellent place to spend the summer. Fish, reflect, pull my life back together, think how I was supposed to go on when I didn't really want to.

I knew from my initial examination that none of Wynona's clothing had been damaged. She hadn't been stabbed with a knife or other object, and she hadn't been shot. She might have been stabbed with a needle; I didn't see evidence, but that was Barry's and the toxicology department's call. There were no signs anyone had strangled her. I leaned towards possibly some kind of poison. Curious, I turned her over to her side. When I'd helped put her in the bag, she was still pliable, so we laid her out straight as though she were sleeping on her back. Now, she was easy to roll over, like a log.

I gently brushed through her hair with my fingers and saw antemortem bruising on the back of her head. It wasn't postmortem trauma, and it wasn't livor mortis. Wynona, my guess, hit her head. Or at least that had something to do with it. She died quickly after the blow but stayed alive long enough for death to leave its calling card. I didn't think she was hit on the head. It wasn't violent enough. I believed she'd fallen on her back. Not disturbing her bagged left hand, I carefully undid the buttoned sleeve of her blouse and rolled it up above her elbow. Sure enough, elbow abrasions. Slight, but there. She had tried to catch herself when she fell. I theorized that Wynona fell backward, hit her elbow (I'd bet the other elbow might have a mark, too), and then hit the back of her head on something. The question was, what? What did she hit her head on? And then the next question was, if it was an accidental fall, which wouldn't be uncommon for someone of the age, declined health, and probable intoxication of Wynona Rich, why didn't someone call an ambulance rather than hang her from the foyer stairway? I put Wynona back together as I'd found her, laid her out as she was before, and took her back to the body cooler. What I'd discovered here was my secret, but the mystery of it consumed me, as these cases always did. As usual, since the loss of my wife, I had no one to talk to. I wondered when, in my lonely desperation, I might start hearing voices.

I left the coroner's office and walked to my Tulane-Gravier apartment. Even at this hour of the morning, it was busy as I made my way through the Medical District, past closed delis and cafes, old historic homes that hadn't yet been consumed, street murals and art. It had a city look to me. I preferred the more haunting feel of Dumaine Street. I must have fallen asleep but awoke a few hours later. An idea had come to me during my nap.

I was back on Dumaine Street by seven. People were active, getting ready for work, taking their kids to school, but there was one house I was particularly interested in: the house across the street from Harry and Wynona Rich. People sometimes think that solving a crime requires convoluted machinations, but like most crimes, the simplest explanation—and the most straightforward methods—are sometimes the best. I was curious who entered Harry and Wynona Rich's house before Wynona found herself at the end of a rope.

The house across the street from the Rich's was stately and timeless. The brick had been painted a muted cream color. The second story showcased a beautiful wrought iron balcony. What I was interested in was on the first floor beside the front door.

A woman, I'd guess in her late thirties, answered the door. I introduced myself and stuck to the facts. "Good morning, ma'am. I hate to bother you. I'm Bill Walton, MLI," I gestured to my nametag, "with the Orleans Parish Coroner's Office and—"

"I was so sorry to hear about Mrs. Rich."

News traveled fast, even in the night.

"Yes, unfortunate," I said. "I want to ask a favor. I have no jurisdiction to ask questions. I don't have a subpoena. You don't have to talk with me. You don't have to help me out."

"What do you need?"

"You've got a Ring camera on your door. Your house is across from Mrs. Rich's house. The police will eventually think about it, probably later this morning, but I'd love to examine the footage from yesterday. Would you be interested in letting me do that? As an MLI?"

I learned several things I didn't know about the Riches from my visit with the neighbor, Gloria McNamara. Wynona was heavily into gambling and drinking. Gloria knew this from her husband, who was friends with Harry Rich. Wynona was going through both alcohol and the Rich family money like water. Wynona was a shadow of her previous physical beauty, but that didn't stop her from having a series of lovers, Stanely Kleminsky, her former walker-bound manager included. The man she allegedly murdered with a dull envelope opener. Gloria knew quite a bit about what was happening across the street. Harry Rich, it seems, after a few snifters of E&J V.S. on ice, had a loose tongue. Or maybe he was lonely like me. With only Wynona to talk with—and she was the problem—it was good for Harry Rich to have someone else like Mr. McNamara to confide in.

Homicide detective Clémence Thibodeaux's phone call interrupted my conversation with Gloria McNamara. Clémence asked me if I was busy. I told her where I was. She didn't ask what I was doing. She said she'd be parked in front of the Rich's house in ten minutes. I asked Gloria if Mr. McNamara, her husband, was around. He'd already gone to work. He was a head chef at Café du Monde. I told Gloria I did my best to stay away from there. I had a weakness for deep-fried dough beignets covered in sugar washed down with café au lait. Gloria had planted the seed, though. After I met with Clémence, I might drop in and have a bite. My waistline didn't need it, but my grumbling stomach did. And maybe I could get a chance to speak with Mr. McNamara. When I saw Clémence stop in front of the Rich home, I finished civilities with Gloria and walked across the street.

"What'd you find?" Clémence asked me.

"That I'm really hungry."

"There's a mitigating circumstance. Wynona Rich had a gambling problem."

I knew that much from Gloria McNamara, but, as usual, I didn't play my cards. I let the detectives do their work. Only when they slipped did I offer any thoughts of my own.

Clémence continued: "She was also going through their money quickly. I spoke with Barry Rosenberg." My boss and the ME. "He already did his post on Wynona Rich. Mrs. Rich didn't die by hanging. Dr. Rosenberg said she died from a blow to the back of the head. He said she had enough alcohol in her system to kill an elephant, but that wasn't what did it."

"Suspect?" I already knew the answer.

"Husband. Mr. Rich." Bingo. I didn't say it, but I knew she was wrong. But she'd get there.

"We need to talk with Mr. Rich. I'll have a confession this morning."

I said, "Let's hope Harry Rich sees it the same way."

Harry was already standing at the front door. He looked like hell.

Clémence: "Mind if we come in?"

We sat and declined coffee—I still had Café du Monde on my mind—and Clémence, never one to beat around the bush, jumped right in. "Mr. Rich. Your wife didn't kill herself."

The blood left Harry Rich's face. I noticed a slight tremor. "I loved my wife," he said.

"You want to tell us about it?" This was Clémence.

"Was she murdered?"

"She was dead two hours before you got the text from her. Did you send the text?"

"How can you tell she was already dead?"

"Investigation."

"What…?"

I interjected, "The body always talks, Mr. Rich. They usually have a lot to say, and everything they say follows a natural order. They're not subjective."

"Did you kill your wife, Mr. Rich?" Clémence asked.

"No."

"Do you know who killed your wife?"

"No."

"Were you a part of hanging her or making her look like she had committed suicide?"

"No." He was shaking now.

"I'm going to forget all the questions up to this point," Clémence said. "I haven't read you any rights, but I want you to know that from this point forward, I will reference your answers, and what you say can and will be used against you.

I'm not charging you with anything. I'm not suggesting anything. I'm telling you, it's against the law to lie to a law enforcement officer. Louisiana Revised Statutes Section 14:133. Obstruction of justice: fines and imprisonment. False reporting of a crime: fines, imprisonment, or both. Later, filing false public records: a felony; up to five years of imprisonment and/or fines. Even with the two million in life insurance you have on your wife, which you wouldn't get because of the Slayer Rule, there's still going to be considerable fines and time in prison. I'm going to ask you these questions again. Did you kill your wife?"

Tears streamed down Harry's face. "Yes."

"Why?"

"She was having an affair with Stanley Kleminsky."

"The man she allegedly killed?"

"Yes."

"Did you kill Mr. Kleminsky?"

"I think I need a lawyer."

Clémence rose. "Then we're done," Clémence said. "Can you get your things? I need to take you to the 8th District to make a statement. Do you want to call your lawyer and have them meet us there?"

"Can I ask a question?" I asked, still sitting across the room from the two on the sofa.

Clémence shot me a glance. "Sure."

"Mr. Rich. If I showed you a picture, could you tell me who the person is? Or would you prefer to have your lawyer present for that?"

Mr. Rich looked back and forth between Clémence and me. His eyes finally settled on an end table photo of Wynona Rich from back when she looked and sang like nobody else. "I can look at a picture," Harry said.

I stood, pulled out my phone, and showed him the screen. He burst into tears. "I think you know where I'm going with this," I said.

"How did you get that?"

"It doesn't matter. But I also know what happened."

Clémence squinted her eyes.

Harry burst into sobs.

"You want to tell us about it?" I asked.

"Yes," Harry said. I sat back down. Clémence did the same. "That's Helen Dupont."

I took over the conversation since I held the cards. "And who is Helen?"

"She and I are…we have a relationship."

"How long."

"About nine months now."

"Did Mrs. Rich know?"

"Only recently."

"You want to tell me what happened?"

He started sobbing again.

"Why don't I talk, then," I said.

He nodded.

"You and Helen Dupont were in the driveway. Wynona came out of the house. I'm not sure you knew Wynona was home. I don't think you did. Wynona was drunk. She staggered. There was an argument. Wynona slapped Helen Dupont, who, in turn, pushed Wynona, who lost her balance, fell backward, and hit her head. Both of you rushed to her, but after examining her, it appeared that she may have been dead. There was a heated discussion. You picked up your wife by her shoulders; Dupont picked up her feet. You both carried her into the house. Pure conjecture: after you got her inside, there was a big discussion. I think the life insurance policy came up. I think the fear of being charged with murder came up. I think you cooked up a plan to make it look like suicide, so no one was charged. Wynona was dead already; what difference did it make?"

"That's not fair," Harry said.

"No," I said. "Nothing about this is fair. But then, Helen Dupont, not you, came from the house, went to the garage, and returned with a rope. One of you sent a suicide text from Wynona's phone to yours. I'd say you sent the text after you both had already made it look like Wynona had killed herself."

"It was awful. I loved my wife. Helen sent it. It was her idea."

"You weren't at Antoine's alone. You were somewhere and then here with Helen Dupont. Helen left in her 2018 Toyota Camry—I have her license number—and left you alone. Five minutes after she left, you called the police."

"I didn't kill my wife."

"I know," I replied. "I have no doubt you loved your wife, loved what your wife used to be. You were sad at what she had become, you became distracted, you felt you needed comfort, someone to talk to, to confide in, but maybe found it in the wrong place. I've been there, done that. Helen Dupont caused an accident, you panicked. Dupont came up with a plan, you were scared, you did what Dupont suggested, and now here we are, you in a chair, me on the sofa. You didn't kill your wife. You did participate in covering up the cause of death, but you didn't commit murder. I can testify to that."

"How did you know all that?" Clémence asked.

"It's my passion," I said. "I see dead people."

"You got it right," Harry said.

"Are you willing to sign a statement?" Clémence asked.

"Yes."

"Do you have a lawyer?"

"No. But I don't need a lawyer."

"I'd advise you to get a lawyer. We can provide one if you don't have one."

"Whatever you think is best. Let's just be done with this. I can't take it anymore."

"We'll ride over to Royal Street," Clémence said. "Do you need to do anything before we leave?"

"Let me lock up, please. I'm not sure when I'll be back."

Clémence walked with Harry. He checked all the doors as he

had probably done a million times since he and Wynona had lived in the house. I'd seen old pictures of them. You could tell. In every shot, Harry Rich was in love with his wife.

As we left, he locked the front door and turned to me. "You don't know what it's like, what it does to you, to lose your wife."

There were many things I wanted to say, but I didn't. Harry Rich was wrong. I did know what it felt like to lose your wife. This case pressed all the wrong buttons in me, and people like Clémence had started asking me too many questions I didn't want to answer.

I got in my unmarked company Ford Transit, watched Clémence pull away with Harry, and I headed toward Moss Street. Minnesota looked awfully good right now. I wanted to thank Barry for letting me hang out in New Orleans these past few months and tell him in person that it was time for me to move on. He'd understand. Barry knew me well. He and I both liked our walleye fresh and pan-fried. I'd ask him if he wanted to visit.

LEVEES

Kelli Stanley

The city was dying.

The air was warm and wet and the wind was picking up. No birds flew. Roaches swarmed up the limestone-washed brick of the carriage house at Dauphine and St. Louis, panicked and confused and looking for high ground like everyone else.

Down on Bourbon, the rum and whiskey were still flowing, drowning out fear, drowning out reason. An occasional whoop sounded more like a scream, and the men and women who stayed in the bar, waiting for the end to come, rubbed rheumy eyes and asked for another round.

Sure, the city was dying. It was dying all the time, every day, sinking a little, sweating a little more, every year a storm, some years a flood, every few years a hurricane so bad that the dead floated in their wooden ferry boats, skeletal smiles to Charon as they waved past the Underworld.

They weren't much impressed with it when they got there. They were from New Orleans, and they'd seen it already.

Jude stuck his rough hands down in the torn pocket of his denim trousers and watched the cockroaches. His back ached and one of his feet dragged while he walked.

He wondered where the roaches were headed.

* * *

He walked down Dauphine, past Ma Bailey's bar, where the red lamps still shone and the cornet was still blowing, not as loudly as the wind off the Mississippi, but the notes were bright and pure and clean and they made his crooked steps a little lighter.

Up ahead more people seemed to be crossing down Toulouse, heading to Bourbon Street or maybe the pharmacy on Chartres. They were dressed funny, stranger than he'd ever seen, like they'd stepped out of something in the movie house, but it was New Orleans, so he didn't give it much mind.

He stopped for a moment and stared at the ramshackle cottages on the left. It was said that an artist, Audubon, lived and worked in one. No one was there, now, only the wind whistling through a broken window and a faded signing advertising palm reading swaying and creaking in the wind. He wondered about the man that had lived there. He'd seen a book one time, filled with pictures, drawings so lifelike you'd swear they'd fly off the page.

So many people in and out, coming and going, some stayed, some settled for a time, and all of them made up New Orleans, Jude thought.

Always been that way. Always would be.

He frowned, the deep cracks along his face deepening and he dug his cold hands further into his pockets and kept walking.

St. Peter was busy, and not just at the gates, preparing for whatever the storm would bring. More people—some dressed even more outlandishly than he'd seen before, like something out of the Bible his mother wrote in when his sister died, or the old school book he'd seen when he was seven or eight—scurried toward the cathedral, ignoring a plaintive *St. Louis Blues* echoing from Preservation Hall.

Probably rehearsal for a funeral march. Maybe getting ready for their own.

The wind was stronger now, and the billowing capes of a

monk flew out behind him, making him look like one of Audubon's birds. No roaches scurried on the walls of St. Louis Cathedral. A voice had joined the strains of the blues from Preservation, singing to the same saint, and it reminded him of Bessie Smith and when he'd seen her dancing in front of the White Elephant Saloon. He'd been a small boy, then, his mama had died, and he never forgot the smile Bessie gave him.

I hate to see that evening sun go down
I hate to see that evening sun go down
'Cause, my baby, he's gone left this town...

The cathedral almost seemed to vibrate, to hum, and inside he could hear other singing, voices upraised in hymns to God, the blues and the gospel combined in pain, feigning hope until hope finally came.

The city was dying.

And this time, Jude knew, nobody thought she'd be back.

A couple of carriages stood in front of Jackson Square, horses flashing the white eyes of fear. Why in the hell would anyone bring an animal down here? Should be in a stable, waiting out the storm. People could make their own decisions, but animals knew better. Ask the roaches.

He stroked the flank of a big bay who was stamping nervously. The smell of chicory coffee and beignets still frying at Café Du Monde caught his nose and he turned to stare at the crowd of roughly dressed men and some Creole women in calico dresses and still others wearing the same strange clothes he'd seen earlier. They pressed forward, trying to buy what they could, a large man in a dirty white apron shaking his head, trying to close up and get out while he still could.

Out of the corner of his eye, he saw a strikingly beautiful, queenly-looking woman in a bright yellow headwrap walk toward the cathedral and he twisted his neck to look again but she'd vanished. He patted the horse again, rubbing his nose, and the gelding blew gentle, warm breath into Jude's creased, dry palm.

A woman's voice broke through the sound of the ever-louder wind.

"He'll be all right. He won't be here for long. LaFitte is stabling him up on Burgundy."

He quickly turned to face her, half-expecting to see the regally beautiful woman he'd spotted earlier. Instead, an Ursuline nun stood before him, wire glasses perched on her nose and a smile stretched across her plain, broad face.

"I'm sorry if you were expecting Madame Laveau. She's been assigned to 17th Street. You may see her on the way."

Jude stared at her. "Do I know you, Sister? You feelin' all right? You should get back to the convent—I know y'all moved up to State street when the canal got dug, but—"

The nun nodded. "That's right, Jude. My name's Rita. Sister Rita Cascia—"

He took a step closer to her, eyes narrowed. "How do you know my name? I ain't never seen you before—and—and that woman, couldn't be no Marie Laveau—she's been dead for nigh on fifty years—"

The nun sighed into the wind and a strange silence followed, with the street noises and excited voices hushed and the only sound palpable not really a sound, just a just-below-hearing level shrieking of the sky and wind and water, uniting in coming destruction.

The storm was coming, the biggest one that had ever been, Jude knew, and it was coming fast. Sound turned on again when a fleshy-faced young man started wailing on a cornet over at Du Monde, hitting warbling high C notes, and the sudden gust carried his tune up past the Cathedral all the way to Tremé.

"What is this?" Jude was demanding now, and he stepped away from the horse while behind him a thin young man in colorful livery grabbed the gelding's halter and started to lead him up toward Dumaine. "That there was Louis Armstrong, used to play down in Storyville before he hit it big with the

Oliver band. What's he doin' here? And what are you doing here? There's a storm comin', one they say nobody ever seen before—you should be back at the convent, Sister Whoever-you-are—"

"Sister Rita." Her voice was lowered but somehow seemed louder than before, loud enough to hear over the wind. She was holding on to her wimple while her train blew around her. "I'm so sorry no one has explained. There isn't much time. Come, let's catch the streetcar. You must get to the Industrial Canal between France and Jourdan—the storm is almost here."

The lines on either side of Jude's face grew deeper. Whatever this was, she was right. The storm was coming in. Better to humor the lady and get out while he could.

They passed Frenchman Street and heard more music, this time a blues piano playing a kind of blue jazz he hadn't heard before. The notes were deep and mournful, like a dirge, but they kept going and so did the nun, her head bent down against the wind, hands on her wimple. A few drops of rain, big ones, were starting to fall.

It was almost five miles to where she said they were going, the canal that had just been dug a few years back, the one that moved the Ursulines to State Street. Nineteen million dollars, it had cost, Jude remembered. Nineteen million dollars. That much money wasn't real, wasn't earned, wasn't sweated, but he'd seen the work when he was a boy, saw them tear up the old houses and the convent and saw the dredger with his own eyes, heard the noises it made as it sucked up silt and forged that canal between the river and Lake Pontchartrain.

The rain was falling harder now, and it was hard to hear anything except the roar off in the distance and the sound of water pounding stone.

"There," Sister Rita gasped, "There's the streetcar. Desire. We change at Cemeteries."

"I was born in the 9th Ward. I know the line. You tryin' to get to Elysian Fields? I thought you were makin' for the Canal..."

"We are." She climbed aboard and smiled at the short, stout, dapper white man with a mustache who wore the conductor's hat. "Sit down."

Jude dug in his pockets. "I had a penny in here—and I ain't seen that this car is the kind we can ride, Sister, so—"

She waved a hand impatiently. "That's the Devil's work, Jude. We don't have much time. Listen, they're all counting on you. The 9th Ward. You're the one—the one to hold it up. The one to keep the canal from breaching."

He stared at her, trying to find sense. What he found instead was fear, a dawning dread. She was telling the truth but he didn't know why and what she said—what she said—"

The conductor clanged the bell. "Changing to Cemeteries," he intoned. "Next stop Elysian Fields."

Jude looked up. "But you—we—we're supposed to get off—"

The nun patted his hand. "We shall. Next stop. He's changing lines to get us there quicker because of the storm."

Jude stretched his roughened, blunted fingers across his forehead and rubbed. Why did he understand this was all—necessary? None of it made sense—none of it should make sense—and yet...

Rita looked at him and spoke softly. "It's the largest, you see. Not once in a century—those come much more frequently now—but once in a millennium. We're the last hope. The last chance."

He raised his head and met her eyes. "Who are you, Sister?"

"Elysian Fields, all out—all out for Elysian Fields!" The soft-voiced white man with the southern inflected drawl pulled a lever and opened the streetcar's door. Rain came down in sheets now, the wind howling, and Jude shrank back into the interior.

The nun put a hand on his shoulder. "You asked who I am.

But you know that already. I'm like you, Jude. I'm a levee."

His brow wrinkled. "A—levee? You mean—"

She nodded. "Against the storm. All of us. The dead. The dead that made New Orleans."

She swept her hand across the streetcar, and he saw it was full of people, speaking so many different languages that it sounded like the music from Ma Bailey's, like Armstrong down at the Café, and they were of all shades and shapes and ages and genders, from children to the men who dressed like women at Club My-Oh-My and women dressed in army uniform and there in the front seat was Marie Laveau, and she nodded her beautiful, elegant head and bestowed a smile on him. Louis Armstrong, smiling cherubically, was sitting next to her.

"It's up to all of us now, Jude. We are the only levees the city has left." She reached out and took his calloused hand in hers. "We won't be back, you know, not anywhere. No more walking, no more memory. This is the last thing we can give her, Jude. We gave her our lives...and now we give her our souls." She shook her head at the expression on his face. "I'm sorry. I thought you knew. You know, you and I were named after the saints of lost causes..."

Jude sighed, deep and long, remembering his father's broken, ill-mended hands and his mother's one dress and the smell of lye soap, remembered his brothers and sisters, the ones that lived and the ones that died, remembered the girls down at May's, selling themselves while he sold coal in Storyville, remembering the river boats, white and gleaming and gliding down the iron-flat river, as wide and grand as an ocean.

He shook his head. "She's always been a lost cause. And she's always dying. But she always comes back."

The nun nodded.

Jude looked around at the assembly. Then he took another deep breath and straightened his back, still scarred from the beating he took when he was fifteen, and he planted his crooked feet, and took his bent fingers out of his torn pocket and he walked, limping less, toward the front of the streetcar.

He nodded toward the conductor and met his eyes. “All out for Elysian Fields.”

THE GENTLEMAN FROM NEW ORLEANS

Charles Todd

I loved the early spring in Somerset. Slowly, the green was returning and the flower buds were about to burst with color. Soon it would be warm enough to spend time in our gardens. I was coming in the front door from my walk when Iris, our maid, came into the foyer. Your mother is in the back and looking for you," Iris announced.

"Thank you, Iris. I will see what she wants," I replied as I took off my coat and slipped off my walking shoes. Even in the sun, the ground was wet and muddy. Good for the plants, but not so good for walking shoes.

Iris handed me a pair of shoes and said, "I will see to these. Go see what your mother wants, Miss."

Iris loved my mother and also liked to be in charge when the Colonel Sahib was not at home. My father served as a regimental Colonel in India and the locals called him that. It became a family nickname ever since, out of earshot from my father, of course.

As I entered the Morning room, Mother was sitting at her desk looking over the household expenses and doing correspondence.

"There you are, my dear. Did you enjoy your walk?"

"The flowers should be blooming again soon, and Demeter is reading the world for Persephone's return," I replied.

"Bess, cousin Melinda has asked you to do her a favor and have a good time while you are at it."

I loved cousin Melinda Crawford and enjoyed her stories from India and around the world where her late husband was stationed. I also knew her favors could be daunting as well.

"What can I do for her?" I replied, steeling myself.

"Don't look so worried dear, she wants you to attend a betrothal party on her behalf."

"That sounds like fun. Where is it being held?"

"Near enough. It is in Bath at the home of Lord Hughes and his wife, Amelia. Their daughter Olivia is getting engaged to Jean Forestall of New Orleans in America."

I started to ask mother if they were playing jazz, but thought better of it.

"What is cousin Melinda's favor?" I knew there was more.

"Apparently, young Mr. Forestall is a nice enough man and seems to have the means to properly provide for their daughter. They just want another opinion. Melinda mentioned your knowledge of American servicemen during the war and thought perhaps you might ask one of them if they know the family. The Forestall name in prominent in banking in America, but Lord Hughes loves his daughter very much."

I immediately thought of Captain Jackson, who flew me to Ireland for my friend's wedding. He was a pilot in the Lafayette Escadrille and later with the United States Army Air Service.

"I can see what I can learn. Will I be attending alone?"

"Of course not, my dear. First, we wanted to know if you could help Melinda. You and I have some shopping to do before anything else."

I knew my mother's love of finding dresses for events. She was good at choosing the most wonderful gowns. I also knew when her mind was set on something and there was nothing to do but agree. I also knew that Simon and Captain knew each other well and I had to tread softly.

Leaning down, I kissed my mother's cheek. "I am certain I

will be in good hands. Tell cousin Melinda I would be delighted to help."

Mother looked up at me and then smiled. "I will let her know. We must get to work on your gown soon."

I knew that look on my mother's face before she smiled. I was being too agreeable, and she was wondering what I was up to.

It was a few days later when the Coronel Sahib and Simon joined us for dinner. I waited patiently for the general conversation to die down.

"I have been invited through cousin Melinda to attend a betrothal party in a fortnight."

My mother looked up but said nothing. It was the Coronel Sahib who spoke first.

"That is very nice of Melinda. Where is it being held?"

"At the home of Lord and Lady Hughes in Bath."

I waited for Simon to say something. He was looking at the Colonel and then at me.

It was the Coronel Sahib who spoke first. "Who will be your escort?"

Still, Simon said nothing. This was not going as I hoped. "I have not thought about that. Any suggestions?"

"Well, Henry can drive the car, but you will need an escort," The Colonel replied.

I could feel my temper begin to rise. Perhaps Simon did not feel he should be considered. I looked directly at Simon. "Are you available that evening to be my escort?"

"Capital idea! What do you say, Simon?" The Colonel Sahib exclaimed.

It took a great deal of self-control to sit patiently waiting for Simon's reply.

"If you don't require my assistance that evening, Sir," Simon finally said.

"Not at all, my boy. Do you good to go out socially."

Simon looked at me. "You don't have anyone else you would like to have escort you?"

I smiled, "Not at all, Simon. You could wear your kilt."

"I doubt that would be appreciated," Simon replied with the hint of a smile.

"Excellent. That is settled then. Clarissa, do you approve?" the Colonel Sahib said, looking at my mother.

"I think that would be very nice," he said.

"So, what brought this all about Bess? I am certain Melinda is doing this for a reason."

"Not really. Olivia Hughes is getting engaged to Jean Forestall, a young man from New Orleans in America. Lord and Lady Hughes are interested in learning more about his background."

"New Orleans. Interesting. What is this gentleman's avocation?" Colonel Sahib asked.

"Apparently, his family is in the banking business. His great uncle was involved in the banking systems for Louisiana and the United States."

"Banking, That is a solid foundation. Does he manage a bank or something?"

Mother spoke up, "That is not clear. He claims to come from a wealthy family who live in a reputable area of the city."

"Hmm. Well, I expect Bess can clear this up."

Now was my chance to ask Simon about Captain Jackson. "Simon, you know Captain Jackson. He flew me to Ireland for a wedding. He is an American. I wonder if you could ask him about Jean Forestall?"

"I will see what I can do. He may be in America now."

"I hope for our sake he is still in England." Turning to my father, I added, "Anything you and Simon can learn would be a help to Melinda."

I hoped that, since this was Melinda's request, her name might help the cause.

"We will see what we can do," the Colonel Sahib replied.

Except for some small talk, we finished our dinner in peace. Finally, Simon headed back to his cottage, and the Colonel retired to his study.

The next fortnight was a whirlwind. Mother had her seamstress over for fittings and choosing material. Even our maid, Iris, was there with her ideas. Her belief that my complexion and auburn hair needed green was well founded. The seamstress explained styles were changing from the Edwardian style to a more modern look. I had seen some of that change when I was in Paris last, assisting Marton Minton with her son. I still believed that short skirts and fringes and tight-fitted dresses were not the look for Lord and Lady Hughes in Bath! But I was grateful that Mother's seamstress was so well informed about the new style trends.

Finally, we settled on a light green dress. It fit the season and was not too modern for Bath. It had a silhouette sheath of powder emerald with an emerald waist that was high, but not as high as the traditional Edwardian style. The sheath top was up to the neck, but there was no collar. The sleeves were long in translucent powder emerald green with embroidered flowers along the arm. The skirt of the dress came to the floor in matching translucent powder emerald green It was pleated and a touch wide with a small train. I felt like a pin cushion statue with the seamstress and my mother fussing around me. It had been a long time since I had been through this experience and it was nothing I wanted to do again. However, the look of joy om Mother's face made it all worthwhile.

In the meantime, I was able to see the Colonel Sahib and Simon at lunch during that time and they had more information about Jean Forestall, the purpose of this extravaganza!

We had decided to have lunch on the veranda overlooking Mother's gardens. After Iris served us, I brought the subject up.

"I hope that Henry won't mind spending the evening driving us to Bath. He is so busy keeping the grounds and making repairs."

"I don't mind driving Bess to Bath," Simon added.

"I won't hear of it. Henry is happy to drive you two and for this event you need a driver and my motorcar." It was obvious the Colonel Sahib had made the final decision.

"I did happen to see Captain Jackson the other day," Simon said.

"Oh!" I exclaimed. "Did he have any insight into Jean Forestall?"

"He got back to me a few days later. The family has quite a reputation in America. Edmund Jean Forestall was from a prominent Creole family through his mother and his father was Irish."

The Colonel's harrumph at the Irish part was definite.

"Well Edmund Forestall was born in 1794 and died in 1879. I found no links to the troubles in Ireland today and the family now," Simon explained. "His banking system, the Forestall System was used through the Americas until the war between the states. His sons continued to work in the New Orleans and Louisiana banking system. A very prominent and philanthropic family."

"What of this Jean Forestall?" I asked Simon.

"That is unclear. He attended Tulane University and was able to avoid the draft for the war. During his last two years of being a student he attended the College of Commerce that was started in 1914. In his early 20's, he is the same age as Olivia Hughes. Most of this information is available in the library in London. I have no knowledge of the man himself or what he is like."

"Well, Simon, that is a great start. Father, did you find anything about this man?"

"Nothing more than Simon I am afraid. He never served in uniform so my sources are not much of a help in this case."

"I understand. Thank you, Simon. I hope Captain Jackson was well. I assume he will be returning to America soon."

"As always, he sends his regards. You know how he is. I don't think he knows where he will wind up," Simon said with a grin.

The rest of our lunch was spent with idle chat and nothing more was said about Jean Forestall.

At last, the big day arrived. I spent most of the afternoon getting ready and dealing with Mother and her seamstress. The dress was beautiful. It was a nice blend of the modern without provoking raised eyebrows.

Iris spent a lot of time brushing and fixing my hair. She put my hair up in a loose somewhat French manner that was complimentary to the dress. The tight buns of years past would not have gone with the dress style.

It was going to be a good two hours' drive to Bath and soon it would be time to leave. I came down the stairs and could tell from the look in the Colonel Sahib's eyes what he thought of my appearance.

"Simon is bound to say you make a bonnie lass in that outfit. Are you pleased my dear?"

"Oh, yes, I am. After all these years in a nursing sister's uniform it feels very different. I don't think Mother has fussed over an event this much since my debutant ball."

The Colonel Sahib grinned, "Henry and Simon have the motorcar gleaming. I hope they had time to get cleaned up and looking smart."

Mother came down the stairs behind me. "Doesn't she look lovely, dear?"

"She does indeed. Now, all we need is the rest of the cast," he replied.

Finally, the motorcar pulled up to the front door and Henry got out, resplendent in a black chauffeur's uniform and cap.

Coming around the bonnet and past the wings, he opened the rear door and Simon emerged. He was dressed in a double-breasted black jacket of barathea with silk lapels, a white evening shirt made from marcella, with a turndown collar, bib detail, and double cuffs, a white bow tie and cummerbund. He wore a pair of beautiful gold and onyx cufflinks with matching studs and pants with highly polished black shoes.

"You two look marvelous!" I cried. I can't thank you both for going to all of this trouble.

"T'was nothing, Miss," Henry replied.

I could see the collar of Henry's uniform was already bothering his neck. Simon, on the other hand, stood there and grinned. I had never seen him in evening clothes except at formal affairs when he wore a dress uniform.

"Simon, that dinner attire looks like it was made for you," the Colonel said.

"It is a wee bit tight in the neck, but thank you, Sir," Simon replied. "Bess, you are quite the bonnie lass in that dress."

I could feel my father's satisfaction without him making a sound. He was right, and he knew it.

"You had best be off then. You want to arrive just at the proper time," Mother said.

With a wave, I headed to the motorcar, where Simon and Henry helped me up into the back seat. Henry closed the door as Simon went around to the other side and got in behind Henry.

I was so impressed with Simon all dressed in his dinner attire, but I did not want to embarrass him. Simon was not that young private I met in India anymore. Tonight, he looked smart.

As Henry made it to the main road toward Bath, I spoke to Simon.

"You look wonderful, Simon. I haven't seen you look so grand since that Regimental Ball ages ago."

"I am hoping not to meet anyone I know," Simon replied.

"Are you ready to meet this man and see what sort he is?"

"I am not really sure what to do. I don't want to drag him into a corner and let you work him over," I said with a smile.

"Any man would love to spend some time with you in your finery."

"Now you are making me blush, Simon. Stop that!" I laughed. "I don't want to stand out. You know me, I prefer the quiet approach."

Now it was Simon's turn to laugh. "You should have thought about that before picking that lovely dress."

"Simon, you know that Mother and Iris had more to do with that than I did. I haven't seen Mother so happy in a long time."

"Bess, you can blame it on your mother all you want. I am sure she had a good time. I was very pleased to see her enjoy herself so much, too."

"I hope I can have a quiet chance to talk to Jean Forestall after all the formalities have subsided."

"You will find a way. Of that I am certain," Simon replied.

After a bit, we settled back and watched the countryside go by and talked about how beautiful it was as the sun set. Before long, Henry turned on the headlamps and we chased the lights along the road. About an hour away, we could see the lights from the outskirts of Bath. We descended into the River Valley of Avon to this historic city located a short trip from Bristol where the Bristol Channel separated Bristol from Wales. I loved Bath with its historic buildings and famous baths. The Georgian architecture made of Bath stone was reminiscent of the height of the Spa Era. Henry glanced at a map and turned east of the city to the Hughes' home. The house was a country home located south and east of the city center.

At last, we arrived at the drive into the country home of Lord and Lady Hughes. We drove down the tree-lined drive and the Victorian Gothic Revival Home came into view. It was beautifully done in granite with a small gothic tower, rounded pinnacles and lancet windows. A long gallery with a large assembly of guests inside came into view and its chandelier's light bathed the manicured lawn.

Henry pulled the motor car up to the entrance and practically leapt out to open the door for Simon before coming around to my door. He took my hand with surprising gentleness as I leaned forward to step on the running board and then to the walk. Simon came behind me, smoothing my skirts as I stepped away from the motorcar. Placing my arm in the crook of his, we stepped up into the entrance where the door was held open by a liveried doorman, and the butler in black tails and white tie and vest ushered us into the house.

The entryway was breathtaking, with a high ceiling and a broad staircase cascading down. The plush burgundy carpet cushioned my steps as I approached Lady Hughes, who welcomed us in.

"I am Bess Crawford, and this is Simon Brandon. We came at the request of Melinda Crawford." I explained.

"Yes, I thought you were. I have known Melinda for many years. Welcome to our home. I hope you enjoy the evening."

"An exciting time for your daughter and your family," I replied.

"It is indeed."

Lady Hughes was a striking woman elegantly dressed in an Edwardian evening gown in a dove grey. Her brown hair was combed up into a tight bun and she wore a beautiful lace stole over her shoulders. She was not tall, but she carried herself erect in a graceful manner. An upstairs maid ushered us to the right and down a short hall to the long gallery. At the far end was a small orchestra playing popular wartime tunes softly enough to provide an elegant background. There were straight-back chairs along the gallery walls except where the tall glass doors faced the lawn. A few tall tables were placed around the room and maids in uniform were passing around silver trays of Champagne. Simon and I accepted our glasses and began to meander through the room. I was looking for the fiancés, as was Simon.

Almost under his breath, Simon said, "I don't think I will know who the guests of honor are until they are presented."

"They may not even be in the room yet. I was looking for Lord Hughes. I expect you are right. Until they are presented to the room, we will never pick them out."

We came to a tall table, and I set my glass down and rested my hands beside it. Simon did the same.

"I think if we stay in one place, it will be easier to see the guests as they move around us. I am glad that this long gown hides my feet. Something tells me we will be standing for most of the night."

"So, I got all dressed up to do guard duty. Some things never change!" Simon said, attempting to hide his sly grin.

And so, we stood sipping our Champagne and enjoying a few hors d'oeuvres that were passed by the servants in upstairs-maid uniforms. Eventually, with great fanfare, they would introduce the betrothed couple along with the parents. I took a chance to look around the gallery. It was a long, beautiful room with another tall pointed-arch ceiling and parquet floors. Sconces with lights adorned the wall and identical sconces were between the large glass doors. At the end of the room, opposite the orchestra, was a large fireplace that would be wonderful in the wintertime. The wallpaper was in white with gold trim to match the rest of the decor. It certainly made a grand impression. In front of the orchestra, there was a white-and-gold sofa on a beautiful oriental style rug and a few Chippendale chairs on either side. Apparently, this was where the couple and the family would be introduced.

Suddenly, the orchestra increased their volume and ended the song with a flourish! At last, the time had arrived. From a door beside the orchestra, Lord and Lady Hughes entered the room, followed by Olivia and her sisters, along with a tall and surprisingly fit young man. Olivia wore a glamorous white gown with gold accents, and her hair was swept up, showing her neck and bare shoulders. The young man wore a double-breasted dinner jacket similar to Simon's, with a white tie and vest. His vest held a watch and chain, and he wore gold cufflinks that appeared to have his initials on them. After a bit of clapping, the room grew quiet.

Lord Hughes stood behind the sofa with Lady Hughes as the sisters sat on the Chippendale chairs. Raising his glass and in a deep voice, Lord Hughes began his announcement.

"Friends, Lady Hughes and I are pleased to present our daughter, Olivia," he turned his glass toward Olivia, "and her betrothed, Mr. Jean Forestall of New Orleans. Please join us as we toast their betrothal and give them our blessing. We sincerely wish them years of happiness in their future, as Lady Hughes and I have found. To the betrothed!"

We all raised our glasses and repeated his toast. "To the betrothed."

"Please come get acquainted with the couple and wish them well. Get to know each other as well. We will be together again at the nuptials," Lady Hughes added.

With that, the introduction was over. It seemed a bit short and formal, but that appeared to be the Hughes' manner. The orchestra began playing softly as the crowd surged toward the happy couple.

"Now we have to bide our time," I said to Simon. "You have to join me when I talk to Jean so his fiancée does not get an inappropriate impression."

"At your service, Miss," Simon said sarcastically.

"At least look like we are having fun. You and I have never been together for a social occasion like this."

"Standing here with you and getting jealous looks from the men in the room makes this worth attending. You are definitely beautiful in that gown and in this light."

"Simon," I whispered, "you promised not to make me blush. There are many ladies here who are very well dressed and attractive."

Once again, we stood there chatting and laughing as the

party continued. At long last, I saw Jean get up from the sofa and move toward the nearest glass door. This was the moment I was waiting for, and Simon saw it as well. He offered his arm, and we took our Champagne and moved in his direction. I felt certain Jean was getting some air and a bit weary from the event. For a moment, I felt bad about interrupting his reverie.

Simon led us out the door and on to the small veranda. Jean Forestall turned as he heard our approach.

"Pardon me, I needed to get some air." He said in an unusual accent. I had, of course, heard of New Orleans, but this was not the southern drawl I had heard during the war. It was partially modified with his educated speech and something new to me.

Simon replied, "We did not wish to interrupt your getting some air. We thought it was a good idea."

"Yes, and on such a lovely evening. I am afraid it is a bit overwhelming with this beautiful home and the history of the area. Where I come from, we think a few hundred years is old and yet in Britain , our history seems new."

"We will have to take you to Scotland if you like history," Simon added.

"I have read about Scotland and the great authors there. It sounds like an enchanted place."

I spoke up. "Congratulations on your betrothal. We wish you both many years of happiness."

"Thank you. Olivia is such a wonderful lady. I am lucky she even considered me."

"How did you meet?" I asked.

"I came to London on bank business and met Olivia at a social event there. Later, we met again when I was in Bristol. We met again many times and got to know each other."

"What brought you to Bristol? Was it banking again? I was not aware Bristol was much of a banking city," I asked, trying to sound curious and yet not pushing.

"Our family has some shipping concerns in New Orleans,

and Bristol does some trade with us. Frankly, it was a good excuse to see Olivia again, to be honest," Jean ended with a smile.

"Do you plan to make your new home in New Orleans?" Simon asked.

Jean smiled again. "And take Olivia away from all of this? I am working to become the agent for the family business here in Britain."

"That would be quite a change for you. What about your family?" I asked.

Jean moved a little closer to us and spoke in a low tone. "I am just a minor member of a very prestigious family. My parents died in a yellow fever epidemic when I was young, and I was taken in by relatives. Britain is my opportunity to make my own mark for both the family business and myself. It is home for Olivia."

I frowned a bit.

Simon took my clue and spoke up. "You must have accumulated some financial security through your family."

"Not up to the standards of this," Jean said, gesturing toward the house. "That is why I was so surprised Olivia would speak to me, much less agree to marry me. She is wonderful, and I love her very much. I will be honest, it will be difficult at first as I get settled in my career. You must understand how much I love and admire Olivia. I will do whatever it takes to make certain she is well looked after and has the life she deserves." Jean stopped and took a breath. "I am a simple, hard-working man who has met the woman of my dreams. I will work as hard as I am able to make Olivia happy in her life with me."

I reached out and laid my hand on Jean's arm. "We are certain you will. You don't even know us and yet you have shared so much."

"Thank you for letting me vent. All of this British formality is a bit much for me. It is nice to tell someone how I really feel,"

Jean replied.

"I am Bess Crawford, and this is Simon Brandon. We live here in Somerset, south of Bath."

Jean shook Simon's hand firmly. "I noticed that Scottish brogue, if that is the right word for your accent."

Simon smiled. "It is indeed. You will be fine. Jean. There is nothing wrong with a hard-working man."

"Well, I must go back inside and see to Olivia. I don't want her changing her mind with all of these fine men who may whisk her away," Jean said in a laughing tone.

"Of course, go be with your betrothed," Simon said as he put his hand on Jean's back and led him back into the gallery.

I followed Simon and Jean thanked us again before he headed to the sofa and Olivia.

Simon and I moved to the house side of the gallery and took a seat. I don't think I had been so eager to sit down since I was assisting the doctors in surgery during the war.

"Well, what did you think of Jean?" Simon asked me quietly.

"For some reason, I like him. He seems wiser than his age and definitely committed to Olivia. What did you think?"

"He seems like a good enough lad. He has his feet firmly planted and is willing to work. I hope it stays with him," Simon replied.

Eventually, the evening grew to an end. We stopped in the foyer and thanked Lord and Lady Hughes for their hospitality and congratulated Jean and Olivia. I felt I had neglected her in my drive to meet Jean. She was a beautiful young lady with a set to her eyes that I liked. She did not appear to be some starry-eyed young girl who had no idea about marriage and making her own home. She spoke with elegance and yet did not come across haughtily. It did not appear that she had been spoiled. I am certain her parents were proud of their daughter, but she spoke with assurance and understanding.

Henry pulled the motorcar up to the door and came around to open the door for me. I stepped up into the car and he closed the door. I waved to our hosts as Simon got in beside me and Henry pulled off into the night.

As we left Bath and headed into the dark Somerset countryside, I could feel my eyelids begin to droop. It had been a special evening. Henry, in his chauffeur's uniform, was a wonder at the wheel. Simon, all dressed in evening attire, looked ever so smart. I felt lucky to have Simon at my side. The last thing I remember thinking before I dozed off was of Simon and whether he could feel about me as Jean felt for Olivia.

TWO SENTIMENTAL GENTLEMEN

Gabriel Valjan

When the good (and not so good) people of New Orleans speak of the day 'two sentimental gentlemen' entered the Hotel Monteleone, they claim the grandfather clock in the lobby choked on a chime and stopped working. Conversations, they said, came to a halt, the lazy hour of illegal cocktails was disturbed, and a lady on stab heels stuttered on the polished marble floors.

The sudden silence in the massive room that day had alerted the clerk at the Front Desk. The smile of hospitality stiffened when he looked at the two men before him. One was a northerner, and his travel companion could only be described as 'swarthy.' His rebellious hair was cut in the slicked-back undercut style, the top brilliant with pomade. The square jaw, eyes blue as the Mediterranean, frame proportionate, made women steal secret looks. He was more handsome than Valentino, whom they had watched on the screen and would likewise never have.

"May I help you?"

"The name is Fawcett. I have a reservation."

"One moment, please, while I consult our ledger."

Eyes everywhere examined them, heads turned to gossip, and lips puckered with either disgust or amazement at their audacity.

"I'm afraid your room isn't available yet."

"No rush, but can we register?"

With the utmost need for discretion, the clerk motioned the Yankee to lean forward. "There must be some mistake. It is one room, one bed," his eyes moved to his left, the other man's right, "and you are a party of two."

"No mistake," Fawcett lied. "The secretary at the Sugar Shed Company, who made the call on behalf of the consortium, must've failed to mention it. Perhaps you know her? She's a petite thing, and she wears her hair in a lovely shingle."

"Afraid I don't," the clerk answered. Surprised, he added, "Consortium?"

"The Exchange."

His smile had turned smug as a lawyer's. "Could you be more specific?"

"On behalf of Mr. Endicott, of the Cotton Exchange."

"I see," the clerk said. "Why didn't you say that in the first place?"

"Because of my travel companion here." Fawcett tilted his head to indicate the gentleman in the burgundy suit next to him. "He's sensitive about the name Endicott."

"And why is that?"

"He claims Endicott had his father murdered."

"Murdered?"

"Lynched with ten other Italians in 1891."

"That unfortunate event happened thirty years ago. He couldn't have been more than a babe in the cradle."

"I know, but you know what they say about Italians and a vendetta," Fawcett said. "I was a mere lad of ten myself, unbreeched, and still wearing my sister's dresses at the time." He used his hand to beckon the clerk forward. The man craned his neck. "My friend here is, how shall I say, touched, but he is in my custody, nonetheless. I'm charged with his transport to DC."

"In your custody? Whatever for?"

Fawcett produced his billfold. The clerk examined the identification and returned it. "I must ask on behalf of the guests at the hotel whether your man here poses a threat to their safety."

Fawcett smiled. "Look at him, in his suit, awful tie, and atrocious hair."

The clerk was not convinced. "May I inquire as to the charge?"

"He's Italian."

"That is no crime."

Fawcett grinned. "It seemed to be the case thirty years ago when Italians were lynched, but I digress."

"Yes, you do, and a lot has changed in three decades."

"Has it?"

"The charge, Mr. Fawcett?"

"Suspected anarchist. He stands accused of trying to form a union on the docks."

The clerk shook his head. "A union, indeed, and in this day and age when employers offer pensions, paid vacations, stock options, and cheap lunches in the company cafeteria."

The man next to Fawcett said through a cough, "Welfare capitalism."

The clerk blinked his eyes. He asked Fawcett, "Your race, the both of you?"

"I thought it was ten years until the next census."

The clerk looked about as patient as a priest inside the box. "The sheriff and mayor have established quotas."

"How 'bout member of the human race."

"Amusing, Mr. Fawcett, but an answer, please."

"My family fought in the Revolutionary War, and the Seven Years' War before that."

"White it is then. A name and race for your man here?"

"Angel Malaparte," the other man said for himself. "I was told the 'o' fell off of Angelo at Castle Garden."

"How unfortunate for you," the clerk said. "I'll write in 'southern.'" He turned his back to his guests to retrieve a key and handed it to Fawcett. The fob indicated the room number.

"Any bags?" he asked.

"We'll manage them until our room is ready," Fawcett said, his eyes on the security man reflected in the mirror behind the desk. "A place you'd recommend for a bite to eat?"

They walked down Iberville Street.

"A secretary at the Sugar Shed made the reservation? You made that up."

"I did, indeed," Fawcett answered. "We have to coax our friend out of his den."

"And that bit about her hair in a shingle?"

"The latest fashion with women. Don't you read the magazines?"

"Apparently not, but I see what you did back there," Angel said, and mumbled something in Italian, which prompted Fawcett to stop walking.

"Don't do that," he said. "I don't know the language, so tell me what you said and translate it for me."

"I'm sorry. Italian has a saying that describes the strategy you used with the hotel clerk. We say, '*Parlare a nuora perché suocera intenda*,' which means, talk to the daughter-in-law so the mother-in-law knows. You spoke to the clerk, so Endicott knows."

"Okay," Fawcett said. "Let's find this restaurant and continue the charade."

They found the recommended establishment for a drink and an early dinner. They argued as to which cocktail came first and tasted better, La Louisiane or the Sazerac. Every hotel and restaurant in New Orleans claimed to have invented the great American drink. Nothing said New Orleans more than serving alcohol in open defiance of the law of the land.

They ordered two House Specials. Served 'up' with a cherry in a chilled glass, the cocktail's ingredients celebrated three nations: American rye, French absinthe and Benedictine, and

Italian sweet vermouth. The Peychaud's bitters from the Caribbean might've been an afterthought.

Angel set his napkin on his lap before he read the menu. The fare ranged from the predictable meat, chicken, and potatoes for the domestic palate to an exotic High and Low menu of fruits from the sea for those who enjoyed Creole and French cuisine. In silence, Angel debated either Oysters Commodore or Lobster Thermidor. He settled on his choice and declared, "Oysters."

"No Thermidor?"

"You know it bothers me, the violence done lobsters."

"How ironic, given the reason we are in town." Fawcett ran a finger down the lists. "What shall I have?"

"You'll order the Filet Mignon Anatole."

"And for sides?" Fawcett asked.

"Bordelaise and fingerling potatoes."

"You know me well, my dear Angel. I am the unadventurous steak-and-potato man."

"I don't know about 'unadventurous.' You weren't last night."

Fawcett ignored the remark and took in the room, the glitter and sparkle of the chandelier some Belgian glassmakers had made the year they fled Napoleon and Waterloo. He marveled at all that was within the Crystal Dining Room, all the sparkle from Baccarat, France.

"Did you see our friend in the glass from the Hotel Monteleone?" he said.

"Yes, I did, and I'm certain he is one of many surprises that awaits us."

Their waiter approached. For some curious reason, he asked Angel if he was Italian. Fawcett drank and listened. He'd heard Italian spoken, but this was not that. He suspected it was Sicilian or some village dialect, as Angel had told him everyone in Italy spoke an argot known only to town and family. At times, he felt as if he was a stranger in a strange land, but he understood the country was changing with each successive wave of immigrants. The sounds he heard in the streets were both alien and familiar, like a rabbi who heard Hebrew from a Jew expelled from Spain.

Before they placed their order, Fawcett requested the waiter bring their friend from Monteleone a Marine Blitz. After the waiter had left, Fawcett said, "The Blitz ought to polish his brass."

Angel raised his glass and replied, "And so it begins."

It had begun.

The tail who'd followed them to the restaurant found himself a phone. After he'd quit the call and left, Fawcett tipped the hatcheck girl. She confirmed for him he had called the hotel and provided a detailed report. He was honest enough to have admitted to the Blitz.

Fawcett paid the bill. He suggested to Angel that he buy peanuts on Royal Street, which he did. The clothes he was wearing drew attention, as did the order, and both were intentional.

Angel found himself a peanut man on the street, next to a cala lady who sold her fried rice cakes with a chant in Creole. The peanut vendor asked for confirmation twice. Angel did not want his peanuts boiled or fried. He wanted them whole and in their shells.

They took their constitutional to the hotel in the Mediterranean style, slowly and leisurely. They entered the Monteleone, and it seemed nobody had noticed, but they knew they had.

With the key in the door to their room, a cleaner beckoned the pair to step inside his supply closet in the hallway. Fawcett and Malaparte stood there still as stones until the little man repeated himself, this time in Italian.

Inside the workman's' office, he handed Angel a stick with a hook at the end and said a word in their language that even

Fawcett recognized in English. When they had returned to the door to their room, the custodian disappeared down the hall and around a corner.

Fawcett used the key, opened the door, and allowed the wood to swing wide like a gate. The room, dark and carpeted, appeared undisturbed. There was a large window, curtained, and His and Hers chairs that framed it like brackets. There was a closet nearest them, a desk next, and the bed with a nightstand to their right. Another door was ajar, and a dull light illuminated the ceramic tiles in the bathroom, the subway tiles of the wall there, white as Ahab's whale.

The phone rang.

"Someone wants to know we're in the room?" Angel asked.

Fawcett disagreed. "The call is to determine if they were successful."

"Successful with what?"

"We'll know once we use the stick in your hand."

Angel went to say something, but Fawcett raised his hand. "Quiet, please."

He tapped Morse Code with his foot so the vibrations worked their way through the carpet. They watched the curtain move.

Angel said, "That's not the steam radiator."

They each slept in a chair, armed. Fawcett had scattered Angel's peanuts on the floor as an alarm. Each chair faced the door, and both men had a view to the bathroom, should someone enter the suite that way.

After they'd collected the peanuts off the floor, they showered and shaved. Fawcett cracked the window open to let the steam escape and lifted the shade to allow sunlight into the room, while Angel relocated their guest from the closet to the bathtub. As soon as the door closed, Angel placed warning signs on the wood:

NE PAS OUVRIR in French.
PA ANTRE in Creole.

They walked downstairs. Fawcett asked for and received a complimentary copy of the *Times-Picayune* from the Front Desk clerk. The man wished him a good morning and handed him a note. Fawcett thanked him and took both the *Times* and the note. The janitor in the hallway passed by. Angel called him over and whispered something into his ear. He tucked a bill into the man's jacket pocket before he entered the hotel's café.

They breakfasted and shared the newspaper.

Fawcett said, "I see you found the workman from last night. You whispered something to him, and I saw you place what I assume is money into his coat pocket."

"I had, and I did."

"May I ask what for?"

Fawcett folded the page. "Our friend in the room needs food."

"Ah, yes. We must be considerate."

"Speaking of communication. The clerk gave you a note?" Angel asked.

"Time and place named."

"Then everything's going according to plan."

If Cotton was king, the Exchange at Gravier and Carondelet Streets was the palace. Here were the offices for the Cotton Exchange, the Louisiana Sugar and Rice Exchange, the Fruit Exchange, and the Mechanics, Dealers and Lumbermen's Exchange.

They were led into a room worthy of a Medici. Two lonely chairs awaited them, and they stood behind them until told they could sit. Two empty glasses and a pitcher of water represented hospitality.

Their host was flanked by five men on each side of him. Behind him sat his father, president emeritus of The Exchange. Against the wall, and behind the ten industrialists were more men, dressed in black, and they were not servants.

Endicott looked like a bald egg in its cup. He invited them to take their seats. He asked how they were finding their stay at the Monteleone. Fawcett responded 'delightful.' While the retinue with Endicott included nobility from the fruit, lumber, and rice industries, Fawcett recognized a man as head of the dock workers from an article he had read in the morning paper. Someone called the meeting to order in a voice that kept all the marble in the great hall cold. Endicott, Junior made an announcement:

"There will be no minutes of this meeting, and, since time is precious, I will dispense with introductions for the gentlemen on this side of the table. Mr. Fawcett, have you worked for members of the Exchange in any capacity?"

"I have not, nor have I ever been on your payroll." Fawcett poured two glasses of water.

Endicott asked, "And your employer?"

"The Bureau of Investigation."

"And the man next to you?"

Angel spoke for himself. "The name is Angel Malaparte, and it's an alias."

"An alias?" A murmur ran down the line.

Fawcett answered. "Mr. Malaparte has worked undercover, in various industries, for the Bureau. He has gathered evidence in each industry the men in front of me own and operate. He last worked as a screwman on the docks."

Screwmen were men who worked the docks and who had created the Dock and Cotton Council to continue the Half-and-Half arrangement between Coloreds and Whites to counter the campaigns the shipowners and planters used to pit one group against the other.

Endicott grinned. "I confess, Mr. Fawcett, I am confused. Is this your idea of blackmail?"

"No. It is insurance. I seek safe passage for myself and for Mr. Malaparte to DC."

The tension in the room could have cracked sugar cane.

"Insurance against what?"

"Violence."

"If I am to understand you, Mr. Fawcett, you seek safe passage for the two of you, so you can arrive in Washington, where you wish to inflict harm on this body?"

"If you or any man here has done nothing illegal, then you have nothing to fear in a court of law."

Endicott, Senior stood up and approached the table. The old man moved of his own power, eyes alert and years left in his veins. The water in Fawcett's glass shivered when the man spoke:

"Men see what they seek, even in a courtroom, Mr. Fawcett. As for wrongdoing, I believe it was the French writer Balzac who'd said that behind every great fortune there's some element of a crime. History bears witness to his observation. Take the founders of this country, for example. They were merchants, and one could argue their enterprise for liberty was nothing more than a ruse to dodge the King's taxman. If their scheme had failed, the lot of them would have been hanged."

"How peculiar it is that you mentioned hanging."

Endicott bowed his head. "You had a man undercover, and we had a spy of our own at the Hotel Monteleone. I was reminded of mob violence and of Mr. Malaparte's connection to it, but that tragedy is long in the past, Mr. Fawcett."

"Mr. Malaparte has lived with the image of twenty thousand rioters gathered outside of the jail that held his father. The unfortunate event may have happened thirty years ago, but what will happen the next time there is profit from hatred?"

"None of us has a crystal ball, Mr. Fawcett."

"There is the rumor that the boll weevil has ravaged the annual crop, and the price of cotton is in decline."

The old man's face twitched. "You needed a spy on the docks to report on a beetle?"

If Endicott had hoped for laughter, there was none. Fawcett reached for a sip of water and sampled it. He held the goblet for them to see it. "Mr. Malaparte said something interesting to me on the way over here. He said that when the price of cotton falls, violence in New Orleans and the American south increases. I'm here, on behalf of my employer, to seek assurances from you that no such violence will happen."

"More insurance?" Endicott placed both fists on the table. "I'm not God, Mr. Fawcett. I can't control all men in all places and what they choose to do in response to the economy. What Mr. Malaparte has said is nothing but conjecture, and need I remind you that the price of cotton plummeted from a dollar to nine cents in 1892, the year after the tragedy?"

Fawcett returned the glass of water to its doily. "And what about the Bogalusa Labor Massacre last year? It seems you and the men here load your coffers either way, yet your employees bear the brunt of economic insecurity."

Great Southern Lumber Company owned the Bogalusa sawmill, the world's largest, and they reacted to attempts by Black and White workers who tried to unionize for better wages. The initial organizer, a veteran of the Great War, Lucius McCarty, was lynched. A private militia of 150 deputies killed four White unionists and two Black men before federal troops restored order.

"What are you implying?" Endicott, Senior asked.

"That you keep your people anxious, that you fan the flames of discord, that Mr. Hearst provided you with the blueprint for organized chaos with his newspapers. Rise or fall, you exploit every opportunity for maximum profit and control. Prices have fallen now, and the boll weevil is the plague. It seems logical that violence should follow, especially since each man here has incentives against unions. Mr. Malaparte can testify to that."

Endicott, Junior rose. "Does your spy here have any proof of a conspiracy?"

"Against unions, yes. Of any other conspiracy, no."

"Can he point to any man in this room and call him conspirator?"

"History speaks for itself, and you gentlemen are the authors of New Orleans."

Endicott, Senior pulled the timepiece from his vest. "I suggest you enjoy your stay in New Orleans, Mr. Fawcett, and return to Washington at your leisure. There is no resolution here. You waste our time with speculation and hearsay from a dock worker. On your way out, please take one of my cards. Should you come to your senses, we can discuss matters like gentlemen."

As Fawcett and Malaparte walked toward the light to exit the Exchange, they accepted that darkness would descend, and it wouldn't be day giving way to night.

Everything that could go wrong did.

Street vendors were slow to take their orders, fast to take their money and slower to make change and deliver goods and services. The waiter in the hotel's restaurant took forever to appear and then would disappear; and the food, when it arrived, was either not the dish they had ordered or worse, cold. Doormen of numerous establishments would see them but fail to open the door for them with the usual hospitality.

At the Monteleone, raucous noises were heard in the hallway, outside their window, and from the rooms above them and next to them. A complaint lodged at the Front Desk would come to naught. Everything conspired to tell them they should leave earlier than planned. When they ignored the hints, events escalated.

On a walk back to Hotel Monteleone one morning, shots rang out. Though the bullets missed their mark, they delivered the message. On a stroll after dinner, foot traffic pushed them down a desolate side street where a car sped up, blared its horn at the last possible second before it ran up the curb, over some sidewalk and barely missed them before the driver cut the wheel and returned the vehicle to the street. A man stood on the running board with a tommy-gun. Since this was New Orleans, he lifted his hat, as if to say, 'Sorry' or 'Next time, boys.'

On their last night at the hotel, the lights turned off, the floor creaked, and shells crinkled and cracked underfoot. Fawcett's first shot found a shoulder, but it was Angel who dropped the intruder dead. The impact spun the man as if to wrap him in his funeral shroud. They stood over the body and recognized their visitor as one of the men against the wall behind Endicott, Junior.

Fawcett said, "It's time. Pack our belongings and fetch our friend in the bathroom."

While Angel collected their things, including the stick and satchel, Fawcett retrieved Endicott's *carte de visite* from the Exchange and pried the dead man's mouth open. He placed the business card between the man's teeth, so it looked as if the deceased had a ticket for Charon's ferry across the River Styx.

The Endicott family lived along River Road, that long, luxurious, and storied stretch of plantation houses between New Orleans and Baton Rouge. The sweat of the enslaved had funded generational wealth. The legacy of the cruelty toward slaves was so great that after The War Between the States no Negro in New Orleans would step foot on any Endicott property. Endicott, Senior was forced to hire immigrants for servants, and since Italians were deemed 'Black' and 'savage,' they numbered the most among those in his employ.

Lemuel Endicott, Senior, was alone in the house that blood had built. It was there in his mansion that he courted ministers, policemen and politicians of rank, and members of the state bar and judiciary. He had invited and feted the leadership of the

Klan from such far-flung states as Indiana and Oregon, where the White Knights had the greatest concentration of members. If the country's hatred for others had become cancerous, Endicott was emblematic of the disease. He sponsored parade floats and marching bands, and donated *gratis* all the cotton used for the massive banners that proclaimed 'America First.'

Fawcett and Malaparte appeared as silhouettes in the darkness, their shadows came into focus for the butler, an elderly Sicilian who had heard a noise outside. He appeared with a sawed-off shotgun, the kind used to kill the *lupo*, or wolf, in Italian..

Angel said two words, "*Una lupara?*"

The old man lowered the weapon. He recognized a countryman, a *paisano*.

They exchanged words in Sicilian that Fawcett did not understand.

Angel reached into his breast pocket and produced identification. The old man stepped closer and read Angel's true name. His face turned pale. He offered him the shotgun. Angel pushed it aside and said in their language. "Save it for when you find a wolf. Where is the man of the house?"

The old man's eyes looked to the ceiling. "He takes his bath on Saturday nights and reads by lamplight."

"Armed?" Angel asked.

"No."

"That's a shame." Angel thanked the man. He told Fawcett to stay put.

"Are you sure?" Fawcett asked.

Angel didn't answer. He made the ascent, satchel with stick inside the bag in one hand, a revolver in the other. He had served in the twilight of the Great War in France and knew how to tread everything from uneven dirt to floorboards in silence. He reached the landing. A glow from the lamp inside the room marked the wood. Angel used his toe to nudge the door open. He waited until the wood ceased to moan.

"Who's there?" Endicott asked from inside the room. Angel heard the water move with the voice. Again, the query. "Who is it?" This time, the water sloshed against the sides of the tub.

Angel appeared in the doorframe and Endicott's eyes widened. "Malaparte. Have you no decency? You're trespassing. I can call the police."

"Be my guest."

"Don't think I won't call your bluff."

Angel set down the valise. "It'll do you no good because I am the law."

Endicott's eyes narrowed. "Fawcett said he was with the Bureau, and the clerk at Monteleone said you were in his custody."

"The clerk never asked to see my identification. He assumed from the way I was dressed that I was—you can say it."

"A dago anarchist."

"I'm sure other words came to mind, words such as 'deviant' or the more genteel phrase, 'sentimental gentleman.'"

"You know a man has a right to defend himself in his own house."

"Second Amendment, I know."

"Why are you here?"

"For justice that's long overdue."

"That was thirty years ago, and times were different."

"Were they?" Angel said. He moved closer to the tub. "You quoted Balzac to us, which made me think of another French writer who had said, 'the more things change, the more they stay the same.'" A question for you, Mr. Endicott. What is the penalty for killing a federal officer?"

"Death, but you and Fawcett are not dead." Endicott's grin was somber.

"It's not for lack of trying. Someone took potshots at us, someone tried to run us over, and then this evening came the undertaker, who obviously failed because I am standing before you."

Endicott acted confused. "'Undertaker'? I don't know what you're talking about."

"The manner of execution in Louisiana?"

"Hanging, why?"

Angel looked at the lamp by which the man read while he took his bath. "I hear electrocution is more humane. You almost succeeded that first night we were at the hotel when your man released a visitor into our room." Angel reached down and raised a water moccasin coiled around the hook of the stick. He held the serpent over the bathwater.

The snake hissed, bared fangs, and revealed its white mouth.

"I want you to understand."

Endicott pulled his legs to his chest. "Understand what?"

"Understand the terror those eleven Italians must've felt inside that jail as a sea of humanity outside screamed for their blood, ropes in hand. Imagine their heartbeats, the horror."

The snake writhed around the stick, and Angel lowered the rod.

"What are you doing?" Endicott asked.

"Putting him on the floor, and giving you a choice those men, my father among them, didn't have. You could wait until the snake climbs up the porcelain and finds familiar water. Cottonmouths enjoy land, but they do love water. You can wait, or—"

"Or what?"

Angel nodded to the light. "Choose a more humane way. It's the choice of poison or electrocution. Either way is easier than hanging from a streetlamp."

Midway down the stairs, he held the grip in one hand, and rested the iron stick against his shoulder like a soldier would his rifle. At the landing ahead of him stood Fawcett and the servant. There was a piercing scream. The lights shuddered and hummed for what seemed an eternity before they returned to a word the president himself liked to use: 'normalcy.'

Fawcett stepped forward. "What happened?"

Angel held up the bag. "Satchel, stick, and snake."

Fawcett's eyes looked northward. "And the snake?"

"Oh, he's fine. Cold-blooded though it may be, the serpent is one of God's creatures, and serves a purpose."

FINAL EDIT

Joseph S. Walker

When my cousin Hal called and asked me to drop by his office, I was surprised he even had my number. Our contacts in recent years were limited to polite nods at weddings and funerals, which suited me fine. Hal was a condescending prick when we were kids. All growing up did was make him a taller condescending prick.

His literary agency was on the fifth floor of a building within shouting distance of MoMA. Maybe that's why the kid at reception had more colors in his hair than a box of crayons. The big box, with the sharpener on the back. The neon hues clashed with an indecipherable black tattoo climbing halfway up his cheek.

It must be exhausting trying to scare old people these days.

Hal's office was lined with blown-up covers of Braden Butler novels and movie posters featuring Butler's most famous character, globetrotting do-gooder Clive Carson. Butler was a household name, churning out two or three bestselling thrillers a year. Every Christmas, Hal sent everyone in the family a copy of Butler's latest. I tried to read one once and quit after a hundred pages, when I couldn't remember a single thing that had happened.

After Kid Kaleidoscope showed me in, established I didn't want a drink, and left us alone, Hal didn't waste time on pleasantries. "Ever been to New Orleans, Ronny?"

I shifted my weight. Hal's office furniture was designed to look good in magazine spreads, not to accommodate the human form. Not mine, anyway. "Nope. I do know all the words to 'Iko Iko.'"

Hal turned a pencil over and over in his fingers. "There's a job I'd like you to do down there."

"I have a job."

"You're a repo man. The deadbeats won't disappear if you take a few days off."

"To do what?"

He dropped the pencil. "Braden Butler is guest of honor at a mystery convention. The last couple of times Bray did events like this, there were...incidents. Young women who claim he took advantage of them."

"Did he?"

"Look, two people go into a room and close the door. Who's to say what happened?"

"Prosecutors? Juries?"

"Not funny. So far, I'm keeping the lid on with a little cash and some NDAs."

"What is it you expect me to do?"

"Run interference. Try to keep him from taking anyone back to his room. Warn them if you have to. At the very least, stick close enough to testify they consented."

I snorted. "That's awfully damn close. Am I supposed to ride around in his hip pocket?"

"I'll register you for the convention. All the action at these things happens at the hotel bar. You'll have a nametag. Nobody will look at you twice."

"Hire a PI or something. An actual security guy."

Hal shook his head. "Can't. Bray won't cooperate with anybody like that. He doesn't know I'm sending you. Says he hasn't done anything wrong and won't be treated like he has."

"Okay, but why me? Hell, send the human rainbow out

there."

Hal fiddled with the pencil again. I resisted the urge to smack it out of his hands. "I thought this might suit you."

That's when I got it. What qualification made me unique in Hal's world? Time. Specifically, time served, on assault and burglary charges. I'm a big guy who looks like he's got that kind of history. Not a lot of us in Manhattan publishing circles. "So, you want me to get physical."

"Of course not. But maybe scare him a little, if nothing else works. Pretend to be the girl's father or something."

I stood. "Threatening a celebrity in a public place? Great idea. See you around, Hal."

"Five grand," Hal said. "Plus travel costs, of course."

I crossed my arms. "Ten."

"Seven."

"Up front?"

"Half now, half if it goes okay."

I sat. You have to repossess a lot of cars to make seven thousand dollars. "All right, Hal. I'll babysit your cash cow."

It was slipping into fall in New York, but Louisiana must use a different calendar. The minute I stepped out of the airport, sweat began streaming from my hairline like I'd had a faucet installed.

The convention was at a big, fairly new hotel on the edge of the French Quarter. I checked in, then took an escalator to the mezzanine and found the registration table. A banner behind it showed Braden Butler, in a black turtleneck, holding up a copy of his latest novel. He looked vibrant and confident, the wavy hair only lightly touched by gray. More like a retired quarterback than a writer.

I gave the relentlessly cheerful registration volunteers my name. In return, they gave me a canvas tote bag, a nametag, and a convention schedule two inches thick. I took an elevator to my seventh-floor room. I knew from Hal that Butler's suite was on twelve. He traveled with his assistant, a younger man named Jimmy Symonds, but Symonds got his own room.

After I cranked the AC and took a cold shower, I paged through the schedule. This was day one. Butler would arrive early tomorrow morning, then participate in various panels, interviews, and signing sessions on days two and three, culminating in a closing banquet the third night. All I was supposed to do was keep him from getting laid the two nights he was spending in town. Should be easy enough. Most days, I keep myself from getting laid without even trying.

I dressed, hung the nametag around my neck, and went exploring. The hotel was crawling with mystery writers and fans. Some tried to read my tag as we passed. I didn't try to read theirs. There was a room of book vendors, a series of conference rooms for panel discussions, and a banquet hall where a couple hundred people watched somebody interviewing a Japanese guy through an interpreter. The bar off the lobby was mostly empty in the middle of the afternoon, but if Hal was to be believed, it would be hopping at night. That's where Butler would hold court, looking for his next conquest.

I made another round, this time paying attention to the hotel employees. All of them, including the maintenance crew, had cards clipped to their breast pockets. When they needed to go through a locked door, they waved the card in front of the electronic lock and it lit up green. That was good. It meant I hadn't wasted five hundred bucks of Hal's money buying a sneaky little gadget from a guy I met the last time I was inside.

I bought a beer and a candy bar in the lobby for a little less than a car payment. Back in my room, I drank most of the beer, then spilled the last drops on my collar. I turned down the sheets, held the half-unwrapped candy over the middle of the bed, and blasted it with the hair dryer until chocolate dripped onto the clean white linen. When it looked sufficiently disgusting, I ate the rest of the bar, flushed the wrapper, and called the front desk.

"Listen, I thought this was supposed to be a classy place," I told the guy who answered. "I went to take a nap and there's shit all over my sheets. It's disgusting. The pictures are going straight into my Yelp review."

In five minutes, there was a knock at the door. I opened it to a young Black woman in a maid's uniform, holding a fresh set of bedding. "I'm so sorry, sir," she said. "I'll fix this up for you immediately."

"Shit happens," I said, moving a little into her space and making sure she got a good blast of beery breath. I grabbed at the stack of linen. "I'll help."

She instinctively jerked the bedding back against her chest. I let my hand go with it and stumbled against her, then back, mumbling apologetic noises. "I'll take care of it, sir," she said stiffly. She turned sideways to ease past me.

"Sure, sure." I backed against the wall, holding one hand up in a pacifying gesture. The other hand was in my pocket, putting the card I'd taken off her chest into a slot on the five-hundred-dollar gadget. I propped my hip against the dresser, crossed my arms, and watched her, my eyes half closed.

The maid stripped the bed, barely looking at the mess, and had new sheets on and the bed made up in about three minutes. When she was done, she gathered the old sheets up in a bundle.

"Please let us know if we can be of any other help, sir."

"Thanks," I said, enunciating like someone being careful not to slur. "Hey, you drop that?"

I pointed at her passcard on the floor where I'd bumped into her. She put a hand to her chest, grunted, and bent to pick it up. "Enjoy your stay, sir," she said, and left.

I gave it ten minutes, then went into the hallway. The gadget was about half the size of a deck of cards, flat unmarked black plastic with a small button on the side. I held it up to my door lock and pushed the button. There was a click, and the lock flashed green. I tried three more doors near mine, and the same thing happened. It's always gratifying when something works the way it's supposed to.

That night, not wanting to give the convention people too much of a look at me, I went out and wandered through the French Quarter. Disneyland for adults. The streets were choked with tourists, streaming in and out of bars and stopping to watch the musicians who seemed to be on every street corner. It was loud and colorful and vaguely artificial, like a giant movie set. The overall atmosphere was enforced gaiety. *Aren't we all having so much fun?*

Sometime after midnight, I was at a bar built around a merry-go-round. I let out a sudden, loud laugh, and the bartender looked at me, startled. "Everything okay, sir?"

"Just had a thought," I said. I finished my drink and put the glass down. "Why am I working for the guy making ten percent instead of making a deal with the guy making ninety?"

"Hell if I know," he said. "Want another to help you mull it over?"

The next day, Braden Butler was being interviewed in the banquet hall at one. I got there half an hour early and took a seat at a table in the front row, a little off to the side. My head throbbed, and despite sleeping in and downing half a dozen Tylenol, I felt sluggish and grumpy. *Fun, fun, fun!*

A woman in her sixties dropped a stack of Butler hardcovers on the table and took the chair beside me. "Is he signing after this?" she asked.

"I don't think so," I said. "There's a signing tomorrow morning."

"Well, maybe he'll do a favor for me." She leaned close. "I met him at this convention fifteen years ago. The first one for both of us. I'm sure he'll remember."

"Who could forget?"

"How about you?" She looked at my nametag. "Ronny. Are you a writer?"

"Trying to be." I looked at her chest. "Angie."

"That's all any of us can do," she said. "What are you working on now?"

"Oh, the usual thing," I said. "Figuring out a blackmail plot."

Braden Butler came in a door at the side of the ballroom, followed by a pale, scrawny man with a leather bag slung over his shoulder. Symonds, the assistant. He was at least a decade younger than his boss, but his hair was thinning and I could see circles under his eyes from halfway across the room. The two of them stopped at an empty table while Symonds poked around in the bag, eventually handing Butler a bottle of water.

"He's certainly kept his looks," Angie said. I grunted. I was more interested in the watch on Butler's left wrist, a chunky golden thing that probably cost more than any car I ever owned. Ninety percent was definitely looking like the neighborhood I wanted to be in.

I managed to stay awake through Butler's interview, but he didn't make it easy. After some opening questions about his childhood and how he developed his plots, it was mostly gossipy stuff about actors I didn't know in his movies, which I hadn't seen. "Just keep writing," he told an audience member who asked about writer's block. "Nothing's going to happen if you don't, but hey." He spread his arms and smiled broadly. "Just look what can happen if you do."

When the interview ended, a knot of people formed around Butler, Angie elbowing her way to the front. I stayed in my seat, pretending to look at the schedule. After ten minutes, Jimmy Symonds pushed his way through, mumbling apologies, and whispered in his boss's ear. Butler raised his arms, probably putting a lot more effort into lifting the one with the watch.

"Sorry, folks," he said. "Got some people waiting, but I'll be seeing you all again."

The fans reluctantly parted, and Butler walked away briskly, Symonds falling into step behind. I followed them down an escalator and across the lobby to the hotel's upscale restaurant. Butler went past the line, waiting to get in without breaking stride. Symonds peeled off, went to a nearby bench, and sat down, pulling out his phone. Apparently, he wasn't invited to lunch. I took a look at the menu, saw a sixty-dollar pork chop, and decided I wasn't either.

I picked Butler up again a couple of hours later, at a panel discussing the ethics of drawing on true crime stories for writing fiction. It was obvious most of the audience was there for Butler. The moderator and other panelists deferred to him repeatedly. He leaned aggressively into his microphone, talking louder than the others and emphasizing his points by tapping his fist firmly on the table. "The writer's only obligation is to the page," he said. "Everything else will be forgotten in time. It's my job as a writer to decide what will be remembered and how. You think anybody today would give a damn about some Kansas family getting butchered decades ago, if not for Truman Capote?"

"Not all of us are Truman Capote," said a woman at the far end of the panel.

"With that attitude, you never will be," Butler snapped. "If you don't think you're good enough to write about anything, *anything*, there are plenty of other ways to make a living."

Afterwards, people immediately surrounded Butler. I loitered in the hallway outside until he broke free, followed him and Symonds to the elevator, and managed to get in their crowded car going up. It was full enough to be a little uncomfortable, and everybody was quiet until a big group got off on eight. Tension eased, and the half-dozen of us left visibly relaxed as the doors closed.

"What's left?" Butler asked Symonds.

"Publisher cocktail hour at six," Symonds murmured. "Then emceeing the awards thing at seven."

The doors opened on twelve. I followed them out and down the hall, pretending to text and wondering what people did to look inconspicuous before cell phones. "I'm taking a nap," Butler said. "Come get me in an hour." He stopped at 1215 and let himself in. Symonds went another two doors down to his own room. I walked on around the next corner. A nap sounded like a pretty good idea. The cocktail thing was probably a private event, and I didn't think Butler would be trying to get any action while he was handing out awards. I had what I wanted—a sense of who Butler was, how he talked and moved. That was all I needed until tonight.

True to Hal's description, the hotel bar was crowded and noisy after the official conference activities ended. People stood in clusters and huddled around tables, leaning in to hear each other over the clamor of voices and zydeco music from the speakers. A few men wore suits, and I saw a sprinkling of expensive jewelry, but for the most part the clothes were casual, the attitudes exuberant and cheerful.

Butler stood with his back against the bar, in the middle of a group of about ten people. I got a beer and sidled into a knot where I could keep an eye on him. Half the people there were watching him while trying to look like they weren't, so I wasn't too worried about getting made.

A stocky man in a tweed jacket with actual leather patches on the elbows shook my hand, looking down at my tag. "Good to meet you, Ronny," he said. "Having a good conference?"

"The best," I said. I remembered my talk with Angie. "What are you working on?" I asked that question a lot in the next couple of hours. It never failed to provide ten or fifteen minutes when all I had to do was smile and nod.

I drifted between conversations. I saw Angie several times, clearly in her element, throwing back her head to laugh or bustling to the bar to get more drinks. Symonds was in a back corner, sitting by himself, barely touching his drink. He had a good view of his boss, and didn't seem much interested in looking at anything else.

Butler never moved from his spot at the bar. He didn't have to. People came to him, cycling in and out as space opened up near him. He was drinking steadily, bourbon being his poison of choice. I wasn't often close enough to hear his voice—Hal was wrong about that—but he was always talking more than anyone else, his arms waving more widely and loosely as the night went on.

It was past eleven when I noticed him paying a lot of attention to a woman who had joined his rotating band of devotees. She was somewhere in her twenties, young for this bunch, with long black hair and a purple dress that came to the middle of her thighs. Butler kept leaning over to say things to her, often touching her bare arm.

Symonds materialized on Butler's other side. He tugged on Butler's arm and said something in his ear, his expression urgent. Butler shrugged him off. Symonds got a bartender's attention, and the man brought him a tall glass of water. Symonds turned back to Butler and pressed it on him. Butler shook his head, but Symonds pushed it into his hands. Apparently, one of his jobs was keeping Butler hydrated. Butler rolled his eyes and drank half the water. He tried to hand the glass to Symonds, but the assistant pushed it back. Butler shook his head in disgust, chugged the rest of the water, and slammed the glass down on the bar. He made a face at Symonds and waved him away.

Most of his admirers had discreetly turned away during the exchange. The woman in the purple dress was still standing beside Butler, but facing the bar. He turned and leaned against the rail, bringing his head down to her level. They talked in low tones, and after a minute Butler began running some of her hair through his fingers.

That was enough of a cue for me. I finished my own drink, nodded to the guy telling me his thrilling idea for revolutionizing the heist novel, and headed for the elevators.

Butler's suite had a kitchenette, a sitting room, and two bedrooms, each with its own generously sized bathroom and full-sized closet. After letting myself in and slipping on rubber gloves, I made a quick pass through, making sure I was alone. One bedroom was untouched. The other had rumpled covers, two empty beers on the nightstand, and a lot of prescription bottles and toiletries clustered around the sink.

I brought a chair from the kitchenette and sat in the closet of the bedroom Butler was using. The only thing hanging in the closet was a suit, probably for tomorrow's banquet. Otherwise, Butler seemed to live out of his suitcase. I pulled on the sliding door until it was an inch from closed and made sure I could use my phone to film through the gap.

Hal would pay seven grand to keep Butler out of trouble. I bet Butler would pay a lot more to keep the things he was planning to do in this room from airing on *Good Morning America.*

Sooner than I expected, I heard the main door to the suite open. I held the phone in place and hit record. There were mumbling voices, then the lights came on in the bedroom and Butler and the woman in the purple dress came in.

To my surprise, it was Butler who looked bad. His face was flushed, and he was lurching more than walking, throwing his legs out in front of himself as he leaned heavily against the woman. Straining, she got him to the foot of the bed, turned him halfway around, and pushed his chest. Butler fell backwards onto the mattress, moaned, and rolled into a fetal position.

The woman crossed her arms and looked down at him. I held as still as I could. After a minute, she shook her head, got a phone out of her purse, and made a call. "He's already out," she said. "Come on up." She hung up and walked over to the window, looking at Butler's view of the Quarter.

In five minutes, the door opened again. Symonds came into the room and looked at his boss. "That was fast," he said. "I guess he had more to drink than I thought. Did he try anything with you?"

"Does it look like any of his fingers are broken?" she said. She hadn't turned from the window.

"All right." Symonds put his leather satchel on the floor. "I'll get him undressed." He went to the bed and shook Butler, who didn't respond. Symonds shook harder, then forcibly rolled Butler onto his back. "Jesus," Symonds said. He propped a knee on the bed and felt Butler's neck. "Lacey, I don't think he's breathing."

"What?" She came to the bed, hesitated, and took Butler's wrist. "No way. I didn't give him that much."

"*You* didn't give him?" Symonds stepped back from the bed, hand at his mouth. "Lacey, *I* was the one dosing him. I put three in his water."

"Well, I put four in his bourbon," Lacey said. They stared at each other over the inert body.

There's a certain art to knowing when to make an entrance. I pushed the sliding door open, keeping the phone held up in front of me. "Smile, kids," I said. "This one is going in the scrapbook."

Symonds yelped and jumped away from the closet. Lacey was made of sterner stuff. Her eyes widened, but she stood her ground. "Who the hell are you?" she said.

I waggled the camera as I stepped into the room. "I'm the guy who just filmed you two masterminds realizing you killed Braden Butler."

"I've seen you before," Symonds said. "You were at the

panel today. And in the bar."

"I get around." I zoomed in on Butler's waxy face. "Don't think you'll be doing much of that in the near future. I wonder what manslaughter sentences are like in this state. What did you give him, anyway?"

Lacey's face was iron. "The same thing he gave my sister two years ago, in San Diego. Back when she could leave her apartment without throwing up."

I stopped recording and tucked the phone in my pocket. "So, you weren't trying to kill him?"

"Of course not," Symonds said. "We're not killers."

"Beg to differ. I get what she's doing here. What's your story? Butler didn't cover dental?"

Symonds opened his mouth, then snapped it shut. "Why should I tell you anything?"

I smiled. "Right now, you've got three choices. You can deal with the cops, who will find my little movie highly entertaining. Or you can answer my questions and do everything I say. Or you can kill me, and hope to hell I haven't already sent the recording to anybody." I took a step closer and let the smile fade from my face. I watched him register the six inches and seventy pounds I had on him. "What's it gonna be, Jimmy?"

He swallowed and looked at his shoes. "I wanted out."

"Out of what, exactly?"

Symonds gestured at Butler's body. "He hasn't written a word in ten years. Terminal writer's block. It's all been me, but I was so wet behind the ears when I started working for him I signed everything he shoved in front of me. I can't tell anyone. I can't publish anything under my own name. I could have quit, but he's Braden Butler and I'm nobody. He could have ruined me with a snap of his fingers."

"Got it," I said. "So, what was the master plan here?"

"Compromising pictures," Symonds said. "Just to get leverage over him. Enough for me to go off on my own, and for Lacey's sister to get the help she needs."

"Very noble." I looked at the body and thought for a minute, then snapped my fingers and held out my hand. "Driver licenses."

They looked at each other.

"Do we need to go over the three options again?" I asked.

Sighing, Lacey reached into her purse while Symonds got out his wallet. I took pictures of both licenses and handed them back.

"Okay, here's the play." I looked at Lacey. "You go back down to the bar. Make sure a lot of people see you. Be memorable. If you have a chance to go back to somebody's room, do it."

"Don't be disgusting," Lacey said. She was rigid with some combination of anger and fear.

"Just trying to give you a solid alibi," I said. I looked at Symonds. "So, you're a writer."

He drew himself up a little. "I am."

"Butler have a laptop?"

"Of course."

"Okay, I've got an assignment for you. A suicide note."

His face twisted. "On the laptop? You think anybody will buy that?"

"I guess that's up to you, Mr. Writer. Make it convincing. He's remorseful about her sister and any other women you know about. He's tortured by writer's block and confesses that you've written all his best books. The interview today made him realize he's a failure. Think you can sell that?"

Symonds bit his lip, staring into space. "Probably," he said. "I mean, yes, I can."

"Put the bottle with his supply of the pills next to the computer," I said.

"What's in this for you?" Lacey broke in.

"I'm just helping you kids out of the goodness of my heart," I said. I slapped my forehead. "Oh, no, wait. Money. I'm guessing that once this story breaks, the publisher will reissue those books with Jimmy's name on them, maybe pay him to write more."

"I suppose you get a cut," she said.

"A big one. But that's only if this works, girl. If you'd rather take your chances with the cops, feel free. Otherwise, the sooner you're back at the bar, the better."

She shook her head, but she moved. After the door closed behind her, I nodded at Symonds. "Hop to it, Shakespeare."

Symonds spent about an hour on the note. I drifted through the suite as he worked. Three times, I had to stop myself from taking the watch off Butler's wrist. The whole house of cards would collapse if this had a whiff of robbery. Whatever beat cop answered the eventual call would probably walk off with it. I wished him well.

"Okay," Symonds finally said. "You want to read it?"

"I'm not really a fan of your stuff. Give me your shoelace."

"Why?"

"Because I don't feel like undoing mine." I did the finger snap thing again. Symonds sighed, sat down, and pulled the laces out of his right shoe.

The hotel door had one of those security locks where a bar on the door catches on a metal loop attached to the wall. I threaded the shoelace through the loop, opened the door, and looked cautiously out into the hall. Nobody there, just the heavy silence of the early morning. I ushered Symonds into the hallway, let the door almost close, then pulled carefully on the shoelace to swing the loop over the bar.

"Clever," Symonds said.

"Don't use it in your next book," I said. "No reason to give anybody ideas." I gave him back the shoelace and pointed toward his room. "Sleep well, Jimmy. I'll be in touch."

***

Myself, I fell asleep quickly that night, and slept soundly. Hal was going to be pissed, of course, especially if Jimmy ended up with some other agent. I was pretty sure I could do without his polite nods, though, and it's not like he shouldn't have seen it coming. I never said I was a nice guy.

Truth be told, I don't even know all the words to "Iko Iko."

ABOUT THE CONTRIBUTORS

JEFF AYERS has been a book reviewer for The Associated Press and Booklist and reviews suspense thrillers for Library Journal, Criminal Element, and firstCLUE. He co-writes the National Park thriller series for Minotaur as A.J. Landau and co-writes the Jigsaw Puzzle Mysteries for Crooked Lane as J.B. Abbott.

ERIC BECKSTROM is a writer and photographer from Minnesota, now based in Bloomington, Indiana. His stories have been published in Bouchercon anthologies (2017, 2022, 2024, 2025), *Black Cat Weekly*, and *Dark of the Day: Eclipse Stories* (ed. Kaye George). One of his first stories, which he adapted for the stage, was produced as a one-act by The Bloomington Playwrights Project.

JAYNE BELMONT is a writer and voracious reader who currently supports her reading habits as a software developer. She resides in the Capital Region of New York State, happily cohabitating with her wonderful husband, three cats, and a handful of ghosts in a very old but lovely home. She is an undercover member of Mystery Writers of America and Sisters in Crime.

DON BRUNS, the editor of *Blood on the Bayou: Case Closed*, is also the editor of *Hotel California*, *Thriller*, *Back In Black* and now *Bat Out of Hell.* He's an accomplished writer with 22 published novels. His novel *Casting Bones*, a New Orleans voodoo mystery, has been optioned for a major motion picture. Bruns has achieved Amazon Best Selling author in a number of categories and is a USA Today bestselling author.

Called a hard-boiled poet by NPR's Maureen Corrigan, **REED FARREL COLEMAN** is the *New York Times* bestselling author of over thirty novels including six in the Jesse Stone series for the estate of Robert B. Parker. He is a four-time recipient of the Shamus Award and a four-time Edgar Award nominee in three categories. He has also won the Authors on the Air Book of the Year, the Scribe, Audie, Anthony, Barry, and Macavity Awards. A former Executive Vice President of MWA, Reed lives on Long Island with his wife.

LARRY S. EVANS II is an executive in the technology business in Houston, Texas. His background is in art, illustration, filmmaking, photography, marketing, and commercial production. He has published cartoons and illustrations worldwide, and both poetry and fiction in regional anthologies and literary magazines. He has worked as a journalist and humor writer. He travels extensively with his wife of 35 years. They have two adult children who are also in the creative arts industry. This is his debut as a Bouchercon author and his first submission to the competition. He and his wife are developing several writing projects.

MICHAEL FERRETER writes traditional crime and mystery fiction. His stories often explore how music impacts our lives and our memories. A former newspaper editor and reporter, his byline has appeared in Midwestern newspapers including the Milwaukee Journal Sentinel and the Omaha World-Herald. He is a member of the Mystery Writers of America and the Midwest chapter. His short story "Music City Row" was published in the 2024 Bouchercon anthology. He lives in the suburbs of Chicago with his family. Read more at MichaelFerreter.com.

BARRY FULTON is a retired diplomat, former Air Force officer, and occasional university professor with overseas assignments in Brussels, Italy, Japan, Pakistan, and Turkey. His latest novel is *The Scorpion and the Bear*. He writes the Thomas Sebastian Scott espionage series: *The Irish Imbroglio, Behind the Seventh Veil, The Lady is Bugged,* and *Flame: Hackers, Artists, Lovers, and Spies*. Fulton is a Senior Fellow at the Salzburg Global Seminar and a member of the Public Diplomacy Council of America, DACOR (Diplomatic and Consular Officers Retired), and Sisters in Crime. Website: Fulton-Pub.com.

JOHN GILSTRAP is the Thriller Award-winning, New York Times bestselling author of over two dozen thrillers, including *Burned Bridges*, the first book in his new series featuring retired FBI Director Irene Rivers, plus *Zero Sum* and 16 additional books in his acclaimed Jonathan Grave thriller series and a half dozen standalones. His nonfiction book, *Six Minutes to Freedom* is currently under development to become a feature film by Netflix. In addition to his writing career, John is an expert in explosives, weapons systems, hazardous materials and fire behavior.

HEATHER GRAHAM is the New York Times and USA Today bestselling author of over two hundred novels, novellas, and short stories. She majored in arts at the University of South Florida, and after several years in dinner theater, singing back-up vocals, and bartending, she stayed home after the birth of her third child and began to write. Her first book was with Dell, and since then, she has written over two hundred novels and novellas including category, suspense, historical, romance, paranormal, vampire fiction, time travel, occult, sci-fi, young adult, and Christmas family fare. Published in approximately twenty-five languages, she has over 60 million books in print. Heather has been honored with awards from booksellers and writers' organizations for excellence in her work. She is the proud recipient of the Thriller Writers' Silver Bullet award for charitable contributions, the prestigious Thriller Master Award, the RWA Lifetime Achievement Award, Distinguished Author Award from the Southwest Florida Reading Festival, the Strand Lifetime Achievement Award, and was Bouchercon 2024's American Guest of Honor. With books selected for the Doubleday Book Club and the Literary Guild, she has been quoted, interviewed, or featured in The Nation, Redbook, Mystery Book Club, People and USA Today and appeared on many newscasts including Today, Entertainment Tonight and local television. Heather loves travel, ballroom dancing, and the water (she is a certified scuba diver!). She has hosted Vampire Balls and Dinner theater to raise money for the Pediatric Aids Foundation and after Katrina created the at-cost Writers for New Orleans Workshop to benefit the stricken Gulf Region. She is also the founder of The Slush Pile Players, presenting something that's "almost like entertainment" for various conferences and benefits. Married since high school graduation and the mother of five, her greatest love in life remains her family. She believes her career has been an incredible gift, and she is grateful every day to be doing something that she loves so very much for a living. Look her up at: TheOriginalHeather-Graham.com.

KERRY HAMMOND is a fully recovered attorney living in Denver, Colorado. Several of her short stories have been published in mystery anthologies and her latest, "Sins of the Father," was nominated for an Agatha Award. One of her stories was featured in *The Mysterious Bookshop Presents the Best Mystery Stories of 2023*. She also enjoys creating downloadable Murder Mystery party games for BlameTheButler.com.

SMITA HARISH JAIN is a two-time International Thriller Writers Award nominee for Best Short Story and has appeared in the Ellery Queen Top 10 Readers Poll. She has more than 20 short stories published or pending publication in Ellery Queen's Mystery Magazine, Black Cat Mystery Magazine, and in anthologies for Mystery Writers of America, Left Coast Crime, and Akashic Noir, among many others. She grew up in Mumbai, India and now works as a university professor, both of which inform her crime fiction.

ALI KARIM is the Assistant Editor of Shots Magazine and writer (Rap Sheet, January Magazine, Deadly Pleasures etc.), former Bouchercon Director (co-chaired programing Bouchercon XLVI, Raleigh, NC, 2015), associate member of CWA, ITW and PWA, and literary judge of crime, mystery and thriller fiction. He has received the Don Sandstrom (2013), Red Herring (2018) and David Thompson (2011) awards for supporting crime and thriller genres. He has contributed to Dissecting Hannibal Lecter, ed. Benjamin Szumskyj (McFarland Press), The Greenwood Encyclopaedia of British Crime Fiction (ed. Barry Forshaw) and ITW 100 Thriller Novels, ed. David Morrell and Hank Wagner (Oceanview Publishing). He is also the Bouchercon 2025 Fan Guest of Honor.

JON LAND is the *New York Times* and *USA Today* bestselling, award-winning author of more than 60 books, including the Caitlin Strong series. He has also teamed up with Heather Graham for a sci-fi series that includes *The Rising, Blood Moon* and the forthcoming *Dark Harbor*. His most recent book, *Cold Burn*, under the pseudonym A. J. Landau, was published by Minotaur in April, the second in the series of National Parks-themed thrillers (after *Leave No Trace*) written with Jeff Ayers. The idea for "Don't Be Scared" came when they happened upon a "bucket drummer" on Bourbon Street last year who became the model for the story's hero.

ROBERT LOPRESTI is a retired librarian who lives in the Pacific Northwest. His stories have won the Derringer Award three times, as well as the Black Orchid Novella Award, and have been nominated for the Anthony. They have been reprinted in Best American Mystery Stories and Year's Best Dark Fantasy and Horror. Two of his books have made the year's best foreign mystery lists in Japan. His novel *Greenfellas* is a comic caper about the Mafia trying to save the environment. He blogs at SleuthSayers and Little Big Crimes. His hobby is writing biographical notes in third person. RobLopresti.com.

DP LYLE is the Amazon #1 Bestselling; Macavity and Benjamin Franklin Award-winning; Edgar (2), Agatha, Anthony, Shamus, Scribe, Silver Falchion, and USA Today Best Book (2) Award-nominated author of 27 books, both fiction and non-fiction. He hosts the Crime Fiction Writer's Blog, the Criminal Mischief: The Art and Science of Crime Fiction YouTube/podcast series, and is co-creator of the Outliers Writing University. He has worked with many novelists and the writers of popular television shows such as Law & Order, CSI: Miami, Diagnosis Murder, Monk, Judging Amy, Peacemakers, Cold Case, House, Medium, Women's Murder Club, 1-800-Missing, The Glades, and Pretty Little Liars.
Website: DPLyleMD.com
Outliers Writing University: OutliersWritingUniversity.com

TIM MALEENY is the bestselling author of the award-winning Cape Weathers mysteries and the comedic thriller *Jump*, which *Publishers Weekly* calls "a perfectly blended cocktail of escapism." His latest novel is *Hanging The Devil*, a global art heist praised by Library Journal for its "relentlessly fast-paced plot with delightful dry humor" in a starred review. Tim has won the Macavity, Silver Falchion, and Lefty Awards, and his short fiction appears in several leading anthologies. The *Irish Times* declares, "If comic crime fiction is your thing, Maleeny delivers in spades."

JONATHAN MABERRY is a *New York Times* bestseller, 5-time Bram Stoker Award-winner, 4-time Scribe Award-winner, Inkpot Award-winner, poet, and comic book writer. He writes in multiple genres including suspense, thriller, horror, science fiction, fantasy, and action, for adults, teens and middle grade. *V-WARS* (Netflix) was based on his books/comics; Alcon is developing his YA post-apocalyptic novels for film; and Chad Stahelski, director of *John Wick,* is developing his bestselling *Joe Ledger* thrillers for TV. Marvel's *Black Panther: Wakanda Forever* was partly based on his work. He's president of the International Association of Media Tie-in Writers, and editor of Weird Tales Magazine. JonathanMaberry.com.

J.M. REDMANN has published twelve novels featuring New Orleans PI Micky Knight. Her first was published in 1990, one of the early hard-boiled lesbian detectives. Her books have won multiple awards, including three Lambda Literary awards, and the Publishing Triangle's Joseph Hansen Award. Her third book, *The Intersection of Law & Desire*, originally published by W. W. Norton, was an Editor's Choice of the San Francisco Chronicle and a recommended book of NPR's Fresh Air.

Pushcart Prize nominee **LIESE SHERWOOD-FABRE** has published mysteries through Belanger Books, MX Publishing, and North Dallas Sisters in Crime anthologies. She is a four-time first-prize CIBA award winner for her series *The Early Case Files of Sherlock Holmes,* as well as a young adult fantasy. A Romance Writers of America (RWA) Golden Heart finalist, she has also received numerous recognitions for her women's fiction. She holds a PhD in Sociology and worked for the US government for forty years, living abroad in Honduras, Mexico, and Russia. She and her husband live in Texas and enjoy spoiling their grandchildren.

CLAY STAFFORD has had an eclectic career as an author, filmmaker, actor, composer, educator, public speaker, publisher, CEO of American Blackguard Entertainment, and founder of *Killer Nashville Magazine*, The Balanced Writer streaming platform, and the Killer Nashville International Writers' Conference. He has sold nearly four million copies of his works in over sixteen languages. ClayStafford.com

KELLI STANLEY was Bouchercon 2024's Historical Mystery Guest of Honor, and is the creator of the Miranda Corbie series (*City Of Dragons*, *City Of Secrets*, *City Of Ghosts*, *City Of Sharks*), literary PI novels set in 1940 San Francisco and featuring "one of crime's most arresting heroines" (*Library Journal*). She's been honored with numerous nominations and awards, including the Macavity and Bruce Alexander, and is a *Los Angeles Times* Book Prize finalist. Kelli has also published a "Roman Noir" series set in Roman Britain and was the founder of Nasty Woman Press, a non-profit publisher of the Anthony Award-winning anthology *Shattering Glass*. *The Reckoning*, her latest book, is a tense, atmospheric and timely thriller set in Northern California's "Emerald Triangle" amidst the marijuana wars and serial killings of 1985. It releases from Severn House on January 6, 2026. (KelliStanley.com).

CHARLES TODD is The *New York Times* bestselling author of the Inspector Ian Rutledge Series and the Bess Crawford series. *A Christmas Witness Novella* (Ian Rutledge Mystery) 10-21-2025 and *A Day of Judgement* (Ian Rutledge Mystery) Spring of 2026 followed by a Bess Crawford Mystery. He has published over forty titles including two stand-alone novels, anthology and twenty short-stories appearing in mystery magazines and anthologies worldwide. His works have received the Mary Higgins Clark, Agatha, and Barry awards and nominations other major awards. He has been a Guest of Honor at Killer Nashville, Malice Domestic and Bouchercon in 2025.

GABRIEL VALJAN is the author of *The Company Files*, and the Shane Cleary Mysteries with Level Best Books. He has been nominated for the Agatha, Anthony, Derringer, and Silver Falchion awards. He received the 2021 Macavity Award for Best Short Story, and the Shamus Award for Best PI in 2023. Gabriel is a member of the Historical Novel Society, ITW, MWA, and Sisters in Crime. He lives in Boston and answers to a tuxedo cat named Munchkin.
Bluesky: @gvaljan.bsky.social
IG: @gabrielvaljan
Web: GabrielValjan.com
Amazon Author page: https://rb.gy/tsntz

JOSEPH S. WALKER is the president of the Short Mystery Fiction Society and the author of more than 100 published crime and mystery stories. He has been a finalist for the Edgar, Derringer, Shamus, and Thriller Awards, and is a two-time winner of the Al Blanchard Award. His stories have appeared in numerous magazines and anthologies, including four of the last five editions of *Best Mystery Stories of the Year*. *Crime Scenes*, the first collection of his stories, is forthcoming from Level Best Books in 2026. He lives in Indiana. Visit his website at JSWalkerauthor.com.

On the following pages are a few more great titles from the Down & Out Books publishing family.

For a complete list of books and to sign up for our newsletter, go to DownAndOutBooks.com.

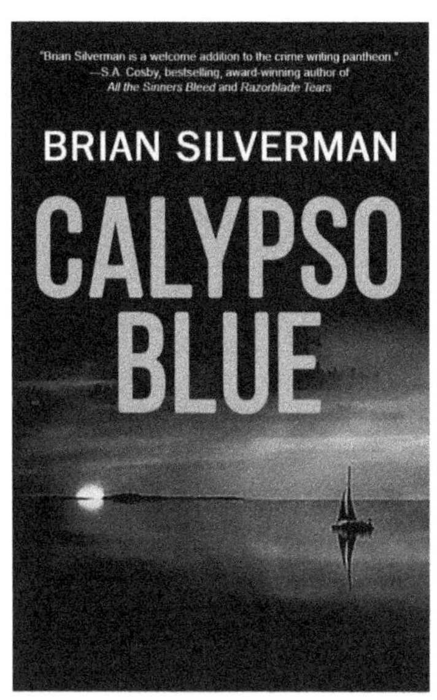

Calypso Blue
A Len Buonfiglio/Caribbean Mystery
Brian Silverman

Down & Out Books
June 2025
978-1-64396-394-5

Bar owner and ex-New Yorker Len Buonfiglio, a hero in his hometown, flees his family and the city for what he hopes is a quieter, idyllic life in the tropics. But when Lord Ram, a world-renowned Calypso performer dies, Len is called in to quiet damning rumors about the man's death.

In his search for the truth about Lord Ram and dealing with the very dangerous mess Maurizio has brought with him, Len soon learns that even on a sunny tropical paradise there is no escape from darkness.

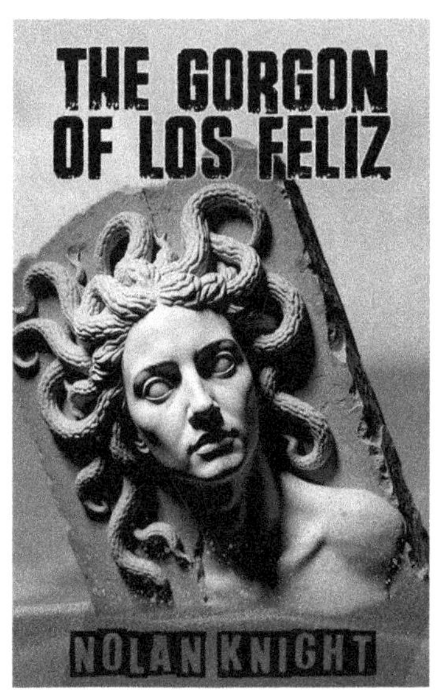

The Gorgon of Los Feliz
Nolan Knight

Down & Out Books
July 2025
978-1-64396-397-6

The Gorgon of Los Feliz is Cameron Kilbride, a bisexual female in her early twenties, newly evicted, hustling a living by rolling tourists on the fringe of Hollywood, stealing cars—*anything* to get by. Enter the affluent Stevensons; Richard and Mauve have lost track of their troubled daughter, Tiffany, and fear she has fallen back into pills, last seen on tour across America with a psychedelic rock band. Desperate to reel her back home, they employ Cam, who makes it her life's mission to find Tiffany for a handsome reward. When she finds their daughter, things soon go haywire, forcing her to steal the girl's identity to bilk her inheritance; however, once she procures this troubled life, the sordid characters in Tiff's world begin to haunt her every step.

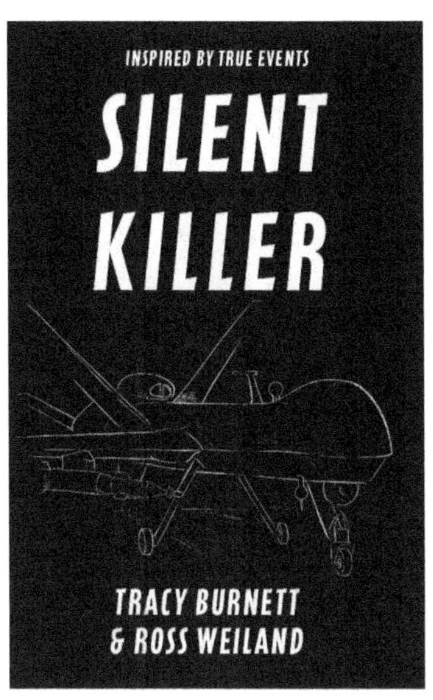

INSPIRED BY TRUE EVENTS
SILENT
KILLER
TRACY BURNETT
& ROSS WEILAND

Silent Killer
Tracy Burnett & Ross Weiland

Down & Out Books
August 2025
978-1-64396-413-3

Gordon Stone is an investigator assigned to the FBI Joint Terrorism Task Force. He's given an insignificant case—a charity scam out of Africa—and ordered to close it.

For Gordon, it's not that simple. Gordon has high-functioning autism. He's socially awkward, but blessed with a superpower—extraordinary focus and attention to detail. That superpower allows Gordon to piece together a disparate puzzle: a Hunter-Killer drone; an illicit drug shipment; a Special Forces operation gone wrong; and illegal immigration linked to 9/11.

When these pieces align, national security is at risk and hundreds of lives hang in the balance.

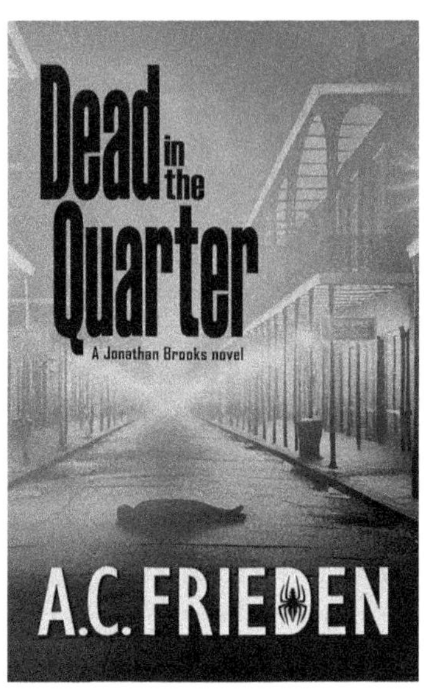

Dead in the Quarter
A Jonathan Brooks Novel
A.C. Frieden

Down & Out Books
September 2025
978-1-64396-415-7

After a celebratory dinner at a Mississippi riverfront restaurant marking his promotion to named partner, attorney Tod Rochon heads home to the French Quarter. In the dead of night, managing partner Jonathan Brooks gets a call from the police: Tod has been found gravely injured. Soon after Jonathan reaches the E.R., Tod is gone.

Driven by suspicion and grief, Jonathan starts digging. But the deeper he goes, the more unsettling the picture becomes—not just outside the firm, but within.

www.ingramcontent.com/pod-product-compliance
Lightning Source LLC
Chambersburg PA
CBHW031138020426
42333CB00013B/428

* 9 7 8 1 6 4 3 9 6 4 2 7 0 *